Olive Borden

D1518845

ALSO BY MICHELLE VOGEL
AND FROM MCFARLAND

*Olive Thomas: The Life and Death
of a Silent Film Beauty* (2007)

*Marjorie Main: The Life and Films
of Hollywood's "Ma Kettle"* (2006)

*Children of Hollywood: Accounts of Growing Up
as the Sons and Daughters of Stars* (2005)

Gene Tierney: A Biography (2005)

Olive Borden

*The Life and Films of
Hollywood's "Joy Girl"*

MICHELLE VOGEL

McFarland & Company, Inc., Publishers

Jefferson, North Carolina, and London

LIBRARY OF CONGRESS CATALOGUING-IN-PUBLICATION DATA

Vogel, Michelle, 1972–
Olive Borden : the life and films of Hollywood's
"Joy girl" / Michelle Vogel.
p.   cm.
Includes bibliographical references and index.

ISBN 978-0-7864-4795-4
softcover: 50# alkaline paper ∞

1. Borden, Olive, 1906–1947.
2. Motion picture actors and acresses — United States — Biography.
I. Title.
PN2287.B6377V64   2010   791.4302'8092 — dc22 [B]   2009054312

British Library cataloguing data are available

©2010 Michelle Vogel. All rights reserved

*No part of this book may be reproduced or transmitted in any form
or by any means, electronic or mechanical, including photocopying
or recording, or by any information storage and retrieval system,
without permission in writing from the publisher.*

Cover image: Olive Borden publicity photo (1926 Fox Studios);
background ©2010 Shutterstock

Manufactured in the United States of America

*McFarland & Company, Inc., Publishers
Box 611, Jefferson, North Carolina 28640
www.mcfarlandpub.com*

In memory of Olive Thomas and Olive Borden.
Same name, same calling, same fate...

Acknowledgments

No book is truly "written" by one individual. It takes a village! So, to my wonderfully faithful, knowledgeable, generous "villagers," all of whom helped me in various ways to get Olive Borden's story told the way it deserved to be — a *huge* thank you!

In no particular order, a round of rapturous applause goes to the following people and places: Kevin Brownlow, Gary Sweeney, David Ybarra, Marilyn Slater, Susan Hatch, E.J. Fleming, G.D. Hamann, Kristine Krueger, Annette D'Agostino Lloyd, Bob King, Benjie Wood, Dr. Levica Narine, Maure Elizabeth Bond, Orin O'Brien, Eve Golden, Lynn Kear, Jim King, Leatrice Gilbert Fountain, Scott O'Brien, Yair Solan, Caroline Yeager, Robert M. Fells, Hugh Munro Neely, Andi Hicks, Dennis Doros, Ben Model, Steve Massa, Gregg Nystrom, David Kalat, Jessica Rosner, James Robert Parish, Steve Starr, David C. Tucker, Linda Armstrong, Terry Mason, Bruce Calvert, Mark Kochinski, Robert Hitchings, Louis Guy, David Menefee, Rosemary Hanes, Laura Petersen Balogh, Paul Green, William J. Felchner, University of Wyoming, AMPAS, American Film Institute (AFI), the Library of Congress — Moving Image Section, Forest Lawn Memorial Park, The Margaret Herrick Library, Milestone Film and Video, Syracuse University Library, George Eastman House, the University of Southern California Cinematic Arts Library, and the Sunshine Mission.

A very special thank you to Edward "Ned" Comstock of the University of Southern California Library Division. I'm forever grateful for the time and effort it took to transcribe the massive Hal Roach Studios payroll ledgers. In doing so, at least thirty films never before attributed to Olive Borden have been included here for the very first time. Thank you.

Ralph Graves, Jr. — I'm extremely thankful for the personal insight you gave to Olive's story. This book would not have been possible without you. In a roundabout way, it was Olive who introduced us; as a result you've become an integral part of our family. Bill Cappello — Thank you for the many hours of research, deliberation and discussion surrounding the various mysteries in Olive's life. You're a true friend. Michael G. Ankerich — Thank you for your generosity in sharing your research, opinions and photos of Sybil Tinkle. William M. Drew — Your profound knowledge of early film and its stars is astounding. Thank you for sharing your thoughts and views with me for this book. Richard M. Roberts — The photo captions would not be the same without your input. Your ability to identify anyone and everyone astounds me each and every time.

My house of testosterone: my wonderful boys! — Matt, Josh, Reeve and Ryan. Mum and Dad — loads of love for everything. The rest of my family and friends (you all know who you are) for your love, support and encouragement on a daily basis. Thank you!

Contents

Preface

My first awareness of Olive Borden came some time in late 2004. I had begun research-
ing the life of another Olive, Olive Thomas, for my 2007 McFarland biography, *Olive
Thomas: The Life and Death of a Silent Film Beauty*. With three common factors; their shared
given name — Olive, their chosen profession — actress, and their tragic deaths, I suppose it
was no surprise to end up finding a misplaced article about Olive Borden amongst my pile
of Olive Thomas research papers.

I'll be honest, I had never heard of Olive Borden before reading that brief article that
nestled itself amongst papers where it didn't belong. The article pretty much covered her
life, career and death within *four* paragraphs, but it was enough bait to entice me to find
out more — eventually. I put the article in an envelope and wrote "Olive Borden?" on the
outside.

Firstly, I found it sad that someone's life, anyone's life, could be wrapped up in four
paragraphs, especially a Hollywood actress. There *had* to be more to Olive Borden's story.
There was something about her that struck me. Her name, her face, her tragic end? I don't
know. Maybe it was all three. Whatever it was, I knew that one day I would investigate
Borden's life and career and honor her time on this earth with more than a mere four paragraphs.

Five years later, after countless hours of research that involved the collation of vintage
newspaper and magazine articles, watching her films, collecting photographs, writing e-
mails, letters and making phone calls, etc., it was clear that my initial reaction to that way-
ward article was a true assumption. There *was* more to Olive Borden's story — a lot more!

With the generosity of many knowledgeable individuals, university archives, libraries
and institutions, the extensively researched filmography contains cast lists, reviews, taglines,
production notes and behind-the-scenes stories and trivia relating to each of her films and
the Hollywood years they encompassed.

The University of Southern California are keepers of the very big, very heavy Hal
Roach Studios payroll ledgers and within those massive pages was a goldmine of information that was jaw-dropping, to say the least. When Ned Comstock, USC librarian-archivist,
contacted me and said, "I think I found something," never in my wildest dreams could I
imagine what that "something" would be.

Almost three dozen Hal Roach shorts (from 1924 and 1925) in which Olive had been
involved were methodically listed (by title and code), along with the dates she worked and
her daily fees for each production. In every sense of the word, these titles were truly "lost"
films because they've never been associated with her — until now.

Sure enough, in one of those shorts, the Spat Family two-reeler *South o' the North Pole* (1924), Olive can be clearly seen in the second reel. There she is playing an Indian squaw. You don't have to squint to find her. She's right there. Clear as day. The payroll ledgers show that Olive was involved in this series for several days per short and her collective salary was the highest throughout this series too. Rule of thumb: The higher the salary, the higher the possibility of seeing her on screen. So, while her appearance in *South o' the North Pole* and the payroll ledgers prove she would have played a distinguishable part in many of the Spat Family comedies, unfortunately, many of them are now considered "lost." With that said, it is a bittersweet find, but nevertheless, Olive was involved in these new discoveries in *some* way. Finally, within this volume, they are now rightly attributed to her.

As far as Olive's film career goes, by 1926 or 1927, Olive had already hit her peak. She achieved her biggest successes during this time: She had a contract with Fox Studios and more money than she ever realized. She was the envied fiancée of one of Hollywood's most desired, most likable leading men, George O'Brien, and she rubbed shoulders with Hollywood's elite and powerful players both on and off camera.

Not unlike many of her peers, when life took a turn for the worse, Olive found refuge in a bottle of alcohol. By the mid–1930s, Olive's career was well and truly over. By the early 1940s she was bankrupt and spending what money she did have on booze. She straightened herself out for a short time and volunteered as a WAAC during World War II. As her contribution to the war effort was announced, a chubby, middle-aged woman with short hair was pictured in uniform in papers across the country. It was Olive. Now in her mid-thirties, she looked much older. The fresh-faced smile, flowing black hair and tiny waist that propelled her to stardom and made her the darling of the silver screen some fifteen years before, was gone. Alcohol had taken care of that.

In her post–Hollywood days, Olive sought comfort in religion. In 1945 she became a born-again Christian. It was around the same time that she moved to the Sunshine Mission, a home for destitute women in the Skid Row district of Los Angeles, California. Her mother, Sibbie, worked in the commissary and Olive helped by scrubbing floors, serving meals and taking care of the many children who called the mission home. She enjoyed her time with the children, organizing pageants and plays to keep them busy, but aside from that one bright spot, Olive's time there was a startling reminder of how low her life had become.

It's hard to believe that none of her Hollywood peers knew of her plight. She may have been too proud to tell them that she was living at the mission, she may have even lied about her whereabouts, pretended she was okay; after all, she *was* an actress. Playing a convincing role was her job; or at least it used to be. But several newspaper reports identified Olive's new home as the Sunshine Mission so it was hardly a well-kept secret.

When she was at her lowest ebb, there wasn't a helping hand extended in her direction, by anyone. No one stepped in to offer her a job (acting or otherwise), his or her friendship, accommodation, money — nothing. Many of her peers still had the power and the money to help her. They didn't. Olive was forgotten.

This book is the first complete biography and filmography dedicated to the life and career of Hollywood's "Joy Girl," Olive Borden. The biography incorporates newly discovered information and sets the record straight on Olive's famous (and infamous) family tree, her marriages, her Hollywood years, her decline into alcoholism and her tragic end. The detailed filmography is the most comprehensive overview of her career ever assembled.

Olive's story is a stark reminder of how fleeting fame can be, how fickle the film industry can be, and how cruel life can be if the wrong path is chosen. Olive's detour to destruction was taken in late 1927. Had she taken an enforced studio pay cut and *not* walked out on her Fox Studios contract, in all likelihood, her career (and her *life*) would have lasted decades longer and had a much happier ending.

Introduction

Olive Borden was just sixteen years old when she (accompanied by her mother Sibbie) traveled on a whim from Virginia to Hollywood with the dream of becoming a movie star. She had no acting experience and little money; her pretty face and attractive figure were her only commodities. Frankly, she was no different than most of the stunningly beautiful teenage girls making their way to Tinseltown, all of them wishing for the same success in the film business, all with odds seriously stacked against them. But Olive was determined. And she succeeded.

Before her nineteenth birthday, Olive Borden was a Mack Sennett bathing beauty (1923), a vamp in several Jack White and Hal Roach comedy shorts (1924 and 1925), and a WAMPAS Baby Star of 1925. She beat the odds and she was well on the way to living her dream.

Olive went on to star alongside Tom Mix, Ralph Graves, George O'Brien, John Boles, Jack Pickford, and many other popular leading men of the 1920s. She was directed by the best of them: John Ford, Allan Dwan, Leo McCarey, Raoul Walsh, Hal Roach and Howard Hawks, just to name a few. At her peak (between 1926 and 1927) Olive was contracted to Fox Studios at a weekly salary of $1500 (converts to approximately $19,000 in 2009). She starred in eleven features in two years. Then came a bitter salary disagreement and a public smear campaign, and in 1927 she walked out on her contract.

Despite the controversy surrounding her decision to leave Fox, she was still in demand and made pictures for Columbia, RKO and FBO. But as the film industry progressed and sound pictures emerged as "the next big thing," many successful careers were left languishing in the shadows. Unlike a lot of her peers, Olive made the leap into sound pictures. She was by no means terrible, but it was soon apparent that her best acting days were behind her.

The transition to talkies was difficult for Olive. She worked tirelessly with a voice coach to eliminate her Southern drawl. She even cut her trademark, long jet-black hair into a bob, the new "do" of the day, and she was cast in a variety of different roles to suit her new look. They were roles the public weren't used to seeing her in. Olive had lost her identity.

Throughout the 1930s, both professionally and personally, Olive's life was in a tailspin. She was cited by the IRS (in 1928 and 1930) for unpaid taxes dating back to 1926 and 1928; and her 1931 marriage to stockbroker Theodore Spector was broadcast all over the country. However, it wasn't the announcement of the happy occasion that made headlines. A year later when it was discovered that her new husband had failed to divorce his first wife, the papers had a field day. Olive found herself caught up in a love triangle!

Spector was arrested for bigamy, the case was dragged through the courts (and the papers) and Olive sought to have the union annulled. Spector was eventually cleared of bigamy charges due to lack of evidence. Olive's annulment was finalized in November 1932 without incident. Ironically, Olive's first film release *after* her annulment was the aptly titled *The Divorce Racket* (1932). It would be her only picture that year. Several lackluster productions followed in 1933, including, *Leave It to Me*, *Hotel Variety* and *The Mild West*.

Her last screen credit was the forgettable *Chloe, Love Is Calling You* (1934); it was a sad, embarrassing end to what once was a promising career. By 1934, Olive had moved to New York, dabbled in vaudeville and stage work, married for a second time, and moved into a small apartment in Long Island with her new husband John Moeller and his father. Olive was miserable but the marriage lasted longer than anyone expected. The couple divorced after seven years.

With two marriages behind her, and no children from either relationship, Olive often reflected on what would have been had she married her steady beau (and widely reported fiancé), fellow actor George O'Brien. Having met on the set of the epic John Ford Western *3 Bad Men* (1926), Olive and George were inseparable for almost four years. But as their relationship fizzled out, there was a good deal of speculation in Hollywood social circles and gossip columns as to what drove them apart. George's parents' disapproval of Olive? Different career paths? Conflicting religious beliefs? The controlling ways of Olive's mother? A culmination of everything? Whatever it was, in hindsight for Olive, George O'Brien was "the one who got away." After their break-up, Olive was seen out on the town with director Marshall Neilan and producer Paul Bern, but neither relationship was very serious. (Source: conversations with Ralph Graves, Jr.)

For most of her life, Olive lived with her "stage mother," Sibbie. Sibbie lost her husband (Olive's father) to typhoid fever early in their marriage, along with an infant daughter; Olive was now all Sibbie had. Her over-protectiveness stemmed from her fear of losing her — to her career, to a man, to death. Eventually, it would be one of those three.

While Hollywood adored her daughter, Sibbie was also adored because she was the mother of Olive Borden. If Sibbie was happy, Olive was happy — and vice versa. Both women lapped up the attention. They went everywhere together — parties, film premieres, costume fittings, location shooting, the film set. If Olive was there, you could be sure that Sibbie wasn't far behind. It was more than apparent that Sibbie was living vicariously through her daughter, but Olive didn't seem to mind. Despite being a grown woman with a feature film contract and a flourishing acting career, Olive still looked to her mother for advice and support in all areas of her life.

One topic that mother and daughter agreed upon was how to spend money as quickly as it was earned. Clothes, shoes, jewelry, antiques, maids, cars; just about everything that money could buy — Olive bought it. But her lavish spending soon caught up with her. When her salary slowed, her spending hastened, and eventually she was forced to downgrade her house, sell her furniture, her jewelry, even her collection of fur coats. Piece by piece, her career, her lifestyle, her money, her pride — all of it was slowly stripped away. This is Olive Borden's story. It has everything.

Everything but the fairy tale ending...

Part I

The Life

CHAPTER 1

Borden Family Tree:
The "Olive" Branch

Olive Mary Borden was born on July 14, 1906, in either Richmond or Norfolk, Virginia, six days before her mother's twenty-second birthday. She was baptized at St. Patrick's Cathedral in Baltimore, Maryland, on September 9, 1906; baby Olive was almost two months old. Her mother Cecilia (sometimes Sybil) Agnes Shields Borden (known as "Sibbie") was born on July 20, 1884, in Norfolk. Olive's father, Harry Robinson Borden, was born some time in 1879, in Fall River, Massachusetts.

Harry's mother (Olive's paternal grandmother), Elizabeth R. Hood (known as "Lizzie"), married Arba Borden on December 31, 1871, and the marriage lasted for about eight and a half years, until her death on July 8, 1880, at thirty years of age.

On November 9, 1884, Arba remarried. His second wife, Canadian born Mary J. Kearney, was only fifteen years old when they wed — not unusually young for the times. However, Arba was thirty-two, more than double his new bride's age. Mary and Arba had three children together. Harry, Olive's father, was almost six years old when his teenage stepmother gave birth to his baby sister. She and her two brothers would be Harry's half siblings: Olive, born February 1886, Arba, born June 26, 1890, and William A. Borden, born February 1893. Harry's father, Arba, died some time before 1910. His wife Mary is listed as a widow in census records after that year.

Looking over the Borden family tree, it appears that Olive was a favorite name passed down through the years. Olive's paternal grandmother was Olive M. Hewitt (born about 1825), and her paternal aunt, her father's half sister, was also named Olive (born February 1886).

Olive's mother, known as Sibbie, was twenty-one and her father, Harry, was twenty-six when they married in Norfolk City on December 22, 1905. The license states that neither had been married previously, and they were both residents of Norfolk. Harry's current occupation was listed as "cook." Harry's parents, Arba and Elizabeth Borden (nee Hood), and Sibbie's parents, Frank (Francis) and Winnifred Shields, were all named on the document.

Looking at the December 22, 1905, date of Sibbie and Harry's wedding, it's a little under seven months to the day of Olive's birth (July 14, 1906). Presumably Sibbie was about two months pregnant with Olive when she married Harry. Pregnancy before marriage was a scandalous, reputation-ruining predicament during those conservative times; and despite Harry making an honest woman of her, Sibbie's "delicate condition" prior to her wedding explains the falsified 1907 birth date that Olive and her mother maintained during Olive's Hollywood years.

Olive being one year younger would protect both of them from the inevitable vindictive chatter and media coverage that would surely ensue if the truth were revealed. "No one could prove them wrong because the occasion of Olive's birth happened 'conveniently' during a year when the state of Virginia didn't legally require the registration of births and deaths. Their little secret was safe. Actually, it was the first of many secrets," said family friend Ralph Graves, Jr.

Olive used her baptismal certificate, dated September 9, 1906, to apply for a delayed birth certificate in 1942. The document was most likely applied for that year because it was needed for her enlistment in the Army. Olive's career was over by the mid–1930s so the revelation of her real birth year would have no significant effect on her livelihood or reputation. By 1942, Olive was making the papers as a former star who was about to join the Army. Apart from that news, the media and the public had little interest in Olive Borden, let alone her true birth year.

Canadian Prime Minister Sir Robert Laird Borden; he and Olive were fifth cousins, three times re-moved.

Aside from her own eventual fame, Olive has some very famous (and infamous) relatives on her father's (Borden) side of the family. She was fourth cousin, four times removed

Silver screen icon Marilyn Monroe; she and Olive were ninth cousins.

Lana Turner before she went blonde. As a brunette she certainly resembles Olive, who was her eighth cousin.

to Gail Borden, the inventor of condensed milk in the 1850s and founder of the Borden Milk Company. The company is still in business.

She was fifth cousin, three times removed to Sir Robert Laird Borden, the eighth prime minister of Canada (October 10, 1911 to July 10, 1920). His portrait is on the Canadian $100 bill. She was also a ninth cousin to Sir Winston Churchill, British prime minister from 1940 to 1945 and again from 1951 to 1955. Olive was an eighth cousin to "The Sweater Girl," Lana Turner, and a ninth cousin to sex goddess Marilyn Monroe (www.ancestry. com).

But, perhaps the biggest discovery of all; Olive was related to one of America's most infamous women — Lizzie Borden! In a rare genealogical occurrence, Olive and Lizzie Borden are related as cousins in not one, but *four* different ways. Lizzie (birth name: Lizbeth Andrew Borden) and Olive are fourth cousins, two times removed through Penelope Read. They are sixth cousins, two times removed through their common ancestors, John Borden and Mary Walker Earle. They are seventh cousins, three times removed through their common ancestors, Ralph Earle and Joan Savage. They are seventh cousins, two times removed through their common ancestors, Richard Borden and Joan Fowle.

Lizzie Borden (1860–1927) was accused of the brutal axe murders of her wealthy father and stepmother on August 4, 1892, in Fall River, Massachusetts. A publicity-hungry reporter penned the below verse to sell newspapers. To this day, over one hundred years since the murders occurred, the catchy ditty is still widely known by the general public:

British Prime Minister Sir Winston Churchill; he and Olive were ninth cousins.

Olive's infamous axe-wielding cousin, Lizzie Borden (1860–1927).

> Lizzie Borden took an axe
> And gave her mother forty whacks.
> When she saw what she had done,
> She gave her father forty-one.

The macabre wording did nothing to deter children across the country from singing the catchy rhyme as they jumped rope and played in schoolyards. In reality, the verse was a slight exaggeration of the truth; nevertheless, the bloody slayings were nothing less than horrific. Lizzie's stepmother, Abby Borden, suffered about nineteen blows of the axe, her father, Andrew Jackson Borden, suffered eleven. Although eventually acquitted of the gruesome murders (due to a lack of evidence), Lizzie was ostracized by the Fall River community. Until a 1904 arrest for shoplifting, she lived a relatively reclusive life. Actress Elizabeth Montgomery (also a real-life cousin to Lizzie Borden and Olive) portrayed Lizzie in the critically acclaimed 1975 television movie, *The Legend of Lizzie Borden* ("The Bewitching Family Tree of Elizabeth Montgomery," James Pylant, *Genealogy Magazine*, 2004).

On her mother's ("Shields") side of the family, Olive was the great-grand niece of Civil War hero General James Shields. In yet another Hollywood connection, Olive's first cousin, actress Natalie Joyce, was the daughter of her mother's sister. Olive and Natalie looked so much alike, they were often mistaken for sisters. Olive's family roots can be traced back to the sixteenth century when her Spanish ancestors were cast up on the Irish coast during the destruction of the Spanish Armada (www.ancestry.com).

Olive's lookalike cousin, Natalie Joyce (1902–1992). She voluntarily retired from films in the early 1930s to marry William Morris Pryce, Jr., and raise a family. She died in San Diego, California, three days after her ninetieth birthday.

It's uncertain if Olive knew of her connection to any of these interesting historical figures. There were many family mysteries in the Borden household. Sibbie always maintained she was a widow. That was a fact. But, during the enormous amount of media coverage spanning Olive's career, both she and Olive never mentioned Harry Borden; it was as though he never existed. A couple of small magazine snippets revealed that he had died when Olive was fourteen months old, with no elaboration about what caused his demise. Furthermore, it was always emphatically stated that Olive was an only child. With confirmation coming from two solid sources (Ralph Graves, Jr., and the 1910 census record), for the very first time it can be revealed, and proven, that Olive Borden was most certainly *not* an only child.

The 1910 census lists Olive's mother Sibbie as "Cecilia Borden — widow" and Olive M. Borden as her toddler daughter. In one column it asks, "Mother of how many children?" She answers — two! The next question is, "Number now living?" She answers — one! The head of the household is listed as Elizabeth White, a seventy-three-year-old widow with seven children, one of which is also deceased. Sibbie is listed as her niece and Olive is listed as her grand niece.

Not long after Olive's first birthday, on September 28, 1907, her father Harry succumbed to typhoid fever. He was twenty-eight years old. He was buried at St. Mary's Catholic Cemetery, Norfolk, Virginia, on October 1, 1907. He lies in an unmarked grave. No photograph of Harry Borden could be located.

By late 1907, two months before her second wedding anniversary, Sibbie was in her early twenties, widowed and grieving the loss of her husband and baby daughter. Left alone to raise Olive, she would rely on the help of family members as she drifted between odd jobs. Olive grew up never knowing her father or sister. She was less than two years old when they died so she had none of her own memories of them. Sibbie rarely spoke of them.

Ralph Graves, Jr., spent many of his childhood years getting to know Olive and her mother. They were frequent visitors to his

A portrait of Civil War hero General James Shields. Olive was his great grandniece.

father's (Ralph Sr.) home. Ralph Jr. gave personal insight into the situation surrounding Olive's late father and infant sister, saying, "Olive knew it wasn't a good idea to ask her mother too many family questions. She didn't like to talk about the past. Her overprotective behavior with Olive no doubt stemmed from the tragic loss of her husband and youngest daughter. Olive was all she had left. Right or wrong, she clung to her for dear life.

"As the years passed, Olive and her mother would become inseparable. It was the two

The 1910 census results showing Cecelia (Sibbie) Borden listed as the mother of *two* children, one living (Olive) and one deceased.

of them against the world. Her mother was very strong-minded, but it seemed, at least to me, to be a mutually dependent, loving relationship."

Olive's early childhood was spent with her Great Aunt Elizabeth; in later years, it's often stated, she lived on her maternal grandfather's Virginia plantation. It seems a little odd that Sibbie's father owned a plantation, yet his young, widowed daughter worked menial jobs (Sibbie was a saleslady in 1910 and a hotel housekeeper between 1917 and 1922) to make ends meet, and traveled to Hollywood (September 1922) with Olive on nothing more than a few dollars and a dream. Furthermore, Baltimore, Maryland, and Norfolk, Virginia, census records list Frank Shields as a plumber in 1860; he was enlisted in the Marines in 1870; and he was a grocer in 1880. Ralph Graves, Jr., said, "It's entirely possible that he owned a small farm later in life, but the term 'plantation' was probably a creative Hollywood embellishment of the truth. The Hollywood publicity machine was notorious for spinning tales about their star players to the public. They did it with everyone."

Olive's childhood was somewhat nomadic. She and her mother drifted between Norfolk and Richmond; later they moved to Baltimore, where Sibbie managed a restaurant. Olive was educated in three Southern convents. At one of them, Olive fell madly in love with a male student, but as a *Modesto-News Herald* article ("That Old Sweetheart O'Mine!" February 11, 1928) stated, "[The] girls and boys were kept strictly separated, [so Olive] never had a chance to meet her first crush, the object of her admiration, whom she saw only through the bars of her convent window."

As a young girl Olive started her education at St. Michaels School in Baltimore. When the new grade school opened in 1920, she moved on to the Sacred Heart School of Norfolk.

Father Waters invited the Daughters of Charity from Emmitsburg, Maryland, to teach in the new school and 180 students were enrolled in grades one through eight in that inaugural year. Sister Ariana was principal and taught sixth, seventh, and eighth grades. The first graduates of Sacred Heart School, according to their records, were Margaret Britt, Julia Forrest, Anita Cofer, Margaret Stevenson and Olive Borden (www.sacredheartnorfolk.org).

Olive went on to finish her education at Mt. St. Agnes Academy, an exclusive school for girls in Mt. Washington, Maryland. Sibbie often worked two jobs to ensure that Olive was educated in the very best schools. She was a popular student: a champion swimmer, tennis player and captain of the girl's basketball team. She spoke fluent French, played the piano, and enjoyed singing blues songs and acting in school plays. Little did she know that the latter would be a vocation that would take her to Hollywood and make her rich, famous, poor and forgotten — all before her thirtieth birthday.

CHAPTER 2

Hollywood, the Early Years

By September 1922, the bright lights of Hollywood and the fame and fortune that it promised was enough of a lure for sixteen-year-old Olive and her mother to take the gamble and head west. Emotionally, physically and financially, it was a big leap to take. As a *Photoplay* (undated 1926) article stated, "The Bordens — just mother and daughter, for Dad died when Olive was a baby — were not poor. Nor were they wealthy. They were at that brave stage where dollars are counted twice, and a roast, after the third day, is made into a stew."

Throughout her schooling, Olive was a competent student, very athletic, and popular with her classmates, but she got bored easily. Shortly after her sixteenth birthday, she abruptly told her mother that she was done with school. Her mother, no stranger to indulging her daughter's whims, supported her decision *but*, this time it came with some advice: "If you won't go to school, you must work, Olive. I do not believe in idling. Work is the most vital thing in life, if you love what you are doing. Tell me what you want to do, and I shall see that you do it" (*Motion Picture Magazine,* untitled article, June 1926).

Olive had always had a dramatic streak. When she said she wanted to be a Hollywood actress, her mother wasn't the least bit surprised. But before Olive tried her luck as a professional actress, she was desperate to go to the Annapolis Prom. Without thinking of the costs involved, she casually told her mother she'd go to the prom, and from there they'd travel to New York for acting auditions. But for Olive to go to the prom, she needed a new dress and shoes. Then there were the traveling expenses involved for their trip to New York. They couldn't afford to do both and Sibbie told Olive she would have to choose. "Not that way [to New York], my dear. We will do things correctly. If you want to go into pictures, we will go to Hollywood. But it will be the prom *or* Hollywood. Which?" There was no decision to make; Hollywood won hands down.

Olive and her mother had both read the sad, deplorable tales of the innumerable girls who took their high hopes and their confident hearts to Hollywood, and who ended up in the cap and apron of a waitress or the ticket booth of a theater. Almost everyone working in the city of Hollywood was an actor or actress, whether they were "acting" or not. Olive and her mother read the movie fan magazines religiously and they knew that beauty flocked to Hollywood — daily. They also knew that many are called and few are chosen. As pretty as her daughter was, Sibbie knew the chances of her hitting the big time were slim. But she was ready to gamble the little money they had on Olive's will to at least try. As they packed their bags, Sibbie chose not to build up her daughter's hopes of succeeding. "It is probably better for you to know disappointment, disillusion and dregs now than later on, when recovery will be more difficult," she said (*Motion Picture Magazine*, July 1927).

The odds were stacked against her, but Olive desperately wanted to be a movie star; and at first it appeared that she would be luckier than most Hollywood hopefuls. Olive and her mother arrived in Hollywood on a Tuesday and by Thursday of that same week she had landed a small part in a comedy at the Christie Studios. It seemed too good to be true. It was.

Olive was directed to do an imitation of a popular leading lady of the day, Lila Lee. With no professional training or acting experience to draw upon, she romped all over the stage and grimaced into the camera. After three days of work, the director let her go. He was brutal in his assessment of her acting attempt: "You'll never be an actress! Go back to school! Go anywhere! But go away!" ("Chicken Southern-Style," *Photoplay*, March 1926). Olive was crushed. "That night I went home to Mother and wept my first tears of disappointment and discouragement," she later said ("Olive Borden: The Joy Girl of the Silent Screen — Part I," Michael Ankerich, *Classic Images* #185, November 1990). Just a few months later, in a June 1926 issue of *Motion Picture Magazine*, Olive told a different account of her failure at Christie Studios.

On her first day, as some of the nicer girls saw Olive struggling with her makeup, they stepped in to help her. "I didn't understand [the makeup]," she said. "I'd never even used powder before, so it was all wrong. After that day, one of the girls told me the studio thought I was terrible, so I marched out and didn't go back. I played an extra at various places, and one day I met a man from Christie's who asked me why I hadn't come back — and it turned out to be all a mistake."

Olive went back to Christie Studios but she only stayed four months. She figured she was being wasted on the comedy lot. Her work there mostly involved her filling up the background, amongst other hopefuls, in the crowd scenes. "I asked for more money and they didn't give it to me," Olive recalled. "I said I'd leave on Saturday unless I got a raise. I didn't get the raise so I had to leave."

Without doubt, Olive's long jet-black hair, dark exotic features and flawless figure put her in good stead for a career in front of the cameras. But with no experience, no connections, and only her good looks and a burning desire to succeed to carry her, Olive pounded the pavement with youthful determination, looking for work. "Sorry, nothing today," the personnel at the casting offices would tell her. The rounds became circuitous and tiresome. There were so many pretty girls — confident girls in limousines and furs and "creations," girls with maids and secretaries and "tips" and things. Hundreds and hundreds of them, each one, it seemed to Olive, more beautiful and more assured than the one before ("Seventy-Five Cents and a Made-Over Dress," *Motion Picture Magazine*, July 1927).

Olive would soak her throbbing, blistered feet in warm salt water each night in preparation for the grueling next day of rejections. Incidentally, Olive was reported to have had the smallest feet in Hollywood. Her 5' 1½" frame weighed a petite 100 pounds and her shoes were specially made to fit her dainty 1½ double A foot ("Film Stars Feet Grow Larger in Ten Years," *Oakland Tribune*, March 10, 1930). While her feet *were* small, they don't appear to be unusually tiny on film or in production photographs (see Olive's bare feet in *Fig Leaves* stills). Women's shoe sizing has changed over the years.

With no work in sight and no money coming in, Olive's mother got desperate and invested the remainder of their savings in a modest confectionary store. An article titled "My Favorite Dish" in *The Hartford Courant* (May 25, 1930) included Sibbie's "Bon Bon" recipe. At the time of the printing, Olive had made it in the movies but she fondly remembered her mother's glorious candy recipes. For holidays, Sibbie would still make some of her famous sweets for the family; each Christmas she would make batches upon batches, pack them in pretty little boxes and distribute them among friends. Olive preferred a special bon bon that she also learned to make. The ingredients were:

1 white of egg

1–2 tablespoons of cold water

3–4-teaspoons of vanilla

2 cups confectionary sugar

Flavoring and coloring as preferred

Olive explained the process: "Put the white of the egg into a bowl and add the water and flavoring. Mix well together. Sift the sugar twice, then add it to the egg mixture, dropping in a spoonful at a time which you fold in well before you add the next spoonful. By the time the sugar is dropped in entirely, the mixture should be beaten into a stiff froth. Pour it out on a board and knead like dough. Shape and color the delicacy as you please."

The Bordens' candy store was near the southern branch of the University of California. Olive sold the lollipops and weighed out the assorted candy. "I stood behind the counter and sold lollipops to hungry students," Olive said. "But lollipops are expensive and students have little money, so after six months we found that most of our transactions were down in red inks in the books" (*How I Broke Into the Movies,* Hal Herman, Yesteryear Press, 1984). The business barely lasted six months. When the store closed, the Borden women were in worse financial shape than ever before.

As the shutters on the candy store closed for the very last time, Olive and her mother had seventy-five cents between them. Olive had a $7.50 (converts to approximately $85 in 2009) studio voucher for a day of extra work but it couldn't be cashed in for another six days.

With the failed business behind them, Olive was determined more than ever before to succeed in the movies. She continued to look for film work on a daily basis. With rejection after rejection coming her way, there was little money to live on and food became sparse. Olive insisted her mother eat her (Olive's) small helping each evening. Olive claimed she wasn't hungry, convincing her mother that she had eaten something while she was out. She had not. After weeks of looking for work and with barely enough food to get her through each day, Olive became so weak that she collapsed in her mother's arms and was confined to her bed. She was diagnosed with severe malnutrition.

Career-wise, it was perhaps the best thing to happen to Olive. A publicity man heard of this "starving" wannabe actress, so desperate to succeed and with so little money she couldn't

An early publicity photograph of Olive.

afford to buy food, that he had to meet her. He tracked her down and afterwards made a point to visit Olive and her mother on a regular basis. Each time he called on the women, he brought a basket of food along. In an attempt to keep their pride intact, the publicity man insisted that he'd be glad to eat with them so long as they cooked the food he brought. He couldn't cook and they couldn't afford to buy enough food *to* cook, so it was an arrangement that put smiles on the faces of all three of them. Within a few weeks Olive was stronger, healthier and had gained a few much-needed pounds — along with a new friend (source: conversations with Ralph Graves, Jr.).

Olive's next film role was in the dramatic feature *Ponjola* (1923), starring Anna Q. Nilsson and James Kirkwood. Olive, uncredited in a bit part, is seen fluttering about with streaked makeup and sad, darkened eyes. She stood out all right, just not the way she intended to! The film's cinematographer, Paul Perry, took her aside and told her to never again hide the smooth lusciousness of her perfect skin. She remembered his advice for the rest of her career.

According to a *Motion Picture Magazine* article (July 1927), someone suggested that Olive try for a part in the "Screen Writers Revue." She tried twice and failed. A kindly girl at the office of application said to her, "Say, Olive, you look too much like a kid. Why don't you put your hair up and dress older and slap on a little makeup?"

Olive thought it over and decided the girl was right. She and her mother went right to work and experimented with different hairstyles. They decided to showcase Olive's cascading black hair and achieved an effect they were both happy with. Next, Sibbie made over a three-year-old dress, cut up a set of Olive's little-girl furs to trim it with, and spent a few cents on lipstick. This time, as an adult, Olive got the Revue.

On April 27 and 28, 1923, the Writer's Review of 1923 at the Philharmonic Auditorium was billed as a "musical-comedy extravaganza." Olive starred in the number "The Shadow of the Pyramids" and for a newcomer, she was in good company. Anna May Wong, Colleen Moore, May MacAvoy, Laura La Plante and Virginia Fox, among others, were part of the same act.

By 1923, Olive had been contracted as one of Mack Sennett's Bathing Beauties. It was an honor given to many of Hollywood's prettiest rising starlets. With Sennett, Olive got between two and four days work a week. It helped buy food and clothes and restore self-confidence! She had weathered her storm of bad luck and was now on her way to becoming a legitimate actress.

In her autobiography *On the Other Hand: A Life Story* (St. Martin's Press, 1989), *King Kong*'s leading lady Fay Wray recalled a day when she was visiting the Sennett studio lot in the early 1920s. "I saw a beautiful brunette girl walking with two men on each side of her. She looked straight at me and smiled a beautiful, friendly smile. My mixed feelings were that she was perhaps a careless kind of person but that she was probably so happy being a movie star that she loved absolutely everybody, including strangers. Her name was Olive Borden, and she was a leading lady of silent films, as well as of the early talkies."

Olive's jet-black hair, milky porcelain complexion and knockout figure were hard to miss; yet despite her exotic beauty she certainly had her fair share of rejections before getting her big break. If Olive had one flaw, she was a little on the "toothy" side but this minor distraction could be easily overcome if she kept her lips together when she smiled. This trivial imperfection did nothing to hamper her film career; in fact, Olive is now acknowledged as being one of the most beautiful actresses of the silent era. She was also one of the youngest actresses to reach leading lady status during the 1920s.

Olive's apprenticeship with Sennett had served her well. By mid–1924, after minor roles in three Jack White shorts (*Neck and Neck, Wide Open* and *Air Pockets*), she was offered a contract with Hal Roach Studios. Olive would appear in a string of comedy creations, most notably in the Spat Family series of shorts, and with her popularity increasing with each new release, she very smartly hired well-respected press agent and eventual radio commentator, Jimmie Fiddler, to represent her.

After she left Christie Studios, before her shorts with Jack White and Hal Roach, Olive said, "I had a terrible all-gone feeling after I'd left. It seemed that I had done a dreadful thing. And I hadn't been out [of work] very long before we found that Mother had invested all our savings in something [the candy store] that lost us every cent. Then it was the case of get something — not try to get it, but

A "toothy" 1920s newspaper caricature of Olive.

A rare original glass movie preview slide for the 1924 short *Neck and Neck.* Olive is pictured on the left with Lige Conley standing next to her. Peggy O'Neil is on the right. This slide is historically significant in Olive's career because it's the first promotional film item that her image ever appeared on.

get it!" I worked wherever I could find anything. I got into the Hal Roach lot and stayed for nine months [March 1924–January 1925], playing vamps, leads, ingénues — all three in my last picture there. The WAMPAS wanted me to be a baby star, and [Hal Roach Studios] wouldn't let me. Mother said: 'We'll see if you can't be a baby star!' and I walked off the lot and became one" ("If You Love Your Work," *Motion Picture Magazine*, June 1926).

On January 22, 1925, it was announced that Olive was chosen as one of the WAMPAS Baby Stars of 1925. WAMPAS (The Western Association of Motion Picture Advertisers) was an organization of movie publicity men who annually selected relatively unknown starlets of the silver screen with the prediction they'd become major stars. The WAMPAS Frolic was an annual party held between 1922 and 1934 (the awards were not given in 1930 and 1933 because of objections of its independence by the movie studios). The starlets were honored at this event and many of them did indeed go on to become leading ladies. In 1925, Olive was selected as one of those future stars along with twelve other potential actresses.

Beth Arlen (the only Baby Star to never make a film), Violet Avon (aka Violet La Plante), Natalie Joyce (Olive's lookalike cousin), Anne Cornwall, Lola Todd, Ena Gregory, Madeline Herlock, June Marlowe, Joan Meredith (aka Catherine Jelks), Evelyn Pierce, Dorothy Revier and Duane Thompson were the rising young starlets for whom a bright future in the motion picture business was foreseen (*The Daily News*, Frederick, MD, Tuesday, January 27, 1925). It was a weak year of predictions. Few of the 1925 WAMPAS starlets had a movie career to speak of. On the contrary, 1926 was a boom year, with Mary Astor, Joan Crawford, Fay Wray and Janet Gaynor amongst the lucky thirteen WAMPAS Baby Stars.

Olive as she appeared in 1924 during her stint at Hal Roach Studios.

After Olive was made a Baby Star, director Paul Bern handpicked her to appear in a fashion scene in Leatrice Joy's *The Dressmaker from Paris* (1925). Olive and the thirteen other lucky women chosen for the scene were promoted in the press as "the fourteen most beautiful girls in the West."

During pre-production, seventy-five people approached Bern, all desperate for work. According to his secretary, he found a place for each of them. When Olive expressed concern that she couldn't afford to buy her own dress for the part, Paul bought one for her ("Tell It to Bern," *Picture Play*, 1925, p. 49). Paul showed his fondness for Olive when he cast her for a second time in his next production, *Grounds for Divorce* (1925). It was an uncredited bit part but it gave Olive the acting experience that she so desperately wanted and needed. *Grounds for Divorce* was released three months

Eleven of the thirteen WAMPAS Baby Stars of 1925. Bottom row (left to right): Violet Avon, Olive Borden, Beth Arlen, Duane Thompson, Natalie Joyce (Olive's cousin). Middle row: Dorothy Revier, Ena Gregory, Joan Meredith. Top row: Evelyn Pierce, June Marlowe, Lola Todd.

after *The Dressmaker from Paris* in the summer of 1925 ("News Notes from Movieland," *The Kingsport Times,* Kingsport, Tennessee, May 17, 1925). Five years later, Olive was often seen accompanying Bern to various Hollywood functions. It appeared to be nothing more than a casual, friendly relationship; they remained in close contact up until his untimely death two years later.

Despite the fact that Bern was seen with many of Hollywood's most beautiful leading ladies and starlets, writer Herbert Cruickshank unflatteringly described him as "a slight man, insignificant in stature, slender in shoulder, only as tall as a girl." But Bern got the last laugh. In 1932 he married sex goddess Jean Harlow, who at twenty-one was half his age. Their romance was tumultuous, short-lived, tragic and filled with more scandal and innuendo than any Hollywood script could ever invent and be believed. The dramatic events to follow became one of Hollywood's biggest scandals: Two months after his marriage to Harlow, Paul Bern was dead! The question arose: Was it murder or suicide?

Today, Bern is infamous for his controversial end and his marriage to platinum blonde bombshell Harlow. His long list of achievements in the film industry is overshadowed by his personal life (and death). While foul play was initially suspected (on September 5, 1932, he was found lying nude on the floor with a single gunshot to his head), his death was eventually ruled a "suicide." An obvious MGM cover up to keep a lid on the messy truth.

Newlyweds Paul Bern and Jean Harlow, circa 1932.

Olive was absolutely devastated by Bern's death. He was a trusted, selfless, loyal friend in an unforgiving city where all three traits were scarce. Around the same time that *The Dressmaker from Paris* was being filmed, casting for *The Happy Warrior* (1925) was underway. Director J. Stuart Blackton was desperately searching for a pretty young brunette with piercing brown eyes and a vivacious spirit. He had heard of Olive and sent for her immediately.

"I needed *The Happy Warrior* so desperately," Olive said in a June 1926 *Motion Picture Magazine* interview. "We [Olive and her mother in-between jobs] had some very low days. Mr. Blackton sat and looked at me. 'No, I don't think she'll do. She's the girl of the book all right, but she has no name.' I cried out: 'I *can* do it! Please let me show you!'

"And he did. And *I* did."

Olive in the bath in one of many risqué photograph shoots that she despised doing. The actress standing looks to be Sybil Seely, whose most notable roles were opposite Buster Keaton.

Prior to Olive's big break in *The Happy Warrior*, she only managed to snare a few extra parts that paid between $12.50 and $25 (converts to approximately $160–$315 in 2009) per week. Sometimes she got as much as $50 and $75 (converts to approx. $630–$945 in 2009) per week — but not often. In a 1926 interview, Olive's mother gave herself some credit for keeping her daughter on the right path to stardom.

"Olive has succeeded in scaling the heights by close application and serious study, but anyone who thinks it is easy is mistaken. There is a place for a girl who has brains and beauty, but she must have an abundance of pluck, and she will do much better if she has a level-headed mother with her" (*Cumberland Evening Times*, January 28, 1926). Olive's mother was *always* with her. Sibbie Borden was the classic example of a stage mother living vicariously through her daughter's achievements. But Olive didn't seem to mind.

CHAPTER 3

Who Was Sybil Tinkle?

"Olive Borden was born Sybil Tinkle..." is the line that begins almost every Olive Borden biography ever written. It proves that if a story is told often enough, the lie *becomes* the truth. The Olive Borden–Sybil Tinkle myth is a classic example.

A case of identity theft, purposeful or otherwise, has caused this misleading piece of information to circulate for decades. In fact, Olive was one of the very few Hollywood stars that rose to fame with the name she was born with.

So, why the confusion?

A young woman by the name of Sybil Tinkle made her way from Texas to Hollywood to become a star. It was the story of many. Some succeeded, most failed. Not wanting to go back home to Texas and admit defeat, Sybil had an idea. And so began the game of pretend.

A rare photograph of Sybil Tinkle. She managed to convince her Texas relatives that she had moved to Hollywood, changed her name to Olive Borden and had transformed herself into a famous film star. Photograph credit: Michael G. Ankerich.

Sybil wrote home and told her family that the studio bosses had changed her name. *She* was now Olive Borden — the movie star! Sybil was a little older than Olive, but not by much. They shared the same dark hair, petite frame and fair complexion, but a side-by-side photo comparison shows them to be two different individuals.

Sybil's family was bursting with pride. Through the art of movie makeup, the Sybil Tinkle they knew was now miraculously transformed into the Olive Borden that the whole world knew. It was a dream beyond comprehension but they truly believed she had made it big in the movies and the Tinkles followed her (Olive's) burgeoning career closely. Before long, their dedication to Sybil (Olive) proved fatal. The events that followed the tragedy would create the identity confusion that would last for decades.

When Sybil's brother, Joe Alton Tinkle, died in a 1928 car crash, ironically while driving home from a screening of an Olive Bor-

den film he truly thought his sister was starring in, the Tinkle family contacted a local
reporter and newspapers throughout Texas
ran the headlines:

Olive Borden's Brother Dies in Car Crash.
Bank Teller, Brother of Star Killed.
Auto Accident Fatal to City Bank Teller,
Kin of Olive Borden.

And perhaps the headline that started the
myth:

Death Reveals Identity of a Noted Actress.

All of the articles claimed that the sister
of the dead man, Olive Borden, was born Sybil
Tinkle in Texas. Local newspapers reported,
"Miss Borden was notified of her brother's
death, but will not return to Texas for the
funeral" (*Houston Press* and other local Texas
papers, April 1928).

Film fan Lee Bailey of Houston saw the
local headlines. She figured it was her public
duty to set the record straight and "out"
Olive's real identity to the Hollywood community. And what better way to do that than

Another rare photograph of Sybil Tinkle.
Photograph credit: Michael G. Ankerich.

to write a letter to the editor of one of Hollywood's biggest fan magazines, *Photoplay*? Ironically, Bailey started out by praising the magazine for giving its readers reliable, correct
answers to their questions, then went on to state (in the April 26, 1928, issue) that Olive
Borden was born in Timpson, Texas, under the name of Sybil Tinkle! Continuing with erro-
neous information about her also living in Lufkin, Texas, and "proving" her statements by
attaching an article from the *Houston Press* (April 23, 1928) reporting on Joe's fatal car accident, Bailey encouraged *Photoplay* to investigate and confirm her story by contacting any
Houston paper for more information.

Bailey proudly wrote that she was "so glad another Texas girl is on the screen" and said
that the state was very well represented out Hollywood way. She said she'd put Joan Crawford, Florence Vidor, Bebe Daniels, Madge Bellamy, Eve Southern, Dorothy Devore, Hope
Hampton, Allene Ray, Jacqueline Logan, Corinne Griffith "and Olive Borden up against
the beauties of any other states!!!"

In all fairness, Bailey's letter to *Photoplay* magazine was based on reports in local Texas
newspapers so she was only relaying what she thought to be true. Little did she know that
her letter, together with some incorrect reporting (thanks to the Tinkle family), would have
enough momentum to muddy Olive's biography for over *sixty* years.

Those who knew Sybil in her pre–Hollywood days remembered her to be a "peculiar"
girl who had a burning desire to become a motion picture actress. They say she was the first
girl in Timpson to smoke and often painted outdoors, clad only in lingerie ("Olive Borden: The Sybil Tinkle Connection," Michael Ankerich, *Classic Images* #209, November 1992).

A beautiful mid–20s era photograph of Olive at the piano.

Census records unequivocally place a young Olive in Virginia and a young Sybil in Texas. Michael Ankerich, author of the article cited above, concluded, "By close examination and through extensive research and interviews with Borden and Tinkle family members, it's clear that Olive Borden and Sybil Tinkle were two different individuals." It took over six decades, but Ankerich's thorough investigation and subsequent *Classic Images* article conclusively cleared up the matter. It was posthumous, but Olive finally got her identity back.

When news of Olive's death made the papers in 1947, Sybil's family thought Sybil had died. Her grieving brother and nephew made their way to Hollywood for her funeral. Once there, a two-decade lie was uncovered: To their horror, they learned that Olive Borden was *not* Sybil Tinkle after all. Confused but undaunted, they continued to search for "their Sybil." After some further investigating, a staff member at a hotel she had been staying at told them she was taken to a TB hospital in California. They were never able to find her.

Years later, the Tinkle family home in Texas burned to the ground. They were only able to salvage a few photos of Sybil. After Olive's death, many members of the Tinkle family still chose to believe that the real Olive Borden was "their Sybil" and related to them. They mourned Olive as their own.

When Sybil concocted the story to "become" Olive, it was a tale woven by a troubled young woman for no other purpose than to make her family proud of her. She had no reason to believe it would go any further than that. However, after the Tinkle family contacted the media following her brother's untimely death — everything changed.

It's not known if Olive knew of the identity mess. At least, she never commented on it publicly; neither did her mother or studio representatives.

CHAPTER 4

"Mix"-ing It Up

Following her lead role in *The Happy Warrior* (1925), Olive was immediately cast in *The Overland Limited* (1925). These two productions introduced Olive to feature film roles. Olive was now nineteen and well on her way to making a legitimate career for herself in the movie industry. One article described her as a "typically southern girl with a rich contralto voice. She drawls her 'a's' and drops her 'r's'" (*The Weekly Kansas City Star*, Wednesday, July 29, 1925). Her distinctive drawl did her more harm than good during her transition from silent to sound films — at least initially. After some serious voice coaching by the wife of director Paul Sloane, her accent was virtually undetectable.

Tom Mix embracing Olive in *The Yankee Señor* (1926). The popular cowboy personality (and top male box office star of 1926) handpicked Olive to be his female lead in the film.

Olive's first film release for 1926 was *The Yankee Señor* with leading man Tom Mix. He particularly wanted a brown-eyed beauty as his leading lady and after seeing Olive in *The Overland Limited* he handpicked her for *The Yankee Señor*. And, she seemed to be a good choice. *The Film Spectator* (March 20, 1926) gave Olive a glowing review: "[Mix] had a fine supporting cast with Olive Borden shining particularly. She portrayed her part as a poor, but proud Mexican girl very convincingly."

Professionally, it would be a big year for Olive as she appeared in six films. The first was anything but an easy shoot. The entire cast of *The Yankee Señor* underwent many days of pain when extremely bright lights were made necessary for the Technicolor sequences. Mix, Margaret Livingston, Kathryn Hill and other members of the cast were badly affected. Olive and Francis McDonald also endured eye pain and headaches, but to a lesser degree. The Technicolor scenes were photographed in

Olive as Manuelita strikes up a conversation with her leading man (Tom Mix as Paul Wharton) in *The Yankee Señor* (1926).

An original newspaper ad for *My Own Pal* (1926).

Olive as Saina with Nigel de Brulier as Rajah Jagore in a scene from *Yellow Fingers* (1926).

a huge Spanish patio built on glass on the Fox lot. In order to obtain the correct lighting arrangements, the production called for eight thousand amperes. Under ordinary circumstances, two thousand amperes would be used. For the better part of two days, Mix and his castmates faced the relentless glare at close range. Mix, Livingston, McDonald, and Olive were obligated to do a lot of dancing in these scenes. There were countless closeup shots and much rehearsing. Many in the cast endured intense pain and it was necessary to administer first aid. At night they were unable to sleep; ice packs were used to help with burning eyes and painful heads. Many of the several hundred extras employed for the fiesta scene were similarly affected; some resorted to wearing dark glasses between scenes. Electricians on the set attributed the pain to carbon fumes, unusually strong lights and intense heat. Despite the discomfort, none of the cast would stop work and, miraculously, the picture was eventually completed ahead of schedule (*Hamilton Evening Journal*, August 21, 1926).

In Olive's next film, *My Own Pal* (1926), she once again starred opposite screen favorite Tom Mix. Olive got little to no mention in many of the New York newspaper reviews. Some of the smaller papers thought she was worthy of a few words; *The Morning Herald* (Hagerstown, Maryland, April 29, 1926) said, "Olive Borden plays the very modern little niece of the chief of police. She will be remembered as the fiery and stubborn little Senorita."

While filming her next picture, *Yellow Fingers* (1926), Olive almost drowned during a scene where her character, Saina, wanders aimlessly toward the ocean. An unexpected wave crashed shoreward and knocked Olive off her feet and into the vast body of water. There was a moment of absolute silence amongst the crew as they watched their petite leading lady get washed out to sea like a helpless rag doll. Olive's mother and the film's director, Emmett Flynn, simultaneously threw themselves into the water to rescue her.

Olive recalled the incident in a June issue of *Motion Picture Magazine*:

> It was during this last terrible storm on the Pacific. We were on location in Catalina. The sea was so rough that the big steamers couldn't dock, but moving pictures can't wait for weather. They had me down at the edge of the island where the rocks stick up in the sea. In the story, I have just discovered I'm Eurasian — my lover has left me and I am frantically trying to wash the color off.
>
> There I was tearing my clothes off as directed, leaning down and bathing my arms in the surf, when along came a wave as big as a house and carried me out to sea. Mother jumped right in, clothes and all, after me. Two of the boys in the company dived in after her — and a thrilling rescue was had by all.

Despite being in shock, badly bruised and soaked to the skin, Olive insisted on finishing the scene and she did! ("Miss Borden Has Narrow Escape in Film Scene," *The Daily News*, July 12, 1926).

During the filming of *Yellow Fingers*, Olive said she had no idea why little boys love

Olive (far right) in another scene from *Yellow Fingers* (1926). Armand Kaliz is seated next to her; the other actors are unidentified. The film was reviewed favorably by the critics.

Like a cobra, Olive seductively emerges from a wicker basket in a publicity still for *Yellow Fingers* (1926).

to run around barefoot all the time because her feet were sore and blistered from hours of dancing minus shoes and stockings on the rough pavement for several sequences in the film (*Hamilton Evening Journal*, June 5, 1926, p. 6).

The September 4, 1926, *Hollywood Spectator* reviewed *Yellow Fingers*: "The film is well staged and provides entertainment of the mildly diverting variety. Emmett Flynn's direction is quite satisfactory. Olive Borden worked well within the limits set for her by those who drew the character. She is possessed with considerable dramatic fervor and in a few years perhaps will give some fine performances of big parts. She is pleasing to look at, but does not possess beauty of the classic sort that has assisted others to achieve fame beyond what their abilities and their few years entitled them to."

After starring in two back-to-back Tom Mix films, Olive was finally getting the exposure that she needed for her career to take off. If she was good enough to stand alone as a leading lady and actually carry a film, now was the time to prove it; and she did. In fact, it was her portrayal of Saina, the Malay half-caste in *Yellow Fingers*, that made critics and audiences sit up and take notice. The *Hamilton Evening Journal* (June 26, 1926) enthusiastically described Olive's personality on screen by saying she was "an actress of the intensely emotional type — joyous and vivacious when the scene calls for impetus and animated action. She could be moody, sad, whimsical and sparkling — all of those emotions were possible according to the type of character she was portraying."

The original glass movie preview slide for *Yellow Fingers* (1926).

Olive in a pensive pose from *Yellow Fingers* (1926).

"To me," Olive explained, "the girls in the picture are real living people. I always try to put myself in their position and imagine how they would feel under the same circumstances. Then I act accordingly. Take little Saina, for example. She has been reared by an indulgent foster father who had pledged his word to her own father, his best friend, that the little girl would grow up to believe she was all white. Both men thought they were doing the right thing — that they were sparing her sorrow and a feeling of disgrace, but they had failed to take into consideration the sharp tongues of the villagers and the working of fate. I put myself into Saina's place, mentally, before going into the scene; in fact ever since the picture started I've lived the character of Saina."

At just nineteen years old, Olive had already made a name for herself as a popular leading lady. But nothing had prepared her for her next role. Both personally and professionally, it would take her young life in a whole new direction.

CHAPTER 5

3 Bad Men ... and One Good One!

Director John Ford was casting his next film, and there was much discussion about who would play the female lead. "How about using the little girl who played with Tom [Mix] — the Borden girl — for the feminine lead in Ford's next picture?" queried a Fox Studio official after seeing Olive's performance in the Mix picture ("Chicken — Southern Style," *Photoplay*, March, 1926). And there it was, Olive was given the female lead in *3 Bad Men* (1926), an epic silent Western, with George O'Brien as her co-star.

"In this picture," Olive said, "I played with such seasoned troupers as J. Farrell Mac-Donald, Frank Campeau, Tom Santschi and Alex Francis. A long-term contract followed, and now, every time I want to feel real serious I buy a lollipop. It makes me feel like Hamlet soliloquizing over the skull in the graveyard." Director Ford was thrilled to have Olive

January 22, 1926: Posing with glasses, pipe and hat, Olive spoofs her *3 Bad Men* (1926) director John Ford in this candid Fox publicity still.

cast in his latest picture and he had high hopes for his leading lady, saying, "Watch that little girl. She has ability and pluck. Some day she will do big things — or I'm not a prophet!" (*How I Broke Into the Movies*, Hal Herman, Yesteryear Press, 1984).

Ford's best (and last) silent Western, *3 Bad Men* was originally intended as a co-starring vehicle for Fox's three big action stars, Tom Mix, Buck Jones and George O'Brien; it emerged with O'Brien as the nominal hero and character actors Santschi, Campeau and MacDonald in the larger roles of the title. With a beautifully staged land rush as its highlight, *3 Bad Men* was a unique blending of the austere and the traditional with the romanticized and the streamlined.

3 Bad Men was Ford's forty-third Western, and it would be his last for thirteen years. His success in other areas (Americana, high adventure, crime) plus the apparent decline of the Western's popularity when sound came in, removed him from the genre for the balance of his contract with Fox. Not until his classic

Stagecoach (1939) did Ford return to the Western genre (*A Pictorial History of the Western Film*, William K. Everson, Citadel Press, 1969).

Orson Welles was once asked to name the three best directors in the history of Hollywood, "I like the old masters," he said, "by which I mean, John Ford, John Ford and ... John Ford." Frank Capra said of Ford, "Jack is half-tyrant, half-revolutionary; half-saint; half–Satan; half–possible; half–impossible; half–genius; half–Irish — but all director and all–American" (*You Must Remember This*, Walter Wagner, G. P. Putnam's Sons, 1975). With Ford as her director and George O'Brien as her leading man, Olive was in the most capable hands. All the ingredients were in place to make a masterpiece, and they did.

Olive was cast as Lee Carlton, the daughter of a Southerner who had come west to seek his fortune. The plot revolves around the eponymous three bad men: Bull Stanley (Santschi), Mike Costigan (MacDonald), and Spade Allen (Campeau). This trio of outlaws, on the lam from the law for robbery and horse theft, befriend Lee moments after her father has been murdered. Settling down with her rescuers, Lee awaits the day of the land rush with a map marking gold deposits. Genuinely caring for Lee and concerned about her welfare, the three men go husband-hunting on her behalf, after first ascertaining that none of them fit the bill. They settle on charming Irishman Dan O'Malley (George O'Brien), a

Olive, J. Farrell MacDonald and George O'Brien in a publicity still for the John Ford Western, *3 Bad Men* (1926).

John Ford, director of *3 Bad Men* (1926), contemplates a scene while on location.

handsome young settler looking for work. The three bad men ultimately sacrifice their lives so that Lee and Dan can reach the promised land. A flash-forward to the couple's happy future includes a ranch and a young son, watched over by the ghosts of his namesakes (*How the West Was Sung: Music in the Westerns of John Ford*, Kathryn Kalinak, University of California Press, September 2007).

The June 1926 issue of *Picture-Play* magazine published a very informative "letter from location" written by Olive during the filming of *3 Bad Men*. She starts with, "Here I am far from sunny Hollywood, in the great primeval, where boulevard stops, traffic cops and cushion roads are unknown, and I love it."

Olive explained that it was her very first location trip and the first time she has ever been away from telephones and bathtubs and "things like that." She admitted she was less than enthusiastic when she got there because Ford had told her such wild tales of the terrible things that still happen in the unsettled parts of the West, and she believed him. She said the Irish twinkle in his eye made her decide to wait and see for herself before getting too worked up about being robbed and kidnapped and all the other cheerful things he mentioned. "To hear him talk," she said, "you would have thought that the uncivilized Indians still scalped three people every morning before breakfast."

Olive said that the biggest thrill of the trip thus far was the last sixty-five-mile lap, made from the end of the railroad line at Victor, Idaho, to their camp at the foot of the mighty Teton mountain range. They traveled by automobile, over roads that she said "would make a good comedy gag — one of those gags where the machine falls to pieces because of the bumps — and the fastest we could 'speed' was five to seven miles an hour, on the good parts." The roads were treacherous and Olive admitted that during the trip she was sure she'd pass out several times, at least! However, the moral support of her mother, George O'Brien and Lou Tellegen saved her from a complete meltdown. Then it was time to travel over the Teton Pass, twelve thousand feet high. She was excited to see the celebrated tree where Trampas was hanged in Owen Wister's *The Virginian*. She jokingly wrote, "There I go giving publicity to Kenneth Harlan, and he works for a different company, but I don't give a rap, I just *adored* him in *The Virginian*."

Returning to the subject of the trip, Olive described how their automobile often skated around thin ledges from which it was possible to gaze over the side of the car and look at a drop straight down the cliff face. She admitted that she was far too afraid of heights to even think of doing such a thing, so she resorted to hearing the commentary of the dangerous drop from the others. With the journey behind them, as they reached the summit of the pass she did look, and from that moment on she couldn't *stop* looking. "I never will forget that sight; the magnificent Tetons, formidable and serene, with snow-capped peaks, and those tremendous valleys, broken only by the winding, twisting course of the Snake River."

Olive said she was initially a little timid about camping in a tent. She explained that at home in Norfolk, Virginia, she and her mother lived in a two-storey house, and in Hollywood, they live in an apartment. So the idea of sleeping on the ground required quite an adjustment. "But after a night or two, I got used to it and now love camp life — even the bugs."

Olive wrote that there is "so much to tell," especially about the land rush scenes, but she'd rather relate the story of how the baby was cast. She explained that Ford, being Irish,

A rare candid shot taken on the set of *3 Bad Men* (1926). Seated in the buggy are J. Farrell MacDonald, Olive and Tom Santschi. George O'Brien is leaning against the side.

tended to have a romantic side to him that was often seen throughout most of his pictures. Every now and then he would think of some little sentimental touch that he must incorporate into a scene to make it just right. And, no matter what it was, "Lefty" Hough, the property man and Ford's right-hand man, managed to find the article or person he required. During the shooting of the massive land rush scenes, Ford was directing away "like mad," she said. Thousands of teams, wagons, riders and drivers were all ready to come thundering down the pass, and the excitement and anticipation was "immense." George, Tellegen, MacDonald, Santschi, Campeau, Olive and her mother were all on the sidelines, covered in dust but thrilled to the core. As they were all excitedly talking about the stirring times of long ago when the real Dakota land rush happened, Ford suddenly yelled, "'Lefty,' where's the baby?!"

Olive said that nobody, not even Ford, had thought of a baby before that minute. Everything stopped and "Lefty" very calmly assured Ford that he would do his best to find him a baby. "You may have to wait a little while. They don't exactly grow on trees around here," he yelled back as he walked off with what seemed like an impossible request to fulfill.

Olive explained how isolated they were on location. Miles from any town, with no one under the age of eighteen in sight let alone a baby. She was sure "Lefty" would come back empty-handed. "But, I didn't know that boy," Olive said. "Lefty" traveled down the road and scouted around, and pretty soon he spotted one of those little covered wagons which prospectors used in the back country. "Lefty" hailed it and sure enough, like magic, sitting up in the front seat was a man, his wife *and a baby*. No more than a half-hour had passed since Ford's spontaneous request for a baby in the foreground of the land rush, and "Lefty" produced a dazed-looking man, a scared little wife and the sweetest baby in the world — out of nowhere. That was the moment when Olive realized that Ford got what he wanted, whenever he wanted it — no matter what!

Olive closed the letter by saying she was crazy about her role in the picture and that the "three bad men," J. Farrell MacDonald, Tom Santschi, and Frank Campeau, and all the rest of them were friendly, "perfect dears." She said that English-born Alec Francis, also in the cast, managed to make "tea hounds" out of Tom and the rest of them; "It is a riot to see those big men, dolled up like hardened pioneers, having their 'dish of tea' every afternoon." Also, "George is perfectly adorable in his role." Her last paragraph said, "Everything is lovely and we are having lots of fun, but Mr. Ford has just sent for me and I must make a flying leap into the saddle and gallop to work. With much love and say 'Hello!' to Hollywood Boulevard for me. Wildly yours, Olive Borden." She wrote a P.S.: "I can ride a horse like a veteran now," and a P.P.S.: "I also won spurs in a race. Isn't that great?"

Olive's view of her new world on location was entirely accurate. The cast and crew slept in tents, ate from chuck wagons and bathed in the river. It was the complete opposite to Olive's romanticized idea of "Hollywood glamour," but she grew to love it. Before filming on *3 Bad Men* was over (it took one year to make), Olive became romantically involved with her leading man. Unlike many of his peers, George O'Brien wasn't known as a womanizer. His relationship with Olive was serious. They were crazy about each other. As their relationship develops on screen, it was also developing off screen. The audience gets to witness a couple falling in love — for real. Unfortunately, Olive and George didn't get to experience a real-life happy ending.

Shortly before pre-production began, Olive was asked about the importance of a man being financially secure and if his bank account would sway her opinion of him. She said, "I never thought much about men folks. It would be mighty nice to have money. But the man would blot out the dollar if all I hear about love is true!" (*Oakland Tribune*, May 4, 1925).

Olive had nothing to worry about. Her new love had looks and loot! After dating steadily for some time, there were strong rumors circulating that Olive and George were engaged to be married. No one was surprised. They had many things in common, enjoyed the Hollywood social scene, were both athletic (Olive would keep fit by sprinting on a daily basis), they had a mutual understanding of the industry they both strived hard to be a part of; and by the mid-to-late 1920s, they were equally considered popular, bankable lead actors. They were, as the popular term went, the Hollywood "IT" couple.

A late November 1929 article in *The Atlanta Constitution* analyzed the O'Brien-Borden romance, stating that it was of several years' standing, with ups and downs for both parties. It even implied that wedding bells were imminent, stating that Olive and George were no longer denying that they were indeed "looking for a house suitable for two."

Olive was less than enthused with George's strange method of wooing his leading ladies. George she could trust. It was the actresses she had trouble trusting! George, the handsome leading man, would court his soon-to-be cinematic female lead off-screen, so she would appear even more besotted with him on-screen. Previous to the shooting of a picture, George would send his leading lady flowers, take her on buggy rides and generally charm her with some light romantic gestures. It was a tactic that he learned from his *Sunrise* (1927) director, F. W. Murnau: Live the role off-screen so it becomes as real as can be on screen. George wasn't known as a ladies man, he was a gentleman and loyal to a fault, so his pre-production wooing was never anything more than an innocent ploy to get a realistic performance from his leading lady of the moment.

Olive knew George's routine well, and while she generally accepted these professional romancings for what they were, when it came to Sue Carol, fiancée of actor-bandleader Nicky Stewart, both Olive *and* Nicky were more than a little miffed at how enamored George and Sue were becoming with each other — for "the sake of celluloid," as George would constantly profess. Incidentally, George and Sue were cast as the leads in the 1930 production *The Lone Star Ranger.*

George O'Brien's muscular physique gave him the nickname "The Chest." After meeting on the set of *3 Bad Men* (1926) and dating for several years, he and Olive were rumored to be engaged. They never married.

Sue wanted to test herself to see if Nicky really was the man for her, and George's off-screen charm was her measuring stick. Nicky was quite prepared to wait out Sue's silliness. As charming as George was, he knew the drill and he knew she'd come back to him. Olive, however, was not so sure about George...

When it all seemed a bit too "real," Olive put a stop to the pre-picture love fest, stepping in and cracking the whip. George was soon brought back to reality by a few harsh words from his fiery girlfriend, and in the end he was pleased that she still wanted to be with him at all, let alone marry him ("Hollywood in Person," Mollie Merrick, *The Atlanta Constitution*, November 23, 1929).

History tells us that George and Olive didn't get to legally seal the deal on their relationship, however, Sue and Nicky did, marrying in 1929 but divorcing a few years later. They had one child together — a daughter. Sue eventually married fellow actor Alan Ladd and they were wed for over twenty years, until his death (January 29, 1964). They had three children.

On the set of *3 Bad Men* (1926), Olive was in her prime and George was a tall, vibrant, handsome man with a build that eventually gave him the nickname "The Chest" because of his buff physique. Due to the desert heat during filming, to the delight of Olive and her two female co-stars, George would often take off his shirt to cool down between takes. "It [George's bare chest] was the only motivation we had to come back the next day," joked his co-star, Grace Gordon (*Chicago Sun Times,* 1926).

Under the heading "Desert Heat Makes Film Players Ill," an October 6, 1925, article in the *Los Angeles Times* reported that Olive and her co-stars Priscilla Bonner and Grace Gordon, three of the picture's four principal actresses (Phyllis Haver was the fourth), were brought home on October 5 because of illness. Olive was reportedly near death from what was diagnosed as a form of paratyphoid. Sibbie also succumbed to a high fever and was bedridden for a time. The entire company evacuated the desert set within a week of the women being brought home and plans were underway to construct a set for the filming of the remainder of the scenes. Grace Gordon had one more scene left to shoot in the desert and she returned after a week of recuperation, when she was strong enough to travel.

Heat, cold and flying dust were blamed for the illness of the three women. The Mojave Desert is usually as dry as its more widely advertised brother, the Sahara, but this time it was wet; a storm raged for days. At the first sign of feeling ill, Olive moved from her tent to the infirmary. The company was housed in tents during the scorching 107-degree days and they were equally uncomfortable when the temperature dipped to frigid lows at night. The conditions weren't much better in the infirmary, which was still a tent! A blanket held by two watchers was held over Olive to protect her from the leaking roof, all the while the gushing water swept back and forth across the floor. To prevent disease, bottled water was supplied to the cast and crew but dust particles contaminated it as soon as it was opened.

Priscilla Bonner recalled her time on the film: "Olive Borden played the lead and she was just so beautiful. I played the character ingénue. But I was all cut out. Olive Borden was so adorable; they used three reels of her and cut out everything that was dramatic in the picture. By the time they got through, it was mostly Olive taking a bath in a barrel" (*Silent Players: A Biographical and Autobiographical Study of 100 Silent Film Actors and Actresses,* Anthony Slide, University Press of Kentucky, 2002).

In the Scott Eyman biography *Print the Legend: The Life and Times of John Ford,* Priscilla continued her recollections on the making of *3 Bad Men*: "They sent the dailies back down to the studio here, and all of the executives saw it and called Ford up and said, 'We want more of Olive!'" So Olive gladly smiled and quirked and shook her beautiful head and shook her beautiful curls and dunked herself a little bit more in the barrel, and the camera went down as far as it dared to, and then it came up again and the whole picture changed from that point on.

Priscilla continued, "John Ford said, 'It's not my picture. I didn't even direct that picture. I just watched while [Olive] acted up.' He would say this to anybody that would listen.... 'I can still direct a picture called *3 Bad Men*, and some day I'm gonna make it. It's a hell of a story.'"

3 Bad Men was remade five years later and released as *Three Rogues* (1931); however,

Ford was in no way associated with the film. Directed by Benjamin Stoloff (1895–1960), Fay Wray played Olive's role of Lee Carleton.

Despite Ford's misgivings, *3 Bad Men*, even by today's filmmaking standards, is a compelling, beautifully shot film. Over two hundred stages, Conestoga wagons, buggies, and broughams and hundreds of men riding horses were an integral part of making the final Dakota land rush scene as realistic as when it happened in 1877. Several of the extras were chosen because they were actually involved in the historical rush. Ford saw no reason to hire extras to reenact it based on what they'd read. Let those who lived it, relive it, only this time he would capture it on film. This somewhat obsessive need for authenticity and eye for detail was something Ford brought to all of his films.

But Priscilla believed that after the studio started interfering, Ford gave up. "He wasn't very nice to Olive," she said. "He was mad at her, he was mad at the executives, he was mad at everybody." Ford felt he had failed in making the picture he was trying to make. He was furious and there was nothing he could do. Priscilla said she just sat around for most of the time and watched them photograph Olive. In one scene, Lou Tellegen attacked Priscilla with a whip. She was sure they'd keep the scene because it was so dramatic, but they cut it out because they needed space to show more of Olive. In the end, Priscilla ended up with a bit and Olive stole the picture (*Print the Legend: The Life and Times of John Ford*, Scott Eyman, Johns Hopkins University Press, 2001).

Ford was notoriously hard on his actors and crew, a trait coming from his need for perfection. If he didn't get what he wanted, he'd yell, curse and fight until he did. His volcanic demeanor brought the best out in all he worked with, whether it was out of fear or otherwise, Harry Carey, Jr., said it best when he commented, "He had a quality that made everyone almost kill themselves to please him. Upon arriving on the set, you would feel right away that something special was going to happen." It usually did (*Company of Heroes: My Life as an Actor in the John Ford Stock Company*, Harry Carey, Jr., Madison Books, 1994).

Olive recalled (*Motion Picture Magazine*, June 1926) a terrifying incident that could have easily killed her. "I couldn't ride," confessed Olive, "so I was to do close-ups, with the horse — presumably — standing still. They put me on the animal, and I — well, you know how we all are, we have to show off! — I sat up as if I knew what it was all about, the way I'd seen the others do. I looked as if I has been born on a horse, they said. I fooled the boys. They thought I had just been pretending I couldn't ride. And then the horse bolted! I stayed with him, though he was trying to throw me when he went dashing across the field, and I was still with him when he took a jump that would make a sensation at a horse show."

Olive's foot, in old-fashioned riding boots; was tangled in the stirrup and she knew if she were thrown, she'd be dragged along and probably killed. After the jump, the horse jarred her foot loose, flung her over his head and proceeded to try and trample her to death. Unconscious, she had no clue of the danger she was in. When she came to, the boys regaled her with horror stories about how the horse started to step on her, pawed the air a minute and then stepped over her before galloping away.

"And a half hour after that, Olive was back at work in a big scene," put in Olive's mother, quietly. "[Fox] made Olive a star in *Yellow Fingers*, but they should have decorated her with a Croix de Guerre and a collection of wound stripes, for a war could scarcely be more hazardous," Sibbie said.

After *3 Bad Men* and her Tom Mix feature *My Own Pal*, Olive was offered a long-term contract with Fox Studios. Now that she had "made it," a slew of people came out of the

woodwork waving their calendars with circled dates and claiming they were the first
ones to discover Olive Borden. There was
Paul Perry, the cameraman on *Ponjola*
(1923), Milt and Jimmie, the press agents
who gallantly introduced her to the press,
Bonney of the casting office, who gave her
helpful encouragement; and of course Paul
Bern, who did *not* want praise or recognition for "discovering" her, but ironically was
the name on the list of people who saw the
potential in her and actually did something
about it by casting her in his films. Then,
of course, there was Fox Studios who
insisted that none of that bunch discovered
Olive Borden—*they* (Fox) did! Olive,
blessed with the diplomacy that only Southern ancestry could bring, was grateful to *all*
of them for their faith in her.

As Olive's star power rose, Fox
attempted to build her up as a professional
rival to, and possible replacement for,
Madge Bellamy. Both had worked hard to
establish themselves at the company by
playing the feminine leads in John Ford epic
Westerns of the '20s, Madge in *The Iron
Horse* (1924) and Olive in *3 Bad Men*.
George O'Brien was the leading man in
both films. The studio established Madge
as their number one flapper in the acclaimed

**Real-life lovers Olive and George in a public-
ity still for *3 Bad Men* (1926).**

Jazz Age drama *Sandy* (1926), directed by Harry Beaumont.

At Fox, Madge had a reputation for being temperamental and she often quarreled with
her bosses. At one point in late 1926, she walked out after yet another heated argument
with studio hierarchy and went to Paramount to make *The Telephone Girl* (1927). Fox likely
had the younger Olive in mind to replace her. The irony is that Olive turned out to be, in
the eyes of Fox, even more temperamental than Madge. At the time of Olive's walkout,
Madge was still under contract, and still arguing with the Fox studio heads. Despite her
tumultuous relationship with the powers that be, she stayed with the studio for another
year.

Just about a year on from Olive's paratyphoid illness, she took sick again. This time
it was appendicitis. After suffering debilitating stomach and side pain, Olive was secretly
admitted to the hospital for tests. After days of monitoring, doctors decided to remove her
inflamed appendix before it burst. The operation was successful but her recovery did not
go as planned. A 1926 *Los Angeles Times* article ("Film Star Discovered in Hospital") broke
the news of Olive's condition and Chief of Police Daniel O'Brien, a friend of the family,
gave the paper a statement: "Yes, Miss Borden is at the hospital. She was operated on last

The original glass movie preview slide for *3 Bad Men* (1926).

Thursday. I am a friend of the family. I have called the hospital frequently. I saw her shortly after noon today. She was in fine spirits and was visible confirmation of the doctor's prediction that she soon will be able to leave the hospital."

An October 23, 1926, snippet in the *Los Angeles Times* was headlined "Olive Borden Now in Critical Condition." The story was brief (nine lines) considering the serious state of her health. It read in part, "Olive Borden, Fox film actress, yesterday was reportedly critically ill, having suffered a relapse following an operation for appendicitis."

Olive's plans for a personal appearance in San Francisco with her beau, George O'Brien, that same evening were canceled because of her ailing condition. Sibbie stayed by Olive's bedside day and night until she improved. After an extended hospital stay and bed rest at home, Olive eventually recovered and got back to work, but it took weeks for her to regain her full strength. There was speculation that the horse-riding accident on *3 Bad Men* was the catalyst for Olive's eventual appendix operation. Olive's back was permanently damaged by the fall and the injury caused her problems throughout the rest of her life. Olive called *3 Bad Men* her favorite movie; but her back pain was a constant reminder in the years that followed of how much she truly suffered for her art.

Hearty applause greeted the "three bad men," J. Farrell MacDonald, Tom Santschi and

Frank Campeau as they arrived for the premiere of *3 Bad Men* (1926). Olive was announced as being unable to attend the screening due to her recovery from an appendicitis operation. Earle Foxe, master of ceremonies, introduced after the cast, Mrs. Alice Whittaker, widow of the author of the book, "Three Bad Men," as the "original heroine of the story you have seen on the screen." In answer to the applause she received, she spoke of the writing of the story which took place when her husband was in the heart of Central America with the temperature at 114 ("Odds-and-Ends of Stage-News," *Chicago Daily Tribune*, September 19, 1926).

3 *Bad Men*, although not particularly well received by the public at the time of its release (it did not recoup its production cost of $650,000; converts to approximately $8 million in 2009) was critically praised for its scope, magnitude, story, directing and acting. In his 1979 biography *Pappy: The Life of John Ford* (Prentice-Hall), Dan Ford (Ford's grandson) said, "*3 Bad Men* is quite possibly his [Ford's] best silent film."

After its premiere, *3 Bad Men* was sent back to the editing room and twenty minutes of footage was cut. When Ford saw the new version, he was so furious at the drastic changes that the additional editing had made to the story, he demanded his name be taken from the credits. It stayed.

Despite Ford's misgivings, *3 Bad Men* is held in high regard as one of the greatest directing achievements of his lengthy career, the undeniable realism and historical accuracy of the Dakota land rush scenes make for a cinematic experience that isn't easily forgotten by someone viewing it for the first time or the hundredth time.

Over eighty years after it was made, *3 Bad Men* has a new, appreciative audience thanks to its recent DVD release. It is now widely considered a classic, epic Western; as it should be. Unfortunately, because Ford's original vision was compromised, he didn't see *3 Bad Men* the same way audiences and critics did. To him, it was an hour and a half of sheer disappointment. Historically, it is an hour and a half of sheer artistry.

An original newspaper ad for *3 Bad Men* (1926).

CHAPTER 6

Adam and Eve,
aka George and Olive

Next was *Fig Leaves* (1926), an elaborate production pairing lovebirds Olive and George as Adam and Eve. Hot on the heels of *3 Bad Men* (1926) and with their relationship now public knowledge, the studio would hype their real-life romance to attract audiences. No amount of money could buy that type of publicity. Both films (*3 Bad Men* and *Fig Leaves*) were released within one week of each other. *Fig Leaves* was a smashing success and managed to make its production cost back in one theatre alone. George and Olive, both on screen and off, were a marketing dream!

The *Los Angeles Times* (May 4, 1926) reported that famous archeologists were assisting Fox experts, that amazing animal effects were built for the specially constructed Garden of Eden and that magnificent sets designed by Menzies would be used in the Eden sequences. As if that wasn't enough, Adrian would design "the most original and vivid array of gowns ever shown on the screen."

Fig Leaves had many elaborate Technicolor sequences. As a number of newspaper reports stated, "Director Howard Hawks endeavored to bring to the screen a carefully planned version of certain events associated with the Garden of Eden. In making this remarkable picture, which was enlivened by a domestic love affair and heightened by a fashion revue which eclipses anything of the kind ever attempted in film-land, Mr. Hawks sought to make every sequence as plausible as possible. He succeeded so well that preview critics pronounced the prehistoric sequences the most gripping shots ever recorded by the motion picture camera" (*Hamilton Evening Journal*, October 2, 1926).

Olive was a connoisseur of fashion and she was thrilled with the lavish wardrobe. "In *Fig Leaves* I wear some gorgeous frocks, intimately feminine, but in my other pictures I have encountered some great rigs as far as clothing is concerned.... Clothing makes all the difference in the world. Men say a girl looks charming in trousers, but I'm sure I felt far from that state. There is something about a gown that is intensely feminine and when you don masculine togs you have a funny sensation. At least, I do. I feel like a rank imposter!" (*Hamilton Evening Journal*, October 9, 1926).

At the time of its release, *Fig Leaves* was highly praised for the splashy, striking production values of the prehistoric and fashion show sequences. The Rube Goldberg devices concocted to adorn the Garden of Eden are disarmingly clever, and the exaggerated animals — dinosaurs, the snake, and a giant ape — seem so homemade as to be endearing. Hawks said he and the cinematographer, Joseph August, had fun devising a way to dissolve

Olive, age 20, as Eve in *Fig Leaves* (1926).

An elaborate full-page magazine ad commissioned by the Fox Film Corporation to promote Olive and George O'Brien's new release *Fig Leaves* (1926).

between the story's two time periods, at a time when lap dissolves hadn't yet become commonplace: They took a beer bottle with a flaw in it, began by shooting through the clear portion, then turned it so the flaw would blur the image.

However, most reviewers commented on the striking fashion sequences. With extravagant sets by William S. Darling and William Cameron Menzies and costume designs by Adrian, who would soon become one of *the* most celebrated designers, the fashion parades, all shot in two-color Technicolor, were spectacles without precedent in pictures, a cinematic equivalent to Ziegfeld's elaborate stage revues. Fox publicity boasted that Olive's costumes alone cost $50,000 (converts to approximately $600,000 in 2009) and *Variety* noted that the salon setting "gives opportunity for the display of a group of lingerie models which comes within an ace of having the sex kick of a nightclub show" (*Howard Hawks: The Grey Fox of Hollywood,* Todd McCarthy, Grove Press, 2000).

Film Daily (July 11, 1927) said,

Howard Hawks wrote and directed this highly attractive little yarn which contains many novel and amusing comedy situations. There is a prologue, which is a real treat, and the only disappointment is that it doesn't last long enough. It shows Adam and Eve in their garden retreat where the deadly serpent tempts the first woman to coax her husband for some new fig leaves and so it goes down through the ages until the coaxing and pleading has become revo-

Phyllis Haver in *Fig Leaves* (1926).

Phyllis Haver (left) in a *Fig Leaves* (1926) scene with Olive.

lutionized into a game of "gimme." This "back to nature" sequence is mighty good comedy and the gag about the prehistoric alarm clock is a corker.

Hawks brings his characters to the modern age, however, and the story continues with Eve asking her plumber husband to "gimme a new hat." And that's where the trouble starts. The wife's pretty neighbor (Phyllis Haver) is the "serpent" of the modern tale and she urges the girl to make her husband provide the luxuries she adores. When he doesn't, the wife works as a model in a fashionable shop and that starts a family riot, which ends peaceably with a reunion of husband and wife when Eve decides she'd rather have her husband than the clothes after all. The fashion show staged in conjunction with Eve's entrance into the modiste shop as a model is gorgeously done in Technicolor and there is a gorgeous amount of it.

After the back-to-back release of two critical and box office successes (*3 Bad Men* and *Fig Leaves*), Olive was the talk of the town. She was Hollywood's newest, sexy leading lady and the public adored her. In the *Chicago Daily Tribune* story "From Model to Film Star in a Year" (March 21, 1926), writer Rosalind Shaffer described Olive's swift rise to leading lady status: "A year ago this month, Olive was working as one of the fourteen models in the fashion show of *The Dressmaker from Paris*. In those days she was the little 'stepsister,' just beginning, while most of the other models were already actresses of established success as picture beauties. So, while Olive walked to work and counted her lunch money, some of the other girls rode up in their double upholstered limousines. Several of these same girls

are models in Olive's present starring vehicle, and Olive admits she
would 'scarcely be human" if she
did not get some satisfaction out
of the deference they are showing
her."

Phyllis Haver, playing the
modern-day serpent in the shape
of a "woman next door," sets her
sites on Adam (Smith) for herself,
and plays on his wife Eve's love for
clothes to disrupt the family
peace. Unlike the serpent in the
Garden of Eden, however, she
fails to shatter the Smiths' paradise.

In 1929, three years after the
release of *Fig Leaves*, Phyllis ended
her film contract with Cecil B.
DeMille and married New York
millionaire William Seeman. She
told DeMille she was exiting
under the "Act of God" clause.
Stunned, DeMille asked, "What
Act of God?" Without missing a
beat, she replied, "If marrying a
millionaire isn't an Act of God, I
don't know what is." DeMille let
her go (www.imdb.com). After
fifteen years of marriage (no children), Phyllis divorced her husband in 1945.

Olive and George were deeply in love during the filming
of *Fig Leaves* (1926). Their off-screen feelings for each
other shine through in this rare series of production stills
for the film.

Haver, one of Hollywood's funniest ladies, took her own life (via an overdose) on
November 19, 1960. She was sixty-one years old. Her housekeeper, Mrs. Graham, found
her body in her plush bedroom. She told investigators, "Miss Haver became deeply depressed
about the recent death of Mack Sennett [1880–1960]." When she had read his obituary, she
was shocked that he had been living in extreme poverty during the last year of his life and
she felt that she had let him down by not helping him (she married and divorced well) when
he needed it most. As he did for many young hopefuls, it was Sennett who gave Haver her
first big break in his Keystone Comedies ("One-Time Bathing Beauty Ends Life with Barbiturates," *Eureka Humboldt Standard*, November 21, 1960).

Unlike *3 Bad Men*, *Fig Leaves* is a little dated, but with that said, it's a charming film
worth viewing for the obvious chemistry between the real-life lovers, the fashion sequences,
and the tacky yet somewhat endearing prehistoric animatronics in the Garden of Eden
sequences.

Adrian had been chosen to design Olive's many outfits for the film. By 1926 he was only a couple of years into his Hollywood designing career and *Fig Leaves* was only his seventh production as costumer, but his unmistakable artistic eye for detail was already apparent.

Throughout Hollywood's golden age, Adrian designed many of Hollywood's most beautiful gowns for many of Hollywood's most beautiful women. However, he is best

As Adam and Eve, Olive and George were naturally required to wear little clothing in the Garden of Eden scenes.

Just as George O'Brien was renowned for his physical gifts, Olive's body was shown to its full potential in most of her films. Together, in *Fig Leaves* (1926), they were the perfect vision of Adam and Eve.

remembered for designing the most iconic piece of movie wardrobe in film history; the unforgettable sequined ruby slippers for Judy Garland's Dorothy in *The Wizard of Oz* (1939). The whimsical Munchkin costumes (made entirely of felt) and the rest of the *Oz* costumes were all Adrian designs too. He was also the mastermind behind Joan Crawford's wide shoulder pads. They eventually became a signature look for her, both on and off the screen.

An almost ballet-like pose that is supposed to imply a leisurely stroll in the Garden of Eden.

Adrian's flair for knowing what suited the female form and his ability to design clothes to enhance assets and hide flaws is the reason many female stars of the day had their own "look" in the first place — Adrian gave it to them. As chief costume designer at MGM (until 1941) he exclusively created costumes for over 200 films for that studio alone. His name was just as well known as any one of the major stars (Crawford, Garbo, Harlow, Shearer, Hepburn, etc.) he repeatedly worked with and his screen credit "Gowns by Adrian" became his signature tag (www.filmreference.com).

Adrian was married to actress Janet Gaynor for twenty years (they had one son) until his death in 1959; however, their relationship was widely known to be a marriage of convenience in an attempt to mask his (and her) homosexuality. Adrian's unexpected demise was initially reported to be caused by complications arising from a stroke that he had suffered at his home on the evening of September 12, 1959, yet there was speculation that he had taken his own life; some reports indicated that his death was eventually ruled a "suicide." He was fifty-six years old (www.wikipedia.org and "Fashion Designer Gilbert Adrian Dies," *Oakland Tribune*, September 14, 1959).

The Academy Award for Best Costume Design began in 1948, after which Adrian only did three rather sartorially undistinguished films. As a result, his staggering body of work was never acknowledged by the Academy, even though he was (and is) considered to be Hollywood's greatest costume designer ("Gowns by Adrian," Stephen MacMillan Moser, *The Austin Chronicle*, June 29, 2001).

Although *Fig Leaves* was a very early

Following the release of *3 Bad Men* (1926) it was no secret that George and Olive were an item. Fox used their relationship to their advantage and as a result, *Fig Leaves* (1926) was a smashing box office success.

Olive (as Eve) receives a sweet kiss by a near-naked George (as Adam) in a production still for *Fig Leaves* (1926).

More dramatic emoting.

Fig Leaves (1926) was released within weeks of 3 Bad Men (1926). It was Olive and George's second (and last) picture together.

Circa 1926: Olive and George, in love on and off the screen.

example of Adrian's work, and there were certainly bigger things to come, the costumes throughout the film have a way of leaping off the screen and Olive wears them beautifully. Olive was positively delighted at the prospect of working with the designer that all of Hollywood was talking about. In an interview prior to the start of production she excitedly said, "Adrian is to design gowns for my fashion show and make me some pretty dresses, I hope. Isn't it funny? A year ago (1925), you talked to me when I was a mannequin in Leatrice Joy's fashion show (*The Dressmaker from Paris*) and now I'm to have my own! The picture business is a great game, if you live through it!" ("If You Love Your Work," *Motion Picture Magazine*, June 1926).

CHAPTER 7

Ralph Graves

Olive and her leading man Ralph Graves traveled to Jasper National Park in Alberta, Canada, for the Irving Cummings Fox feature *The Country Beyond* (1926). It was their second time together as male and female lead, the first being the 1925 two-reeler *Good Morning, Nurse!*

In a letter (July 21, 1926) to notorious film fan and collector Charles "Chaw" Mank, Jr., Olive mentioned returning from Canada after doing exterior scenes for *The Country Beyond*. She predicted it would be a "very good picture."

Olive thoroughly enjoyed her time in Canada; she wrote that it was "indeed a very beautiful country." Canada obviously thought of her in the highest regard, literally. In honor of her time there, after filming ceased on the picture, a peak in Jasper National Park was named "Borden Peak" after her. When the film was released, Olive received rave reviews for her performance.

The Sheboygan Press (November 26, 1926) said, "A fine story of absorbing interest, containing pathos, humor and action in just the right proportions with a star whose winsome beauty captured the hearts of yesterday's audience, this latest Fox feature proves splendid entertainment. Olive Borden plays the part of Valencia, Curwood's bewitching girl of the Canadian wilds.... In the latter sequences, Miss Borden is seen in some very stunning gowns of a kind that enthrall both men and women."

"[Olive is] at her best" was the verdict of the *Hamilton Evening Journal* (December 31, 1926). "For Miss Borden is equally bewitching and charming as the unsophisticated girl of the Canadian

Olive looking happy and relaxed on the set of *The Country Beyond* (1926). The film was shot on location in Alberta, Canada.

Olive with her leading man, Ralph Graves, in *The Country Beyond* (1926).

An original glass movie preview slide for *The Country Beyond* (1926).

wilds and as the premiere dancer who takes New York by storm. Two strangely contrasting roles which would seem beyond the histrionic ability of any one actress, but Olive Borden is a sensation in both."

Three years later, in February of 1929, Olive would make another feature with Ralph Graves, Columbia's *The Eternal Woman*. Around this time, Ralph's son Ralph Jr. was a young boy in awe of his father's beautiful leading lady. Now eighty-six years old, Ralph Jr. still has fond, vivid memories: "I met her when I was six years old, probably around the time *The Eternal Woman* was in production or newly completed. I called her Aunt Olive. She would often come over to our house and swim in our pool. She adored the water. My grandmother Graves told me I had an enormous crush on her and every time she left our home she would kiss me on the cheek."

Ralph Jr.'s mother was actress Marjorie Seaman. Ralph Graves, dashing leading man, had met the beautiful Marjorie when she was playing in D. W. Griffith's *Dream Street* (1921). He was the male lead opposite Carol Dempster. They married and later that same year, Marjorie played the feminine lead in *Free Air*, an independent production directed by Edward H. Griffith from Sinclair Lewis' novel, filmed entirely on location in Minnesota. The film was released the following year (1922). She was pregnant by then and in early 1923, she died from the effects of the complicated birth of Ralph Jr.

An original glass movie preview slide for *The Eternal Woman* (1929).

Following five years of being a widower, Ralph married for the second time. Virginia Goodwin, a non-professional from a socially prominent family in San Diego, was his bride. Their April 1928 wedding was a secret and only disclosed to the press two months later in June. Ralph and Virginia had one child together, a son, Jerry, born in August 1929. In August 1932, Virginia divorced Ralph, charging mental cruelty, and was awarded custody of three-year-old Jerry. In 1934, just two weeks before Ralph wed for the third time, Virginia married Frederick Tudor Scripps, the nephew of famed publisher E. W. Scripps. According to Ralph Graves, Jr., his half-brother Jerry endured a childhood of abuse at the hands of his stepfather. The torment of his abusive childhood plagued him. He committed suicide when he was in his early twenties.

Ralph took his third plunge into matrimony with Betty Flournoy, a St. Louis co-ed who was then working in films. After a whirlwind romance of only four weeks, they were married in Yuma in June of 1934. Ralph Jr. learned of his new stepmother, along with the rest of the world, via the newspaper announcements (source: conversations with Ralph Graves, Jr.).

Ralph and Betty had three daughters. Betty Jr. was born in July of 1935, Carla followed in May of 1938 and Barbara was born in November of 1946. Baby Carla died in a freak accident when she was four months old. The tragedy made newspaper headlines worldwide. "Ralph Graves Child Died of Strangulation: Baby Killed When Accidentally Caught in Carriage Netting," declared the *Los Angeles Times* (September 10, 1938). The baby was left on a patio with Bessie Leonard, the nurse in charge. The carriage was covered with mosquito netting and the baby became entangled in it and was strangled to death. Leonard told Mrs. Graves that she had turned her back for a second and when she looked again, the infant was partially out of the carriage, its delicate neck caught in the netting. When Leonard screamed, Mrs. Graves ran from the house and released the baby. The women worked frantically to revive her, meanwhile calling a doctor, but when Dr. Crombie Nixon arrived at the West Los Angeles home, the baby was already dead. Stunned by the tragedy, Mrs. Graves was taken to Cedars of Lebanon hospital and put under heavy sedation.

Ralph Jr. lost his biological mother at birth and he did not have a close relationship with either one of his stepmothers. However, his memories of his Aunt Olive are happy ones. Having a child of her own was Olive's dream. She greeted all children with a smile and genuinely enjoyed their company. Unfortunately, Ralph Jr.'s recollections of his father are quite the opposite. Even after all these years, the memories of an absent, self-absorbed father remain. Ralph Jr.'s primary caregivers were his maternal and paternal grandmothers. "Grandmother Graves" and "Grandmother Seaman" is how he still lovingly refers to them.

In a letter to me, dated July 6, 2008, Ralph Jr. said, "Nothing you could say about my father would surprise me. We didn't get along too well. I was not close to him." Understandably, he did not wish to elaborate. As he told me, "Despite everything, he was *still* my father" (source: conversation with Ralph Graves, Jr.).

And, despite a less than perfect marriage, Ralph and his last wife Betty remained together until his death. Ralph Graves, veteran of over one hundred fifty films, succumbed to a heart attack in Santa Barbara, California, on February 18, 1977 (age 77). His third wife, Betty, died a little over a year later, in April of 1978.

Ralph Jr. said that he can still picture Olive swimming in their pool as if it were yesterday:

She was always smiling, happy, vibrant and full of life. She was stunningly beautiful in person. Her mother, Sibbie, would almost always accompany her to the house and I got the feeling, even as a young boy, that her mother was very, very controlling. The typical "stage mother" that is so often talked about; she was exactly that. Aunt Olive would swim laps and her mother would sit by the pool, watching, until she was done. Mrs. Borden (Sibbie) was heavy-set, but in her own way, she was also a very attractive woman. Olive never seemed bothered by her mother's constant presence. I was young, but from my childhood perspective, they seemed extremely close.

Nearly all the leading ladies and starlets of the day would come to our house. I remember Marion Davies and Fay Wray being there often, also Viola Dana and Barbara Stanwyck too. My father would

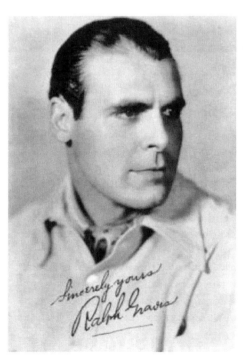

Ralph Graves, Olive's leading man and long-time friend.

A magazine ad promoting *The Eternal Woman* (1929).

bed almost all of the pretty actresses that frequented our home but there was never anything romantic between him and Aunt Olive. I don't know why. She was as beautiful, if not more beautiful than all the others. It wasn't because he wasn't attracted to her, I know he was, but there seemed to be a respect for her that he didn't have for any of the others, so their relationship remained platonic. Don't get me wrong, he wasn't always happy about this arrangement [*laughs*].

My father was so used to having any woman he wanted. He wasn't used to rejection. But, he gradually realized Aunt Olive was untouchable, out of his reach. He didn't push the boundaries with her. She was always very clear about what she wanted and what she didn't want. For whatever reason, she just wasn't interested in my father romantically. But, his bruised ego eventually healed and they remained friends.

CHAPTER 8

Hollywood's "Joy Girl"

Olive's film career spanned a decade. Her most prolific years were 1926 and 1927; and she made eleven feature films during that two-year period. *The Monkey Talks* (1927), directed by Raoul Walsh, was based on an internationally successful stage play of the same name and showcased Olive as Olivette, a petite acrobat of the Folies Bergeres in Paris.

Jacques Lerner, a well-known animal impersonator, created the original role of the "talking monkey" in the Paris stage version. Lerner studied the art of primates for over fifteen years, first as a hobby and later with serious intentions of becoming a professional animal impersonator. He played the part of the talking monkey on the Paris stage for two years. Lerner was brought to America by the producers to reprise his role in the silent film version. Lions, tigers, elephants, camels, a variety of monkeys and bears — in fact, almost all of the wild animals housed at the world-famous Selig Zoo in Los Angeles — were borrowed for the picture.

Unfortunately for Olive, most of the praise was reserved for Lerner and many critics panned her performance as Olivette. The *New York Herald-Tribune*'s Harriet Underhill wrote (April 2, 1927) that Lerner "should be the star of the piece, for he gives a remarkably fine performance. But the producers have chosen Olive Borden for this honor. Miss Borden is a self-conscious young woman, who purses her lips, arches her insteps and is thoroughly irritating all the time. If this is acting, make the most of it!"

As the film begins, we see a small troupe of circus actors who, because of a series of misfortunes, are deprived of all their worldly possessions. It doesn't take them long to hatch a clever scheme to get them back on their feet and "in the money" again. One member of the troupe, a dwarf tumbler, will be disguised as a monkey, taken to Paris, and advertised as "Jocko" (Jacques Lerner), the "monkey who talks."

After all parties enthusiastically agree to the scam, we jump forward and see the "monkey talks" performance playing to packed houses across the country. However, in order for their scam to continue, the men must reclusively situate themselves away from other performers so the real identity of the talking monkey is never found out.

In a "beauty and the beast" plot twist, the "monkey" falls in love with Olivette (Olive), a beautiful acrobat of the traveling show. Olivette is intrigued by the talking "monkey" but even after "Jocko" tells her that he loves her, she remains completely clueless that he is a man dressed as a monkey.

Despite their initial pact to stay away from the other performers to maintain the secret of their act, Olivette spends time with the men, and "Jocko," away from the stage, and still she believes the monkey is real. "Jocko" maintains his monkey get-up around Olivette, bow-

A publicity still autographed in 1929.

Olive in a dramatic scene from *The Monkey Talks* (1927). George Eastman House has a complete print of the film but it shows extensive nitrate damage.

A scene from the highly acclaimed feature *The Monkey Talks* (1927) with Olive and monkey impersonator Jacques Lerner.

ing his legs, lengthening his arms, stooping and swaying just as a monkey would. Yet, when he's alone with his friends, he stretches himself out, takes off his mask and broods about the love he cannot have.

Despite his misery, "Jocko's" desire to disclose his true identity to Olivette, at the cost of hurting his friends and destroying their livelihood, proves too great a sacrifice. He puts his feelings for her aside and continues to perform (as the monkey) to audiences who give him rapturous applause for his ability to speak like a human. Because of the success of the talking monkey act, a plan is cooked up by the evil lion-tamer to steal "Jocko" and replace him with a *real* primate. Before the switch is discovered, the real monkey makes his way to Olivette's dressing room. She has no reason to believe that it is any other monkey but "Jocko" paying her a friendly visit. As always, she approaches him without fear. When the real monkey attacks, she screams, desperate for someone to come to her rescue before she's mauled to death.

A powerful climax is reached when "Jocko" escapes his captors and sacrifices himself (and his identity) to protect Olivette from the rampaging beast. As "Jocko" slips away in Olivette and Sam's (Don Alvarado) arms, Sam, who has also been in love with Olivette but has not pursued her due to his staunch loyalty to "Jocko," is free to reveal his love for Olivette and they live happily ever after.

Because of the nature of Olive's onscreen circus profession, she is often scantily clad throughout the picture. It was a welcome change for the male audience attendees who were

The Monkey Talks (1927) film poster.

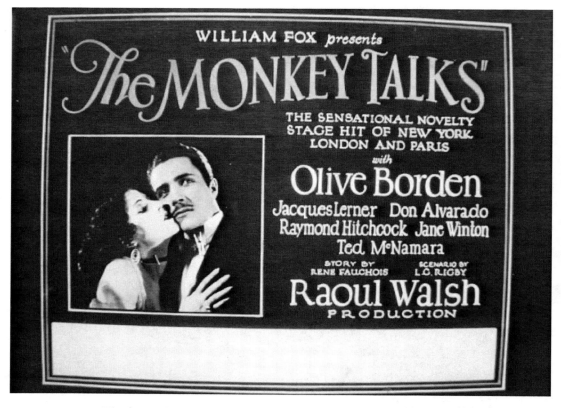

The original glass movie preview slide for *The Monkey Talks* (1927).

used to the conservative fashions of the day. Few cared what Olive was doing or how she was acting, so long as she was on the screen. Olive's curvaceous figure did every costume justice and for the first time in her career, she was not just an actress — she was a bonafide sex symbol!

On the night the theatre sequences were being filmed, hundreds of extras were employed. When Olive made her first stage entrance, she was to perform a rigorous dance number. Director Walsh was shouting his praises at Olive and the extras for their enthusiastic performances. Olive stumbled but she regained her footing and continued dancing with such ease that Walsh thought nothing of it. The scene wasn't marred by her mistake so he kept on filming.

Thrilled with the take, Walsh yelled, "Cut!" and Olive dropped to the stage floor the moment she heard the word. The concerned extras swarmed around her. Walsh hurried to the stage and discovered Olive in great pain. She had badly turned her ankle midway through the routine. "If only you'd have stopped," he said with great concern. "What pain you would have saved."

"Well," Olive replied, "I've been in such positions myself on the stage and you know the show must go on. I forgot everything when the music started. The lights, the people ... and everything were so real — I just did what I have been trained to do — to finish" ("'The Show Must Go On,' Cries Olive Borden, Injured During Filming of *The Monkey Talks*," *The Daily News*, 1927).

Olive in a scene from *The Monkey Talks* (1927). Olive's state of undress made this film a popular choice for male moviegoers.

Olive and her leading man, Don Alvarado, cradle wounded Jacques Lerner in one of the final scenes from *The Monkey Talks* (1927).

As of 2009, the George Eastman House in Rochester, New York, is the only film institution known to hold a print of *The Monkey Talks*. It's complete but at least half the footage is barely visible due to extensive nitrate damage. Preserved on safety stock, it won't decompose further; however, a digital restoration is needed to bring much of it back to a viewable state. The assistant curator at George Eastman House, Caroline Yeager, said such extensive restoration would "cost a fortune" and because of the time and expense, a restoration effort will *not* be planned any time soon.

Ironically, four years after the release of *The Monkey Talks*, the *Los Angeles Times* (July 12, 1931) ran a sultry picture of George O'Brien's future wife, Marguerite Churchill, with a caption, "*The Monkey Talks* is a thriller of the old school. Marguerite Churchill plays the heroine in the new version, the role enacted by Olive Borden in the silent picture." The sound version of the film was never made, but it's interesting to note that the two main loves of George O'Brien's life were cast in the same role, just a few years apart.

Olive's next part was in the Harry Beaumont Fox feature *The Secret Studio* (1927). Olive plays Rosemary Merton, a young woman with a college education and a flair for the arts. A March 13, 1927, *Los Angeles Times* article printed the bold headline:

Introducing Olive Borden — Flapper

The term "flapper" was used in the 1920s to describe a young woman with bobbed hair, heavy makeup and short skirts. A party-loving, sexually free, reckless, liberal, independent woman was — a flapper! It was the popular 1920 Olive Thomas film *The Flapper* that introduced the term. Joan Crawford, Louise Brooks, Clara Bow, Colleen Moore, Leatrice Joy, Bebe Daniels and, eventually, Olive Borden, just to name a few, all made a career for themselves using the flapper image.

Author Jeanine Basinger explains the term in her book *Silent Stars* (Knopf, 1999):

> The flapper wasn't a siren or a vamp or a femme fatale. She wasn't innocent, and she wasn't maternal. She was a naughty, grown-up girl who wanted to play with boys, to cause trouble, to be mischievous. In fact, the movie flapper was a logical extension of the movie tomboy, that cute little girl who dug for worms and stole cookies in the earliest silent films. It was completely logical for the rule-breaking tomboy-girl of the teens to grow up to be a flapper, because breaking the rules was what a flapper was all about. The first step of liberation for females on-screen were inevitably safe enough for the audience to watch comfortably, and the flapper fit the bill.

An original newspaper ad for *The Monkey Talks* (1927).

Olive was given high praise for her performance in *The Secret Studio*. As usual, her attractive features were complimented, along with her slender, shapely legs. An article in the *Los Angeles Times* (March 13, 1927) states that she does some very convincing work in the role, and predicted that it should go a long way toward establishing her as one of the "flappiest flappers" of the films. As a whole, *The Secret Studio* was deemed to be "an excellent one of its type and will be pleasing to many."

Norbert Lusk (1883–1949), a New York correspondent for the *Los Angeles Times*, thought otherwise. In his review, published a few months later, he disagreed with the above-

As Rosemary Merton in a lobby card scene from *The Secret Studio* (1927). Olive is in the center; the other actors are unidentified.

mentioned article completely. "Ten years ago it would have been considered 'daring and artistic,'" he stated. "Unfortunately, today finds it a terrible picture..."

Olive was featured ahead of everyone else in the credits but Lusk thought her acting was atrocious and felt that she had no business being top-billed. He said she gave a "writhing performance in which she apparently attempts to emulate an eel. She is irritating beyond belief and the free display of her pretty figure does not mitigate the utter ineptitude of her flings at expressing anything but coyness" (*Los Angeles Times*, June 19, 1927). This review is not unusual for Lusk in relation to one of Olive's films. For some reason, he took immense pleasure in tearing strips off her every performance, even in films where other notable critics raved about her talents.

Lusk worked as a film critic for the *Los Angeles Times* for two decades. He was also a critic for the *New York Morning Telegraph* and *Picture-Play Magazine*. He died due to a heart ailment in 1949, at age sixty-six. He was exceedingly influential, so no star wanted to rub him the wrong way; apparently Olive did at some time. Whatever she did, he never forgot it and he never let *her* forget it each time one of her films was released.

Mae Tinee of the *Chicago Daily Tribune* (June 21, 1927) reviewed *The Secret Studio*, with praise going to the cast, the director and the photographer. "You suspect that the yarn was written for the express purpose of providing Olive Borden with opportunity for the

A lobby card for *The Secret Studio* (1927). Pictured: John Holland (left), Olive and Ben Bard.

display of her teeth and her beautiful figure — you don't object — reason being that the teeth are mighty white and the figure very lovely."

The heroine (Olive) goes to New York to make a name for herself and poses for an artist who turns out to be a rascal and *almost* completely ruins her reputation and her chances with the noble, rich young man who loves her for the flowering innocence that has, in the great city, set her apart from the other girls he knows.

A February 3, 1927, article in the *Los Angeles Times* reported that Olive had just returned to New York to realize her dream of seeing her name in lights in Times Square. Her two latest features, *The Monkey Talks* and *The Secret Studio*, had just been released and the movie-going public adored her. Four years prior, in an almost "fairy tale moment," Olive had stood on a corner in Times Square and asked her mother if she thought she'd ever have her name in electric lights over a theater. Now, upon her return east, Olive was met by the press and swarmed by photographers. Finally, she had fame. She had her name in lights. She had her dream — Olive Borden was a movie star!

Those early comedies for Christie, Roach and White had served Olive well. In a July 1927 issue of *Motion Picture Magazine*, Olive admitted just that. "Comedies," she said, "are the best training school in the world. They teach you never to say 'Can't.' When a director tells me to do something today, no matter what it is, I *try it*."

Because Olive learned (and truly believed) early in her career that there was no such word as "can't" and that nothing was impossible, she succeeded in many areas of her life. It might not always work out exactly as planned (she found that out too) but she couldn't be faulted or criticized for never giving something a go. She was a go-getter!

Olive admitted she always worked hard with anything she tried. A job was a serious undertaking to be learned from. Whether it was her school work, sports, playing the piano, or making candy with her mother, Olive gave the task at hand 100 percent. Acting was no different. No one spared her when she first entered the business and even at the height of her career, few still spared her. Being an actress was hard work, but she admitted, "I love it!" When she first arrived in Hollywood she said, "There wasn't anyone *to* spare me, you see. I was there on my own. I was there to work and to make good. There wasn't any influence behind me, no 'pull' and certainly no experience."

Olive confessed that she didn't have beautiful clothes, money, a maid or even a "foot in the door" that so often helps some Hollywood hopefuls over the first rungs. But the hard road taught her that a girl *can* get there, and get there sturdily and honestly and independently, if she really means business. "It *is* a business to me, and everyone knows that it is. Now we have a home in Beverly Hills and I have my bungalow dressing-room ... oh, they all have them, but mine is the nicest ... and I have Mother, who has stood by me through thick and thin" (*Motion Picture Magazine,* July 1927).

A title card for the Allan Dwan–directed *The Joy Girl* (1927).

Fox Films announced on February 2, 1927, that Olive would play the lead in their new Allan Dwan-directed production, *The Joy Girl* (1927). An article in the *Los Angeles Times* (June 7, 1927) praised Olive for snaring the female lead, saying, "The star role has gone to Olive Borden as a reward of merit to the young actress who has worked unceasingly for the past year." Along with her co-stars Neil Hamilton, Mary Alden, Marie Dressler and Helen Chandler (the article stated), Olive would soon be leaving for Palm Beach, Florida, where they would remain for three weeks shooting exteriors, and then to Fox's New York studios to film the remaining scenes, all of which were interiors. When the train, known as "The Joy Girl Special" (because the entire cast and director Dwan were on board), arrived in Palm Beach, it was met with fanfare worthy of traveling royalty. When all members of the cast stepped off the train from New York, Olive was met with the fans' loudest cheers of all.

Olive had to learn how to smoke for her role in *The Joy Girl* and she admitted to the *Chicago Daily Tribune* (February 1, 1927) that she was appalled by the prospect: "I thought it was a bad habit and I don't like to acquire bad habits. We have to do things like this for the sake of art, but it will only be for this one picture."

Jewel Courage (Olive) is the very pampered daughter of Mrs. Courage (Mary Alden), who is married to Mr. Courage (William Norris), a clerk. Jewel's doting mother, deter-

Another lobby card for the silent comedy *The Joy Girl* (1927). Pictured (left to right), Mary Alden and William Norris play the on-screen parents of Olive's character, Jewel Courage.

mined for her daughter to have all of life's luxuries that she herself never possessed, gives Jewel the best of everything and is her slave. She will not permit Jewel to work, though Jewel, a genius at designing hats, is constantly being sought by a fashionable milliner to join her establishment. However, Jewel and her mother have other ideas; the main objective is for Jewel to marry a rich man. This she sets out to do with great gusto. The remainder of the story surrounds Jewel's adventures in snaring herself a wealthy husband.

Reviews for *The Joy Girl* were favorable. Mae Tinee of the *Chicago Daily Tribune* (September 21, 1927) said, "The title role is handed skillfully by Olive Borden who has great, witching eyes and a lot of unbobbed, wavy dark hair. Miss Borden is not 'perfectly beautiful' to my way of thinking, but she has much charm. This with the eyes and hair, and a knowledge of what clothes to wear — and how — make her a screen personality to conjure with. Her heroine in this picture is an appealing and attractive one."

Before she left for Florida, Olive was the honored guest at a tea party given for her by the screenwriters of New York. Norbert Lusk, the acid-tongued *L.A Times* reviewer, noted in his column that Olive confided to the press that she was quite worn out from a day of fittings at the costumer's. Lusk sarcastically added that any fatigue was entirely of Olive's own doing because of her "inability to wear ready-made clothing" (*Los Angeles Times,* February 13, 1927).

There are a couple of versions of how Marie Dressler was cast in *The Joy Girl.* By her own account, Dressler remembered director Allan Dwan phoning to tell her he wanted her to play a small part in an Olive Borden picture that he planned to shoot in Florida. She said, "I was not at all keen about it." However, Dressler's companion and personal astrologer, former actress Nella Webb, said, "You're going! If I have to ship you by freight." Marie gave in, but she wasn't happy about it.

Allan Dwan came up with a different version. In Peter Bogdanovich's 1971 biography *Allan Dwan: The Last Pioneer,* the director insisted he was lunching with his studio manager at the Ritz Hotel when he saw a woman sitting alone at a little table. He asked his companion if the woman could be Marie Dressler. Upon further inspection, neither could quite make a definitive judgment. The men eventually called the headwaiter to the table to confirm their suspicions. Yes, said the waiter, it was certainly Miss Dressler. She was a resident at the hotel. Dwan proceeded to write a note: "Dear Miss Dressler, I'm an admirer of your work in the theatre. I'm a director of motion pictures and I'm interested in whether you would care to play in a picture of mine which is to start immediately."

The headwaiter handed Dressler the note just as she was ascending the stairs to the main floor. She read it, staggered slightly, then grabbed the stair rail, as if she was about to faint. "Well," recounted Dwan, "I thought she's either had a drink too many or she isn't well." Then a bellboy came to see me and said, "Miss Dressler would like to know if you'd see her before you go — she's in her room." Dwan said he was guided to a floor that consisted of rooms used only for the servants of guests at the hotel. In one of these rooms sat Marie Dressler. According to Dwan, Dressler told him that he had saved her life by sending her that note. "I've just had my last meal downstairs and I was going out that window. I'd reached the end of my strength. The world was through with me and I was through with the world. But this looks like new hope" (*Marie Dressler: The Unlikeliest Star,* Betty Lee, University Press of Kentucky, August 28, 1997).

Marie had the time of her life in Florida. Her part as Mrs. Heath was small (her scenes were shot in a day and a half), but she was back in front of the camera after a nine-year

Olive in a romantic pose with leading man Neil Hamilton in *The Joy Girl* (1927).

absence. Her film career was not only rekindled, she was as popular as any of the pretty actresses half her age — and weight! Marie later won a Best Actress Oscar for her performance in *Min and Bill* (1930), along with another Oscar nod two years later (a Best Actress nomination for her role in *Emma*). She worked steadily until 1933 with her last film being *Christopher Bean*. She succumbed to cancer on July 28, 1934, at age sixty-five. If Dwan's story is true, his note with the offer of an immediate job not only saved her career, it saved her life.

Dwan (1885–1981) became one of Hollywood's most prolific directors. By the end of his career, he figured he'd directed about 132 features and over 200 shorts. All told, with writing and producing thrown into the mix, Dwan had been a part of the creative process on about 1400 films! *The Joy Girl* would be the only film that he and Olive worked on together.

Olive's love of fashion was well known. Her wardrobes were massive walk-ins, big enough to house her clothes, shoes and fur coats. The press described the outfits she wore socially in great detail and she would never wear the same dress twice. Being labeled as a spendthrift bothered her but Olive worked hard for her money and she felt she had the right to spend it on whatever, and enjoy it *with* whomever, she pleased. She did just that. No one could accuse her of being frugal, yet many felt it their business to call her finan-

Olive posing in a beautiful lace gown, circa 1927.

cially foolish. *The Bridgeport Telegram* (Friday, November 4, 1927), reporting on what the stars of the day enjoyed collecting, stated that "Olive Borden takes great pride in her collection of dolls from all nations."

Socially, Olive and her mother were often seen out together at lawn parties, film premieres, luncheons, promotional events, etc. Both women dressed to impress. They enjoyed the attention of eager fans waiting to greet them, and the media often described their outfits and the particular event they were attending in newspapers the following day. Myra Nye's *Los Angeles Times* society pages (May 8, 1927) mentioned the Borden ladies attending the premiere of Janet Gaynor's Academy Award–winning spectacle *Seventh Heaven* (1927). Olive was described as wearing a Parisian gown of silver sequins with a skirt of silver fringe sweeping to her dainty ankles; pearl earrings and necklace; corsage of orchids; and wrap of white ermine with white fox collar. Sibbie was wearing chiffon velvet with a skirt of black sequins; a black velvet wrap with a white fox collar and cuffs.

Hollywood had a habit of labeling their actresses with tag lines; Mary Pickford was "America's Sweetheart," Jean Harlow was "The Blonde Bombshell," Theda Bara was "The Vamp" and Clara Bow was "The It Girl," just to name a few. So, after her lead role in the 1927 film *The Joy Girl*, Olive's tag line was set in stone. From that moment on, Olive Borden became known as Hollywood's "Joy Girl."

CHAPTER 9

George's *Sunrise*, Olive's *Pajamas*

By the end of 1927, Olive's career was about to take a major detour; however, her relationship with George O'Brien was still solid. Or so it seemed. The *Los Angeles Examiner* (November 30, 1927) reported on the premiere of F.W. Murnau's Academy Award-winning masterpiece *Sunrise* (1927). Olive accompanied George, who was the male lead in the film (opposite Janet Gaynor) to the premiere. Looking beautiful in a white satin gown that was heavily beaded in crystals, and wearing red slippers adorned with rhinestone buckles, Olive was met with "ooohs and aaahs" as she proudly walked arm in arm with her now widely reported fiancé. An ermine coat with white fox collar, a gift from George, kept her warm. George's parents came to town especially for the opening of their son's new film (*Los Angeles Times*, November 30, 1927). For Olive, both personally and professionally, the *Sunrise* premiere was the end of a very long, very emotional, bittersweet road.

George was widely praised for his performance in *Sunrise* and Janet Gaynor won the

Circa 1927. Olive was 21 years old.

Best Actress Academy Award for this film, *Seventh Heaven* (1927) and *Street Angel* (1928). The very first Academy Awards ceremony of 1929 (May 16, 1929) was held at the Hollywood Roosevelt Hotel, in the Blossom Room. There were 250 people in attendance and tickets were $10 apiece (converts to approximately $125 in 2009).

Films opening in Los Angeles between August 1, 1927, and July 31, 1928, were eligible for nominations. At the time, an actor's entire body of work within a one-year span was the determining factor behind winning the individual awards. Gaynor was bestowed the first Best Actress award for her outstanding work in all three films. *Sunrise* also won Best Unique and Artistic Production (the only year this award was given) and Best Cinematography (Charles Rosher and Karl Struss). The Best Picture honor went to *Wings* (1927); the World War I air combat picture starring Clara Bow, Charles "Buddy" Rogers and

Richard Arlen has the distinct honor of being the only silent film to win a Best Picture Academy Award.

Despite critical and industry acclaim, and today's opinions that *Sunrise* is one of the greatest silents ever made, if not one of the greatest *films* ever made, it did poorly at the box office. With the advent of sound, it got lost in the shuffle and hype of the talkies. Warner Bros. released *The Jazz Singer* (1927), the first part-talkie feature film, two weeks after *Sunrise* hit theaters.

Aside from the luxurious fur coat that George gave Olive to wear to the *Sunrise* premiere, he often surprised her with jewelry and trinkets to make her happy. It was no secret that Olive had a large collection of fur coats and expensive jewelry. An undated newspaper clipping said that Olive was once so highly insulted that a salesgirl had offered to show her a fur coat that cost less than $3,500 (converts to approximately $45,000 in 2009), she walked out of the store and never went back.

The Los Angeles Times (June 3, 1927) reported that a 23-year-old thief by the name of Arthur Carlson had finally been caught after a string of robberies netting him up to $100,000 (converts to approximately $1.2 million in 2009) in goods. He broke into Olive's Beverly Hills home and stole $9,000 (converts to approximately $112,000 in 2009) worth of furs, clothing and jewelry that were stored in an antique trunk. He took it all— including the trunk! Olive was devastated. It took her quite some time to feel comfortable and secure living in her home again after the robbery.

After months of trying to capture the career criminal (he had two prison stints for previous robberies), police were transporting him on a Southern Pacific train when he escaped via a bathroom in one of the train cars. Police fired four shots as Carlson bolted from the fast-moving train. None of them made contact. He was recaptured near Modesto, California, walking along the roadside looking to hitch a ride.

Carlson ended up confessing to

Olive in a scene from *Pajamas* (1927) with Jack J. Clark.

fifty-two robberies, most of which were in homes of the Beverly Hills motion picture colony. He was convicted on two counts of robbery, each of which carried five years to life in prison. Much of what Carlson had stolen had been sold on the black market and was never recovered. However, Olive was lucky enough to get most of her beloved items returned to her.

In her next film, *Pajamas* (1927), directed by John G. Blystone (her second film with him), Olive played Angela Wade, the daughter of a rich man. It was a change of pace for Olive, the only other film that remotely touched a rich girl angle was the Allan Dwan–directed *The Joy Girl* (1927); in that production she merely posed as a rich girl. *Pajamas* is a comedy focused on the marooning of two young people, who detest each other, in a forest into which they have been plunged through an airplane mishap (*Los Angeles Times*, July 10, 1927). Fox built a complete home to match that of a Long Island, New York, millionaire's residence. Complete with a garden and swimming pool, the set was reportedly one of the most attractive interiors ever designed for a comedy-drama.

During the filming of *Pajamas*, Olive's daredevil streak took over once again and she insisted on doing her own stunt. Director Blystone reluctantly agreed. It just wasn't worth arguing with Olive when she had her mind set on something. In the air scene, the camera plane flew out of control and dove directly toward her ship, missing it (and her!) by inches. Since the scary incident, and much to Olive's dismay, studio officials insisted a $25-a-day (converts to approximately $300 in 2009) stunt double would stand in for her on risky scenes. Any chance of their leading lady getting hurt meant production being held up for weeks, costing the studio thousands of dollars. Hiring a stunt double was money well spent (*The Ogden-Standard Examiner*, Wednesday Evening, August 31, 1927).

Pajamas was released (October 23, 1927) about a month after the New York premiere of *Sunrise*. As the ad (pictured) shows, Fox intended to team George and Olive up for a third time. It never happened. In fact, strangely, there are only three components to the *Pajamas* promo ad that stayed the same: the title, the studio and Olive as the leading lady. Arthur Housman, Marjorie Beebe, Barry Norton, Ben Bard and, most importantly, George O'Brien never appeared in the final film. Allan Dwan was replaced by John G. Blystone as director.

F.W. Murnau personally chose George for the male lead in *Sunrise*. In fact, he was the first actor to be cast in the film. William Fox beckoned Murnau to make him a "masterpiece" at *any* cost,

The director of *Sunrise* (1927), F. W. Murnau.

A rare ad for *Pajamas* (1927) that promotes Olive's lover George O'Brien in the lead role. He was replaced with Lawrence Gray. Allan Dwan, the director, along with the rest of the advertised cast were also replaced. The title, studio (Fox) and Olive as the female lead were the only three elements that remained true to this ad.

George O'Brien as "The Man" and Janet Gaynor as "The Wife" in one of the many visually stunning scenes from *Sunrise* (1927).

assuring him that he would have full creative control. That also meant he had his choice of Fox stars for the leads. So (as the story goes), George was already cast in *Pajamas*, but it had yet to be filmed, when Murnau, the great German expressionistic director, handpicked him for the *Sunrise* lead. There was no greater honor and there was no competition. Murnau won. Olive lost. Dwan dropped out as director because he lost his male lead. The rest of the supporting cast fell away because of scheduling conflicts, and Blystone, as the new director, recast the picture to his own tastes.

However, it went one step further than that. It was announced, for weeks, in official Fox studio publicity that Olive was to play the coveted feminine lead of "The Wife" in *Sunrise*. Fox desperately wanted to pair Olive and George up again, if not in *Pajamas*, then why not in *Sunrise* (1927)?

At first, Murnau liked Olive's look and agreed to the pairing; however, he was unaware of Olive and George's personal relationship off camera. When he found out they were a couple, without warning and with little explanation, Olive was advised she was dropped as the feminine lead. The part was going to Janet Gaynor instead. At the time, Olive was a major star and Gaynor was a rank newcomer. However, Murnau being the "temperamental artiste" that he was, refused to have George and Olive distracted onscreen by their off-screen relations. Murnau was also concerned that Olive was too set in her acting ways. Gaynor was a newcomer, a clean canvas and more easily molded into the demure character of "The Wife" that he wanted. "Olive knew that *Sunrise* was her lost opportunity," said Ralph Graves, Jr., "and she had to stand by and watch her man garner great success from it. She couldn't just walk away and forget. Her film [*Pajamas*] was completely thrown for a loop when O'Brien was taken from it. She felt used and abused by O'Brien, Murnau and the studio."

Olive hid her bitter disappointment and without a word of resentment she helped Gaynor with her wardrobe and gave her the reading material and preparation notes that she herself had already studied and written for the part (*Motion Picture Classic*, July 1928).

Olive despised Murnau for his assumption that her personal relationship with George would in any way affect either of their performances. After all, they had previously starred in *3 Bad Men* (1926) and *Fig Leaves* (1926). The public adored them as a couple and Fox was banking (again!) on the additional publicity that their off-screen relationship would bring to the picture.

Murnau had a strict German work ethic. He seemed to have an unusual hold over George, and Olive didn't like it one bit. He worked like no American director she'd ever seen. For two weeks prior to the filming of *Sunrise* he cut George off from his family and friends, Olive included. George was under strict instructions that he could only speak to and see Murnau and his valet. No one else.

The role of "The Man" in *Sunrise* was particularly challenging with many deep, dark, conflicted feelings involved. Murnau wanted George to *become* "The Man" and he couldn't do that with his girlfriend in tow, onscreen or off. Murnau wanted George to lose his jovial, "good boy" persona for a role that was quite the opposite. It would be the most challenging task of his career. Murnau demanded the isolation, George, being the amiable guy that he was, didn't question the master. He trusted it was for the best and he did what he was told. Olive was furious. "Olive did nothing to hide her dislike for [Murnau]. I remember my father telling me that he listened to Olive for many hours venting about 'that director,'" said Ralph Graves, Jr.

Murnau took to training his actors like a football coach would train his players. All members of the *Sunrise* cast were subject to his obsessive supervision, even in matters of physical health and socialization. One challenge for George and Gaynor was Murnau's strict order to frame no words with their lips nor utter a sound while they worked before the cameras. *Sunrise* was to be a picture of any nationality, a worldwide masterpiece, and since pictures are things of action, everything that is done before the camera must be interpreted by the eye.

"He made me isolate myself from my friends to completely lose my own personality for two weeks before he was ready to shoot scenes," George said. "During that period I saw nobody but him and the valet and I wore no clothes other

The dashingly handsome George O'Brien.

Olive Borden, Fox star, chooses to do the Black Bottom in the horn of a saxophone just for the sake of doing something radically different.

than those which my part called for." George even rowed an imaginary boat for two hours in his library before he took hold of the real oars on location for the dramatic boat scene (*Syracuse Herald*, August 18, 1927).

George went to Germany and Paris to visit with Murnau, and Olive naturally thought she'd be going along with him. When George informed her that he'd be going alone, Olive was angry and devastated. Ralph Graves, Jr., said, "My father said she still talked about missing out on that trip years later. He got the sense that she was more sad than bitter, but she never got over that lost opportunity."

Ironically, in an October 23, 1927, *Washington Post* interview, around the same time that George's *Sunrise* and Olive's *Pajamas* were released, Olive gave an account of her perfect man. It sounded like she was describing George, but one has to wonder if her last few words about him traveling was a public dig at George for doing just the opposite. She said her perfect man must be the sort who understands moods and is kind, and he must have a sense of humor about himself and other people. "I never thought it would make much difference if his hair were dark or light, if only he were tolerant and the color of his eyes wouldn't matter as long as there were laugh lines around them."

Olive said that since she arrived in Hollywood, she hadn't changed her mind about his traits, looks and personality but she'd been too busy to do much dreaming about men. Sometimes between shots on the set, when things got a little boring, Olive admitted that her active imagination would conjure up an apparition of this ideal man, sitting quietly in the midst of all the rush and confusion, usually smoking a well-worn pipe. On location, she thought of him as being as much at home in a khaki shirt and field boots as he was in the tailored clothes of the city. He would be the sort who could adapt himself easily to any environment, and be a good companion dancing at the Ambassador Cocoanut Grove or riding horseback out in the San Fernando Valley.

"But I think above all," she said, "he must be an adventurer who always longs for the far places of the earth. To paraphrase Edna St. Vincent Millay, the poet, 'There isn't a train he wouldn't take, no matter where it's going' and of course, he'd take me along."

Olive's ideal man was George O'Brien and he left her behind. For Europe—for *Sunrise*...

Opposite: **Olive dancing "The Black Bottom" in the horn of a giant saxophone, circa 1927.**

CHAPTER 10

Broken Dreams

The *Los Angeles Times* (August 18, 1927) news item "Fox Buys Story for Star" announced that Winfield R. Sheehan, vice-president of Fox Films, had purchased the rights to the well-known Viennese operetta *The Dollar Princess*. The article stated that Olive was lined up for the starring role. Olive never starred in the film. In fact, Olive's association with Fox would soon be a thing of the past. Her career, as she knew it, would never be the same again.

Olive was becoming resentful. She was resentful at Fox for allowing Murnau to steal, not only her leading man for *Pajamas* (1927), but her lover too; she was bitter at Fox executives for pulling her from the coveted lead role of "The Wife" in *Sunrise* (1927); and despite none of it being directly his fault, she was angry at George for letting all of it happen. After George's return from Europe, the once inseparable pair were seen less frequently together. "She deeply loved O'Brien," said Ralph Graves, Jr., "but she felt he let her down badly with the whole *Sunrise* fiasco."

By late 1927, Fox advised Olive they were cutting her salary (at her peak in 1926 she was earning $1500 per week). It was nothing personal. Many studios cut their actors' salaries around this time period because the advent of sound pictures was imminent. The "talkies" were a new and unknown quantity. The studios had no idea who'd make the crossover and who wouldn't. Voices, heard for the first time by filmgoers, often didn't match the characters and personas the actors had established over many years.

Many highly regarded silent actors careers were ruined by the sound era. It was a different acting style; there was less emoting involved because speech was now a factor in helping to tell the story. Several silent film stars with thick foreign and regional American accents were not well received by the early sound recording equipment. Greta Garbo and Marlene Dietrich survived because they were considered sensual and exotic. But Pola Negri, Anny Ondra, Vilma Banky, Norma Talmadge, Clara Bow, and many others were finished. Like many of her peers, Olive found the transition from silent to sound films problematical at first. The stars who once captivated their public's attention with dramatic, muted performances, were all of a sudden laughed at whenever they opened their mouths.

Popular and beautiful silent actress May McAvoy had the distinct honor of starring opposite Al Jolson (paid $75,000 for his role, equivalent to almost a million dollars in 2009) in what's considered the first feature length talkie, *The Jazz Singer* (1927). The aptly worded sentence, "Wait a minute, wait a minute, you ain't heard nothin' yet!" were the first words spoken by Jolson in the film. He was right. It was the beginning of a new era, a period of revolutionary change that no movie-going audience will ever likely experience again.

The Jazz Singer has musical sequences and "partial" sound; so it's technically part silent/

part sound (less than 350 spoken words), but it *was* the groundbreaking film of its time and it's still referred to as the "first feature-length talkie." A silent version of the film was also released to play in theaters that had not yet invested the $20,000 (converts to approximately $250,000 in 2009) it cost to wire a movie house for sound.

McAvoy had no speaking scenes in the film. But the following year, in the "partial talkie" *Caught in the Fog* (1928) when she did speak, her voice was soft, almost girlish, with a lisp! Needless to say her career was over.

Dolores Costello also spoke with a lisp; she sounded very similar to her granddaughter, Drew Barrymore. After two years of voice coaching, Dolores managed to overcome her speech impediment and made a handful of sound pictures, most notably *Little Lord Fauntleroy* (1936) and *The Magnificent Ambersons* (1942). Her final film was *This Is the Army* (1943). While Dolores worked to improve her speaking voice for the talkie era, her film career was ultimately ruined by the harshness of the abrasive early film makeup. Her delicate skin was so severely damaged, it took hours to camouflage. Costello passed away (emphysema) on March 1, 1979, in Fallbrook, California, at age seventy-five.

Olive had a distinctive Southern accent. Like Costello, she worked tirelessly with a diction coach. She was determined to lose her twang for the sake of the new era in film. As a result, she achieved moderate success in sounding more refined and several newspaper articles actually praised her speaking voice. It is wrong to assume that talkies ruined Olive's career because she adapted very well.

Sound or no sound, Olive took the salary reduction at Fox personally. She felt she deserved every penny and she refused to take a dollar less than she was getting. She was insulted, angry and heartbroken of the mere suggestion of a pay cut. Olive walked out on her contract because she was sure they'd beg her to come back. Her bluff backfired.

Instead, Fox waved goodbye, shut the door behind her and later told the newspapers that she was "temperamental." It was yet another slap in the face. No contract *and* public humiliation. On November 10, 1927, Louella O. Parsons reported that contract negotiations had been underway for several days without an agreement being reached. She announced that Olive will "leave the Fox organization when her present contract expires, about the end of November." Olive's career was far from over, but she lost momentum and confidence. Without a doubt, it was the beginning of the end. Olive was only twenty-one.

There was media speculation (*Motion Picture Monthly*, undated, 1928) that Olive was in an enhanced emotional state because of George leaving for Europe without her; and maybe somehow that played a big part in her not negotiating with Fox. No newspaper articles specified the exact time of George's trip to Europe. It was a "needle-in-a-haystack" moment that answered the question "Was George in Europe, with Murnau, when Olive and Fox parted ways?" A letter written by George's secretary, G. De Courcy, dated August 12, 1927, gives the valuable information that completes the timeline. Within this letter, De Courcy responds to a fan request for a photograph and apologizes on George's behalf for not having any new photos made because he has been working steadily in New York and hasn't had a chance to have any new ones taken. But, "on his return from Europe, when he answers your letter, he will forward new photographs." So George was in Europe — in mid–August of 1927. He would have been away and back at least two months *before* Olive's contract negotiations began. It's confirmed. His absence had no bearing on her decision to leave the studio. However, Fox's pandering to Murnau and the studio's reluctance to fight for her place in *Sunrise* was, without doubt, the beginning of her bitterness toward the powers that be at Fox.

Louella O. Parsons reported in her column on October 12, 1927, that John Ford had specifically asked for Olive to be the leading lady in his new romantic silent drama *Hangman's House* (1928). "Olive Borden is being considered for the lead," she said. "At least John Ford wants her, and these directors usually get the stars for their pictures that they want."

Hangman's House was set in Ireland and starred Victor McLaglen, Hobart Bosworth, Larry Kent, Earle Foxe and a then-unknown John Wayne. June Collyer played the female lead because Olive walked out on her contract and was no longer in the Fox stable. Disappointed, Ford had no choice but to look elsewhere for his leading lady. Ironically, as part of the 2007 "Ford at Fox Collection," *Hangman's House* was released on the same DVD as *3 Bad Men* (1926) as a double feature. Had Olive taken the Fox pay cut, *Hangman's House* would likely have been her next role with the studio. Ford wanted her and if Olive was still a contract player, he would have gotten his way.

Ford went on to become one of the most influential directors in the history of American cinema. During his illustrious career that spanned an astonishing *seven* decades, he received countless awards for his directing, including four Best Director Academy Awards. Had Olive taken the pay cut, stuck with Fox and played the lead in yet another film with the master at the helm, it's obvious her career would have taken a very different path.

Just as her contract at Fox ended, Olive took delivery of a made-to-order gunmetal Lincoln convertible. The specially built Lincoln, ordered through Stephen S. Nerney of Hollywood, was the only one of its kind on the West Coast at that time. It was her third car. Despite being unemployed, Olive's extravagant spending continued. In fact, it seemed to get worse. Depressed at not having a job, she bought cars, jewelry and furs to make herself happy. Within months, the world she had worked so hard to build was about to come crashing down around her.

Olive had always enjoyed interior decorating. She designed her own home from top to bottom and helped many of her friends with theirs. She had often thought about opening her own shop and working for clueless, but wealthy, homeowners who needed help designing their interiors. With her Fox contract behind her, now was the perfect time to make that career change but Olive was too depressed to make the transition from actress to designer. She spent her time brooding at how poorly Fox had treated her. In the meantime, she had no income and no job offers, and her lavish lifestyle was starting to catch up with her.

It became painfully obvious that Olive could no longer afford to stay in her luxurious $65,000 (converts to approximately $810,000 in 2009) Beverly Hills mansion at 627 Hillcrest Road. She reluctantly made arrangements for its sale and Olive and her mother moved to a smaller residence in Santa Monica. Her four housemaids — gone. Her chauffeur-driven limousine, on standby 24-7 — also gone. Mandy, her loyal cook, stayed on, as did Lila, her personal maid. They were the only hired help that Olive could still afford and insisted she couldn't do without.

She tried to convince herself, and the public, that she was much happier in her new, smaller home, saying, "It's much nicer being in a little house. Now I can sit in my bedroom and call to Mother and she can hear me. It used to be that I had to write her a note. What's the use of a big house with only two people to live in it? What's the use of all the pomp and ceremony when you're not the type you're playing?

"Look here, I was never a grand lady. I couldn't be what they wanted me to be. And the more I tried, the bigger fool I was. How could I have dared to give myself such grand airs when I was making such bad pictures?

"I'm not that exotic, vampish type. I don't want to be a great dramatic actress. I'm not sophisticated. Why should I try to play sophisticated roles? I've two ambitions. On the screen I want to be a good comedienne. And off the screen I want to be a real honest-to-God woman!" ("Olive in Quest of Her Soul," Helen Loring, *Photoplay*, December 1929).

Piece by piece, most of Olive's antique furniture was sold, and one by one, her beloved collection of fourteen fur coats warmed the bodies of other women who could afford the luxury of owning them. Olive knew downgrading was an admission of failure, but it was all she could do to pay the mounting bills. After all, Olive was now $40,000 (converts to approximately $500,000 in 2009) in debt and unemployed!

As Olive sat in her walk-in closet, with most of her designer clothes, fur coats and fancy shoes gone, she suddenly remembered a low-heeled pair of English walking shoes that she came to Hollywood wearing. She found them, slipped them on her much-photographed feet and took a deep breath. She had finally come back down to earth. It was with an almighty thud, but her feet were now firmly on the ground — literally! It was back to basics and a long way from the fanfare that she once enjoyed as Fox's little darling of the screen.

As Olive prepared to move out of her house and liquidate most of the treasured possessions that the riches of a successful career had given her, she was now without a film contract, without an "entourage," without a job, and forced to sell it all to make ends meet. A future of uncertainty lay ahead and the only "realness" that remained was the personality that she had arrived in Hollywood with — that of a sweet Southern girl. She was never the "temperamental, haughty, movie star" that Fox demand she be. She was still "Ollie" and she swore she would never again be told how to act offscreen by any studio or anyone — ever again!

The furniture that Olive owned, and didn't owe on, was shipped to the new smaller residence in Santa Monica. She kept her radio because she believed when she was at her lowest, she could turn it on and whistle to it, and it would keep her courage up. Her bookcase, packed with many expensive first editions, never read (she never had time), would also go with her. Time was all she had now. Finally she could catch up on her reading, and she did just that, for it would be close to six months before she returned to acting.

Ironically, the most important piece of furniture she took was a small desk with a big burden! The desk was so crammed with overdue bills, they were overflowing from the drawers. But, they were bills that Olive had every intention of paying — somehow.

Not surprisingly, many willing gentlemen with bulging bank accounts offered to come to her rescue with proposals of marriage and money to help her out of her predicament. That was the easy way out. But Olive didn't take it. She graciously thanked every one of them but declined all offers of "help" and continued on figuring out how she was going to meet those bills on her own without giving up the independence that she worked so hard to achieve. Sitting by herself on moonlit evenings when other girls were out at the Cocoanut Grove, or the Biltmore, she found the magic answer. To get out of debt, she had to get further into it!

She took out a mortgage on a business building that was self-supporting. The rent gave her enough money to pay off the monthly mortgage and the little that was left over was enough to live on and chip away at the unpaid debts. Together with the money she earned on several independent productions during 1928, it only took her a year to pay off the building. And, not long after that, almost all the bills in her desk were stamped PAID in bright red ink. Olive was by no means wealthy, but she was just about debt-free and she

Olive in a dramatic scene from *Come to My House* (1927).

did it all on her own. If only she'd thought more about how to invest her money when she had it, her lavish lifestyle need never have downsized along with her career.

Shortly after Olive proudly climbed out of her financial hole, she sat down with reporter Walter Ramsey. She leant across the table and said, "Know what I really want to do? I want to go to Paris to live. I've heard that a person can get along on about a third of what it takes to live in this country. And they live more slowly over there — more enjoyably I think" ("She Can Take It: Olive Borden Has Character As Well As Curves," *Motion Picture Classic*, November, 1929).

Christmas Day 1927 and Olive's last Fox feature, *Come to My House*, was newly released. By early 1928 it was circulating throughout theatres in most cities and towns across America. Around the same time there was a rumor going around Hollywood circles that she and the studio might reconcile. A *Los Angeles Times* article (February 19, 1928) entitled "Star May Return to Fox Films" printed an exclusive interview with Olive on why ties were severed with the studio. To her dismay, Fox had publicly stated that Olive was "difficult" and "temperamental." A very ugly smear campaign was brewing. Olive put on the bravest of faces in an attempt to cling to her good reputation and save face with her public.

The *Los Angeles Times* article mentioned the ongoing confusion surrounding the breakdown between Olive and the studio. Here was a star on whom hundreds of thousands of dollars had been spent for exploitation, whose dozen-odd vehicles had been moneymakers at the box office, literally walking out on the company which indubitably had "made" her. And all of Hollywood asked, "Why?"

The article gave Olive a chance to tell her side of the story. It was important for her to make a candid, honest, public attempt to protect and restore her reputation and secure her future in the industry. Fox was on the warpath and, because of the studio smear campaign, Olive's name was very quickly becoming mud!

Olive emphatically stated that she was perfectly willing to renew her contract, but she wanted a chance to do something worthwhile and they wouldn't let her have it. She was weary of being told by directors, "We'll have you do everything, be everything, in this film." She was allowed no say in the selection of her stories, just plunged into one after another, rushed to Canada and New York and Florida, hurried through three whole pictures in the time it took Murnau to make *Sunrise*, and in two years, she was never offered a real vacation.

"I have been criticized on the score of 'putting on the dog' because I used my car for driving short distances — from set to dressing-room, and so on. The stages, many of them, are across the street from the little bungalow I occupied. Obviously, I could not run back and forth in bathing suits and other scanty outfits. When Fox first began its program of expansion, I was told that important plays and books had been purchased for me, even that I was to go abroad to act in them. Just as suddenly, the plans were changed; and that left me exactly where I was before."

Incidentally, Olive's forthright explanation did nothing to get her foot back in Fox's door, so to speak. Despite rumors, there were never any renewed contract negotiations. Olive Borden and Fox Studios were history.

While *Come to My House* was Olive's last film for Fox, she still put her heart and soul into the production. While filming the fast-paced boat scenes off Catalina Island, Olive refused a stunt double and insisted on being in the shots herself. Olive was cutting through the waves in a powerboat when it struck a cross wave and tipped to one side. Olive was thrown over against the end of the boat, but she didn't let go of the wheel. One of her expensive earrings was knocked off during the commotion and when she docked the company searched for the piece of jewelry but it was nowhere to be found. Olive shrugged it off and stated, "Well, it's better the earring going overboard than me!" (*Sidelights of the Stage and Screen*, January 18, 1928).

After the production was complete, Olive and her mother enjoyed some beachside rest and recreation. They took a house at 905 Ocean Front in Santa Monica. The *Los Angeles Times* column "The Society of Cinemaland" (February 19, 1928) reported that Olive had been "quite ill" and she and her mother would remain at the temporary home for at least three months until she was well enough to travel abroad to France and Italy for another three-month break.

Despite not having a long-term studio contract, Olive continued to work steadily and her next few films were for a variety of studios. A *Los Angeles Times* article of October 19, 1928 stated, "Olive Borden is planning to go to Europe just as soon as she completes her present F. B. O. picture, *Love in the Desert*, which George Melford is directing. Accompanied by her mother, Miss Borden proposes to spend two months in Paris, Berlin and London."

Before the trip, Olive attended the premiere of the Michael Curtiz epic *Noah's Ark* (1928) at Grauman's Chinese Theatre. Following the film, a party was held at Bess Meredyth's house. *The Los Angeles Times* (November 25, 1928) ran a one-page story on the star-studded event; under the headline "A Hollywood Party!" it reported that Olive had arrived with George O'Brien (who also starred in the picture) as her date. George's leading lady in the film, Dolores Costello, accompanied the couple to the lavish event.

During the filming of the climactic flood scene for *Noah's Ark*, the volume of water used was so overwhelming that three extras drowned, another was so badly injured that his leg needed to be amputated, and a number suffered broken limbs and other serious injuries. Director Curtiz was so excited by the realism, he continued to shout directions at the sea of drowning people and kept cameras rolling. Thirty-five ambulances attended the injured. The chaotic scene was reminiscent of a war zone. Costello caught a severe case of pneumonia. John Wayne and Andy Devine appeared among the hundreds of extras in the flood scene (*Stunt: The Story of the Great Movie Stunt Men*, John O. Baxter, Doubleday, New York, 1974).

Olive complained that watching the film had exhausted her and she'd shed tears through most of it. "I don't know how on earth Olive managed to weep so much and yet look so fresh and lovely," remarked one party guest. "I never could do it." It was also noted that Olive had almost heaved herself out of her tight-fitting dress at the highly emotional moments of the picture.

In the highly acclaimed Kevin Brownlow/David Gill–produced thirteen-part series *Hollywood* (1980), Olive and George are seen for a brief few seconds at the *Noah's Ark* premiere. They're in good spirits, laughing and looking excited to be greeted by so many adoring fans.

Olive and George were constantly by each other's side. They'd rarely miss a film premiere, a charity event or a lavish Hollywood party held by their peers. They even attended Rudolph Valentino's West Coast funeral on Tuesday morning, September 7, 1926. Lon Chaney, John Gilbert, Montagu Love, Malcolm McGregor, Antonio Moreno and George were ushers.

The two went their separate ways by December of 1929; many people suggested that neither one of them really got over each other completely. For close to four years they were the most perfectly coiffed and happiest couple on the social scene. Their parting took many by surprise. There was never a solid explanation for the break-up; the strongest rumor circulating was that George's strict Irish-Catholic family did not approve of Olive's hard-partying ways. George was a dedicated son and closely connected to his family; for George, breaking off his engagement to Olive with the feeling that his family knew best was not an

Studio head Jack Warner, with leading man George O'Brien and leading lady Dolores Costello on the set of *Noah's Ark* (1928).

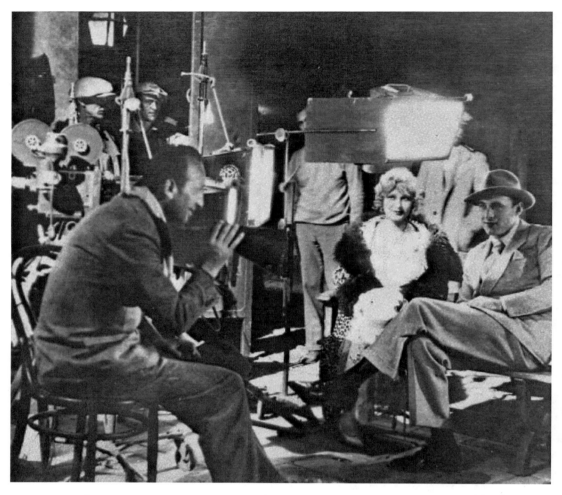

George O'Brien and Dolores Costello look to Michael Curtiz for direction on the set of *Noah's Ark* (1928).

inconceivable notion. And Olive had her own problems with a meddling parent (Sibbie). Olive was rarely out of her mother's sight. Sibbie was definitely the third wheel in Olive and George's relationship.

In a March 1926 issue of *Photoplay*, Sibbie insisted that George was "just a dear good friend." Looking at the date of the article, at that point in time, that may well have been the case. Olive (in the same article) also dismissed tales of a "relationship" by waving her hands in denial of anything romantic between herself and George. However, there was no denying the burgeoning romance that blossomed and flourished in the months and years to follow.

Disapproving parents aside, the early cracks in Olive and George's relationship initially surfaced due to professional reasons when George began the arduous creative process imposed on him by *Sunrise* director, Murnau. Firstly, George being pulled as the leading man from Olive's *Pajamas* because Murnau handpicked him for the lead in *Sunrise*. Secondly, Olive being pulled as the female lead from *Sunrise* because Murnau refused to direct

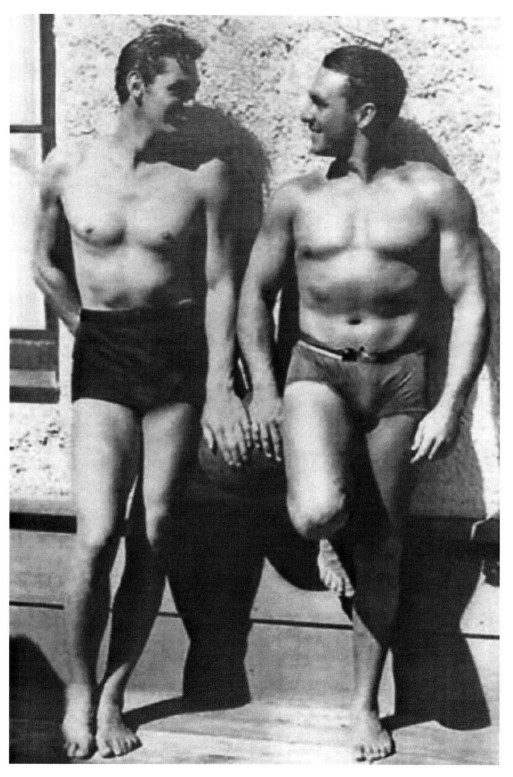

Johnny Weissmuller (left) aka "Tarzan," showing off his famous physique, and George O'Brien, proving why he earned the nickname "The Chest."

actors involved in a personal relationship offscreen. Thirdly, the enforced separation for two weeks prior to filming so that George could "lose himself" and become "The Man," his intense character in *Sunrise*. And lastly, George's solo trip to Germany (and Paris) to meet with Murnau in August 1927. These were all contributing factors toward the eventual split.

Despite their relationship weathering the "Murnau storm" for nearly three more years, Olive felt betrayed by George. Her antipathy toward Murnau caused many arguments between them. Olive felt that George's personality transformation for the role of "The Man" never really left him. He changed and they parted ways. "Olive told my father that O'Brien played 'The Man' in *Sunrise* but when it was over he was no longer 'the man' that she knew," said Ralph Graves, Jr. "Their relationship problems began with *Sunrise* and his parents and Olive's mother were more pressure points, yes, definitely. But I don't think it was one particular incident that broke them apart. It was a number of things. It got too much, for both of them. They were arguing all the time so they thought it best to split. Two good people, both of them, just honest, good decent people who under different circumstances probably would have made it."

On July 15, 1933, George O'Brien married actress Marguerite Churchill. They had three children together. Daughter Orin has played double bass for the New York Philharmonic Orchestra since 1966. In its prestigious 125-year history, aside from the occasional female harpists, Orin was the first woman to join the 104-member orchestra full-time. Asked about her father's romance with Olive for this book, Orin claimed her father only ever mentioned Olive Borden in passing as one of his co-stars; never as a love interest. Orin's brother Darcy was an award-winning novelist and professor of English. Darcy passed away in 1998, two years before his mother. A third child, Brian, died in infancy.

George and Marguerite separated in February of 1948, just four months after Olive's death, and were divorced on July 15, 1948, their fifteenth wedding anniversary. Marguerite sobbed as she told Judge Otto J. Emme that since her husband's return from service as a Navy lieutenant commander, their life had not been happy. "His attitude toward me changed," she cried. "He said he regretted very much having to take up married life again with its responsibilities. Sometimes he locked himself in his room. Often he disappeared for days at a time." The couple split their $300,000 (converts to approximately $2.7 million in 2009) in assets and O'Brien was to pay monthly child support for Orin (thirteen) and Darcy (nine). Neither of them ever remarried.

Churchill died of natural causes in Broken Arrow, Oklahoma, on January 9, 2000. She was eighty-nine. By the early 1980s, as O'Brien's health deteriorated, he became bedridden (following a stroke) and remained that way for the last few years of his life. He died in Tulsa, Oklahoma, on September 4, 1985. He was eighty-six. For his contribution to the motion picture industry he was awarded a star on the Hollywood Walk of Fame at 6201 Hollywood Blvd.

In a personal letter written to author Michael Ankerich in 1994, Darcy O'Brien *did* recall his father's romance with Olive, and stated, "Before my mother, she was his great love." He said she had a rather wild reputation; his father's ex-secretary, who also doubled as a stunt rider in his silent Westerns, personally told Darcy, "Olive was in debt to the stagehands," but he gathered that she meant that on a monetary or friendship level — not sexual. Darcy said that when Olive died, his mother did urge George to go to her funeral. He didn't. Despite his mother's blessing, Darcy presumed (knowing his father) that he stayed away out of respect for his mother's feelings. She didn't *really* want him to go and he knew it.

Without a doubt, the war(s) had a devastating effect on George's psyche. If *Sunrise* truly shifted his personality, as Olive suggested, the war(s) certainly finished him off. Following his service, he found it extremely difficult to readjust to civilian life. The role of husband and father was suddenly too much for him to cope with. He even found difficulty in returning to the role he knew best — that of an actor.

In 1917, during World War I, George (age eighteen) enlisted in the United States Navy, serving on a submarine chaser. He also volunteered as a stretcher-bearer for wounded Marines and was decorated for bravery under fire. Following his first round of military service and his successful silent film career, George's good looks, athletic build and expert horsemanship allowed him to fit into the popular genre of talking Westerns with ease; he became one of the top five Western stars of the era. With World War II brewing, George abandoned his film career (prior to Pearl Harbor) and re-enlisted in the United States Navy. He served as a beach master in the Pacific and was again decorated several times for bravery under fire. This time he left service with the rank of commander (www.imdb.com).

With two world wars behind him and his marriage in trouble, he found it even harder to return to acting. His long-time friend, director John Ford, stepped in to help and cast George in several of his films of the late 1940s, including *Fort Apache* (1948) and *She Wore a Yellow Ribbon* (1949). George also served in the Naval Reserve in both the Korean and Vietnam Wars. He retired with the rank of captain in 1962. He was recommended for the rank of admiral four times.

As Darcy confessed, Olive held a very special place in his father's heart. His post-war personality change was further heightened by Olive's untimely death just months before he and Marguerite Churchill separated.

CHAPTER 11

The Most Misunderstood
Girl in Hollywood

Because of the continued hate campaign directed at Olive in the media following her Fox walkout, writer Hal K. Wells of *Motion Picture Classic* took it upon himself to write an article in her defense. He genuinely liked her and he felt she had been wrongly represented following her Fox contract breakdown. He started his July 1928 article by saying, "I am growing most thoroughly tired of hearing about that very temperamental and ritzy little actress — Olive Borden — because no such person exists, or ever did."

Wells had conducted Olive's first ever interview a few years prior and claimed he got to know Olive rather well from that point on. Following her Fox walkout, the newspaper and magazine article claims she was "volcanic," "impossible" and "temperamental," and of making the lives of film associates and the press miserable with her "high-hatted" ways, were, according to Wells — all "Bunk!" He explains that when Olive first sprang from comparative obscurity to the lofty heights of Fox stardom, the executives formulated two main policies for her future career path: First, to present "clothes-horse" sequences in all her pictures to show off her perfect figure to the greatest advantage; second, to create a new star personality, a combination of Gloria Swanson, Alla Nazimova and the Duchess of York.

The first policy was carried out with "grim thoroughness." Never for more than two reels was Olive seen more than half-dressed. The lingerie sequences, leopard skin sequences, bathtub sequences (and any other scenario a writer could concoct to showcase her in a form of undress) were written — and she obliged. Olive hated her scantily clad scenes but she did them because she was told they would most certainly make her a star. She tried to make good on the second production policy too, but her personality was her own and she wasn't about to change it — not even for the sake of becoming a film star.

She had been instructed by the studio to be aloof and coldly impersonal on set. They wanted to give her the reputation of being "temperamental" — that was Fox's premeditated plan. She was called into the office of one of the Fox executives and firmly told that it was no longer "in character" for her to speak with such "menials as the electricians, stage hands, and prop boys."

Olive tried half-heartedly to do the Duchess act for a few days, then refused point-blank to continue snubbing her friends among the studio's workers. Wrote Wells, "That is one serious flaw in Olive's character for any peace of mind in Hollywood, where 'yessing' the powers that be has become one of the fine arts. Olive couldn't 'yes' C. B. DeMille himself, unless she happened to mean 'yes' at the time."

Olive Borden has forsaken the cloistered confines of the Fox lot to become a freelance artist. Independence, we call it. But Olive, if the pose below counts for anything, is hipped on the idea

Hesser Photos

A Ripe Olive

with French Dressing

A 1928 magazine ad promoting Olive as a freelance artist following her Fox walkout.

Olive in a publicity shot showcasing her tiny waist, circa 1929.

In spite of her refusal to play the temperamental role, somehow that reputation still managed to attach itself to her. Wells said, "It [the 'temperamental' rep] represents a serious menace to both her happiness and her career."

Olive did have one fatal personal characteristic that helped build that "temperamental" reputation. She suffered from extreme shyness amongst strangers. She was often frightened half out of her wits when forced to meet a group of people she'd never met before. And, like many people with the same affliction, her glacial temperament in that particular situation gave the people meeting her the impression that she was snobby or "high-hatted."

One instance brought up in the article was an afternoon tea at the Ritz in New York. Fox wanted the Eastern magazine and newspaper people to meet their new star, and the Ritz ballroom was hired for the affair. After waiting around long past the time the writers were told Olive would appear, they were finally greeted by "a strangely flustered young actress who fluctuated between icy dignity one minute and almost kittenish coyness the next." As a result, many of those writers went back to their desks and wrote scathing pieces that were "almost savage in their disapproval."

Wells said that Olive did not even know until fifteen minutes before that there was to be a tea held. She was rushed into the ballroom to confront the waiting crowd without even learning whether the affair was in her honor or someone else's. None of the studio publicity men were available to help. Olive didn't know what to do. She did know that it was vitally important that she make a favorable impression upon the assembled writers, most of whom were seeing her for the first time.

The best way to refute her reputation of being "temperamental" and "hard to work with" is to rehash a few facts. Wells gave the following three examples of Olive's good-natured, committed work ethic.

The incident when she was thrown from the galloping horse on *3 Bad Men* (1926). She went right back to work with little complaint and worked through her pain. For months afterward she concealed her sore back and side and went gamely ahead making pictures until she was hospitalized with appendicitis. There was speculation that she may have damaged her appendix in the fall. Subsequently, she had her appendix removed and was hospitalized for weeks. Her back gave her constant pain for the rest of her life. "I think that horse-riding accident may quite possibly have been the beginning

Olive on the cover of the February 1928 issue of *Picture Play* magazine.

of her drinking to numb the pain of her permanent back injury," said Ralph Graves, Jr. "I remember how much she loved the water, she loved to swim, mostly because it helped ease her back pain. I had a couple of nice photos of her and me by the pool. Wish I could find them now. I've looked everywhere with no luck."

Wells brings up the *Sunrise* (1927) debacle and Olive's sudden replacement in the lead role by Janet Gaynor. He said Olive was anything but bitter and temperamental over being pulled from the role. She was hurt and disappointed, but she did not let her emotions or "temperament" get in the way of helping Gaynor prepare for the role that she herself had already studied for. She was completely professional and did what she felt was right, going above and beyond what most actresses would have done in the same situation.

Olive was also labeled "temperamental" because she demanded a car take her from her dressing room to the stage, just across the street. It does sound like ridiculous "diva behavior" *until* you learn that the street she was to cross was the busy Western Avenue, one of Hollywood's busiest roads, and that Olive's costume was nothing more than a skimpy nightgown. She was well within her rights to ask for door-to-door transport in order to maintain her modesty and her dignity.

Wells ended his article by saying, "It's high time that the myth of the Borden temperament and ritzy airs be laid forever to rest. It has already brought enough heartache to its helpless victim. I've written this brief story without Olive's knowledge or consent. She is very distinctly not the whining type. She'd rather take a sound spanking than even hint to anyone how savagely the situation has really hurt her."

Hurt her it did — personally and professionally. The mud slung by Fox stuck. It was almost a case of, "If we can't have you, we'll make sure no one else does either!" For the years that followed, Olive had no choice but to prove her temperament and her work ethic — all over again.

CHAPTER 12

They Have Voices!

By 1929, the scandal and negative publicity surrounding Olive's separation from Fox was finally dying down and her career seemed to be back on track. She now had a four-picture deal with Radio Pictures (RKO). *Half Marriage* (1929) was the first "all-talking" feature of the proposed four to be released for the studio. It was also Olive's first all-talking role. Her voice recorded well and she was naturally charming throughout the picture.

After her Fox walkout, Olive picked up three films with F.B.O (*Gang War*, 1928, *Sinners in Love*, 1928, and *Love in the Desert*, 1929); a one-time engagement with Tiffany Stahl (*The Albany Night Boat*, 1928); and three films with Columbia Pictures (*Virgin Lips* and *Stool Pigeon*, 1928; *The Eternal Woman*, 1929). *Gang War* and *Love in the Desert* were particularly significant because Olive's voice was heard, albeit briefly, for the very first time. Both productions inserted a few lines of dialogue and various sound effects in post-production. At the dawn of all-talking pictures, silent films were being peppered with speech, gunfire, footsteps and screams. Within a matter of months, Olive and the rest of her inaudible contemporaries would leave silent film behind — forever.

Cinematographer Joseph Walker photographed Olive on two films, *Virgin Lips* and *The Eternal Woman*. In his autobiography *The Light on Her Face* (ASC Press, 1984) he clearly remembered the strictness of Sibbie and the tight reins she held on her daughter: "Olive's mother, a large woman with dyed red hair and unmistakably Irish, trusted no one on the set; she watched us cagily and wouldn't allow her attractive daughter out of her sight."

When the more permanent offer came from Radio Pictures, Olive gladly accepted. Unfortunately, the four-picture deal became a two-picture deal. *Half Marriage* and *Dance Hall* (1929) were Olive's only two films for the studio. However, *Every Week Magazine* reported in 1929 that *three* of Olive's four pictures for RKO were completed. One of Olive's "completed" RKO pictures, aside from *Half Marriage* and *Dance Hall*, was said to be called *Tanned Legs* (1929), directed by Marshall Neilan and starring Arthur Lake, Olive's leading man in *Dance Hall*. However, the eventual leading lady was little-known newcomer June Clyde — *not* Olive.

In *Half Marriage*, Olive stars as the wealthy party girl-art student Judy Page. After one of the many wild (and somewhat wacky) parties that appear to be held quite often at her Greenwich Village apartment, she elopes with Dick Carroll (Morgan Farley), a young, poorly paid architect employed by her snobby father. Following their hasty middle of the night nuptials by a very accommodating over-the-border country justice of the peace, they spend their first night together as man and wife and wake up blissfully happy.

Judy's mother (Hedda Hopper) ruins the fun when she arrives unexpectedly and insists

Olive as Ann Hardy and Daphne Pollard as Mabel in the FBO feature *Sinners in Love* (1928).

that, since her school is now closed, Judy must immediately return to the Page country estate with her. Before answering the door, Judy hustles her secret husband out onto the balcony. She dresses, quickly straightens the room and regains her composure before letting her mother and Tom Stribbling, a slimy, smooth-talking wannabe (parent-approved) husband of Judy's, into her apartment.

Hiding on the apartment balcony with drapes drawn to prevent him from being seen, Dick listens, and sometimes sneaks a peek, as his lovely bride willingly agrees with her mother about returning home. Judy quickly packs her bags to leave the city without him. Before leaving, Judy manages to usher Tom and her meddling mother out of the apartment ahead of her. There's just enough time to say a quick goodbye to her bemused husband. She kisses him and promises to call him — soon.

After three long weeks apart, and while her stuffy parents are away, Dick finally visits Judy at the family home. With their marriage still a secret, Dick has words with Tom after he pays too much "attention" to Judy, his *wife*, at the country club dance. Frustrated and angry at Dick for keeping such close tabs on her, Judy storms out of the dance. Dick follows her and they begin to argue about the state of their relationship. In the heat of the moment, both agree that their "Half Marriage" (since only they know about it), was a huge mistake. Judy tells Dick to meet her at her city apartment at nine the following night to

Olive with Eddie Gribbon in a scene from *Gang War* (1928).

discuss what to do about their situation. When Tom gets wind of their evening rendezvous, he instantly assumes Judy is a loose woman and decides to make his own moves on her. Tom sneakily intercedes and sends a telegram to Dick, canceling the meeting.

With Dick out of the picture, an intoxicated Tom shows up at Judy's apartment unannounced. When he forces himself on her, a struggle ensues and Judy runs out to the balcony to escape his unwanted advances. As it happens, Dick sees the pair struggling on the ledge from the other side of the street. Within seconds, Tom loses his footing and plunges six stories to his death. Dick immediately races to Judy's apartment to help her. Hysterical and in shock, Judy repeatedly screams, "I killed him! I killed him!"

When the police start asking questions, Dick does all that he can to protect Judy. He gallantly takes full blame for Tom's death. However, after the police delve further, and just as Judy's concerned parents arrive at her apartment, the truth is revealed — on two counts.

Judy is cleared of any wrongdoing in Tom's death due to self defense; and a happy ending is had by all when Judy's secret marriage to Dick is revealed and given the full blessing of her society parents.

Olive's performance in *Half Marriage*, along with the film in general, received a scathing review from the *Chicago Daily Tribune* (August 27, 1929). The photography was called "okay," the quality "inferior" and the direction "not good"; the in-depth review didn't get

The original glass movie preview slide for *Sinners in Love* (1928).

any better. "Olive Borden is utterly disappointing. Richard Tucker and Hedda Hopper struggle nobly with stupid situations. The day is only one quarter saved by Ken Murray who is a clever entertainer and almost succeeds in injecting some pep into the aimless and haphazard offering. Minor roles are played — and that's about all you can say for them."

It's a little puzzling to see that Ken Murray gets a small dose of half-hearted praise by the *Chicago Tribune*, especially since he has one of the most annoying roles in the film. His long-winded jokes, deplorable singing ("You're Marvelous" at the country club dance) and unaccountable desire to grab an unsuspecting man on the dance floor, spin him around and then flip him over his shoulder borders on the bizarre. This tactic happens on several occasions throughout the film. Maybe that's the injection of "pep" the newspaper is referring to? He may now be a dated entertainer, but Ken Murray had a brutally honest saying about Hollywood that was true then and is still true now: "Hollywood is a place where you spend more than you make on things you don't need to impress people you don't like!" (www.imdb.com).

Despite having a rather prominent part in *Half Marriage*, Olive's other co-star, Anderson Lawler, went without a mention in most reviews. Unfortunately for him, it was a pattern followed for much of his career. *Half Marriage* was one of two films that Lawler made during 1929 and it was the beginning of a rather miserable career path that limped along for a decade or thereabouts, ending in 1939 with *Torchy Blane in Chinatown* (1939). Lawler died twenty years later (April 6, 1959) at age fifty-six (www.afi.com).

Lawler's disdain for his role as Tom Stribbling in *Half Marriage* stuck with him long after the film was released; he perhaps even blamed it for his lackluster future in Hollywood, saying, "The fucking high point of my career was in *Half Marriage* in 1929. What crap! I jumped to my death from an upper floor when I learned I was losing Olive Borden in the film. Who writes such crap, and for me no less? My mother was convinced though. She took a train all the way from Alabama to Hollywood to see if I had survived the fall" (*The Secret Life of Humphrey Bogart: The Early Years [1899–1931]*, Darwin Porter, Blood Moon Productions, 2003). Lawler's acting "career" aside, by the early thirties the homosexual actor became more noted for his role of escort to some of Hollywood's most beautiful women. Kay Francis, Tallulah Bankhead, Marlene Dietrich, and Constance Bennett, just to name a few, all "used" Lawler as their token date when they were in need of a man to accompany them to a premiere. There was no romantic pressure and Lawler was always the life of the party. Being a professional date wasn't exactly the role he wanted to be known for, but as fate would have it, Lawler's eventual "fame" came from being "seen" with someone famous.

Olive received mixed reviews for her *Half Marriage* performance mainly because of the less than stellar material she was given to work with. However, her "naturalness" and "vocal abilities" in her first speaking role were often noted by critics, despite the poor script.

Dance Hall also received mixed reviews but audiences loved the peppy dance hall theme, and as a result it played to capacity houses throughout the country. *Dance Hall* is a simple, endearing tale of young love,

An original newspaper ad for *Gang War* (1928).

Olive on the cover of *Motion Picture Classic*, March 1929.

Olive was featured in a magazine photograph spread wearing this elaborate costume and labeled a "modern Southern belle." Her latest movie release was promoted as *Companionte* which was the working title for *Half Marriage* (1929).

heartbreak and the usual happy ending that many early Hollywood films were known for. Tommy Flynn (Arthur Lake) is a young, "gosh-darn-it" type of guy who lives at home with his doting mother (Margaret Seddon). A regular at the local dance hall, he's an exceptional dancer, with trophies to prove it. This cash-strapped shipping clerk is also head-over-heels in love with Gracie Nolan (Olive), a bubbly, wide-eyed dance hall hostess who partners up with him in the nightly dance competitions. Despite being financially challenged, Tommy intends to ask Gracie to marry him; however, the dashing, older, smooth-talking stunt pilot Ted Smith (Ralph Emerson), who Tommy naively believes to be his friend, sweet-talks Gracie and steals her heart. As Tommy searches for Gracie in the bustling dance hall so he can propose to her, he finds Ted snuggling with Gracie in a corner. Crushed, Tommy soon realizes his love for Gracie is one-sided.

Ted is about to fly out of town on a ten-day mission and he asks the good-natured yet broken-hearted, Tommy to watch out for Gracie while he's gone. Of course, he agrees. A couple of days into Ted's trip, a newspaper headline

An ad for *Half Marriage* (1929) from the 1930 edition of the *Motion Picture Almanac*.

announces that his plane has gone down and he's yet to be found. When Gracie reads the headline, she collapses. Tommy carries her to his home and calls a doctor, who diagnoses Gracie as having a "heart condition" due to nervous shock. "She must rest and stay calm for a couple of weeks," he says. Tommy convinces his mother that Gracie is to stay with them until she completely recovers. As the weeks roll by, Gracie regains her strength. But, when Tommy makes a brief visit to the dance hall, he finds out that Ted is alive and well and has been back in town for two days. Out of fear of losing her again, Tommy chooses not to tell Gracie the news. When Gracie finds out that Ted is alive, she's furious at Tommy for keeping the news of Ted's return from her and she accuses him of being "selfish." Determined to make things right, Tommy storms out of his house to get Ted. When he arrives at Ted's home, Ted is "preoccupied" with Bee (Helen Kaiser); it's clear that Gracie is a fling of the past. Bee answers the door to Tommy and pretends, as per Ted's wishes, that he isn't home. When Tommy asks Bee where he could possibly find him, she tells him that he may be at the dance hall later. Tommy runs into Ted and Bee at the dance hall later that evening, confronting him about his treatment of Gracie, and a fight breaks out.

Olive posing with blonde hair for her role as Gracie Nolan in *Dance Hall* (1929).

Tommy comes off worse for wear and Ted and Bee are ordered to leave. On their way out, they run in to Gracie. Ted tells her that he was never really serious about her and figured she wasn't serious about him either. He makes light of the situation and tells Gracie that he and Bee are a couple. He then brazenly asks if they can still be "friends." Gracie tells Ted what she thinks of him and, after he and Bee leave the dance hall, she has a good cry on the shoulder of Bremmer (Joseph Cawthorn), the protective dance hall proprietor.

When Gracie finds out that Tommy is nursing a bruised face (and ego), she rushes to his side. She apologizes for the way she's treated him, confesses her love and tells him that she knows he's been loyal and wonderful to her all along. They kiss. The happy ending is topped off by Gracie and Tommy being employed as the new pro-dancers at the dance hall, for $200 (converts to approximately $2,500 in 2009) each a week!

Olive's cousin Natalie Joyce, who could easily pass as

The original glass movie preview slide for *Dance Hall* (1929).

her twin sister, appeared alongside her in *Dance Hall*. She only
has a brief scene, helping Tommy
up off the floor after his fight with
Ted, but there she is, unbelievably
similar in looks and voice as her
well-known cousin. Olive traded
her signature dark locks and went
blonde for the film. Melville
Brown, director of *Dance Hall*,
stated that most dance hall girls
are either blondes or redheads and
he wanted Olive to really look the
part (*The Capital Times,* October
30, 1929).

One review said, "The picture has been produced with sincerity and intelligence... *Dance*

A blonde Olive with her cousin, Natalie Joyce, in a publicity still for *Dance Hall* (1929).

A besotted Arthur Lake in a scene with Olive from *Dance Hall* (1929).

Hall boasts one of the most competent all-around casts ever to be assembled for a talking picture. Olive Borden, more bewitching than ever before in her newly-blonde tresses..." (*Hamilton Evening Journal*, May 24, 1930).

The *Ogden Standard Examiner* (January 22, 1930) reported on Olive's change of hair color and the confusion it would have caused prior to a new system the studio implemented specifically to avoid mistaken identity. It was the classic moss-grown gag about the studio gateman who halted the star as she entered the studio because he could not recognize her in makeup. Olive Borden, wittingly or not, did it. She arrived in her car, her brunette bob transformed to a vivid blonde for a new role, and otherwise made up so that he did not resemble Olive in the least. A studio press agent standing nearby figuratively pulled out pencil and paper, gloatingly. The gateman, however, failed to play his part. He did not recognize her either, but a new system made such recognition unnecessary. He glanced at the studio badge on the car and turned to his list. The badge, No. 175, could belong to no other car than Olive Borden's. And that was that. The press agent departed disappointedly.

As previously mentioned, *Dance Hall* fared much better with audiences than *Half Marriage* and was generally praised by the majority of the nation's critics for being a "fascinating picture" acted with "brilliance and sincerity" (*Chicago Daily Tribune*, January 7, 1930).

Despite regaining her status as a darling of the silver screen, Olive never really got over the fact that Fox dubbed her "temperamental." She continually tried to explain their interpretation of the word and defend her personality. That was her mistake. She should have just let it go and moved on. She couldn't. It ate her up.

Olive had always refused to be a "yes" girl. If she didn't like something, she'd say so. At the completion of each picture, all the people connected with the film would get together and tell one another what a great production it was — even if it was terrible. It was that type of fake adoration that got under her skin. If Olive didn't like her pictures, she'd say so in no uncertain terms. Hollywood people were all about patting one another on the back when they were together and then walking away and stabbing those same people in the back to advance their own careers. Olive despised that behavior, and because she spoke up and had an opinion she was labeled "temperamental."

If a director started tearing his hair out and shouting at her over a scene not done to his liking, Olive would simply turn and walk away until he had calmed down enough to speak to her properly. Directors could be just as difficult as actors and actresses, sometime more so, yet the stars were usually blamed for any on-set blow-ups. Directors were beyond reproach. Actors and actresses were a disposable commodity. Olive learned that rule the hard way (source: conversations with Ralph Graves, Jr.).

A comic recess between Arthur Lake and Olive Borden in "Dance Hall," screening at the R-K-O.

A Joe Grant cartoon of Olive and Arthur Lake from the *Los Angeles Evening Herald*, during the release of *Dance Hall* (1929).

The *Jefferson City Post Tribune* (January 31, 1929) printed an interview with Olive where she explained her formula for choosing the pictures that she wanted to do. "If I don't like a story or part," she said, "I just don't do it. But when I get something I like, I work like the devil. Consequently, I am accomplishing far more than I ever did before and I'm not working half as hard."

She said when she left the Fox lot a year earlier, she was so nervous she didn't know whether she was temperamental or not. So she moved to the beach for three months and became just a kid again, doing things kids like to do and enjoying herself generally. Then she came back and went to work because she wanted to prove to herself that she was not temperamental.

Before Olive's "comeback," she made one very drastic change. She cut her hair! A December 1929 issue of *Photoplay* recounted Olive's unexpected makeover. Olive had always taken great pride in her long, black hair. It had a habit of winding seductively over the nape of her neck; it was part of her signature look. With-

Olive cut her trademark long hair in an attempt to revamp her image when "talkies" became the new Hollywood trend. Despite only being in her mid-twenties, Olive's best acting years were behind her.

out a doubt, she was known for her hair as much as her figure. She still had her famous figure, however, after her contract was cut; she decided it was time that her hair was cut too.

In mid–1928, Olive sat trembling in a barber's chair and watched her long locks fall to the floor. She was afraid to go too far so she only allowed it to be cut to shoulder length. It pleased her, but the change was not drastic enough. "Okay, go a little shorter," she nervously told the barber. And he did. The result was a boyish bob. Olive had reinvented herself ("Olive in Quest of Her Soul," Helen Loring, *Photoplay*, December 1929).

Olive received critical praise for her vocal ability in *Half Marriage*, her first all-talking role, yet she still worked tirelessly to improve her diction and tone. Olive was distinctly different from other actresses of her time. She wasn't classically beautiful, but she was easy on the eye and she had a sparkling charm that was hard not to like. With the introduction of sound, her full personality was projected and she jumped off the screen. Audiences had a taste of what to vocally expect from Olive's two films before *Half Marriage* when she and her *Love in the Desert* co-star Hugh Trevor had a few lines at the beginning and end of the film.

"All this was experience," Olive explained in a *Los Angeles Times* interview (April 11, 1929). "We are, all of us learning something new [talkies]; I appreciate now that we do not begin to progress until we realize how little we actually do know."

From Morgan Farley, opposite whom she played in *Half Marriage*, she said she gained a knowledge of how things are done on the stage. In return, "I taught him not to put a ghastly pale makeup on his face for the camera," she said. Let's hope that Farley took Olive's makeup advice in his future roles. He looks decidedly anemic in *Half Marriage*.

Next, Olive spent three days doing screen tests for the First National production *The Squall* (1929); however, the Warner brothers had Myrna Loy under contract and were lobbying hard for her to get the part. Much to Olive's dismay, Myrna won the part of Nubi, an exotic gypsy girl who runs away from her cruel master and is taken in by a family of farmers (*Los Angeles Times*, December 25, 1928).

William Beaudine directed Olive in her last feature film for 1929. *Wedding Rings* is a tale of two sisters, the younger Eve (Olive) having always taken anything she wanted from the elder, including her sweethearts; and the elder sister, Cornelia (Lois Wilson), having never really objected to her sister's thieving ways because she's never loved any of the men her sister has snatched away. However, Cornelia gives Eve fair warning, if she were to ever fall deeply in love, she would fight her sister tooth and nail for the love of the right man. When she meets a wealthy, middle-aged man and falls in love, the battle for his affections begins. Dialogue and sound effects in *Wedding Rings* were said to be the clearest the talking screen had yet produced. Both Olive and Lois Wilson were credited as having delightful singing voices.

The Charleroi Mail (February 28, 1930) gave Olive a glowing review for her performance in *Wedding Rings*: "Olive Borden, always vivacious and attractive, is amazingly clever

Olive (left), H. B. Warner and Lois Wilson in a promotional still for *Wedding Rings* (1929).

Olive with director Edward Sutherland. They worked together on *The Social Lion* (1930).

as selfish, jazz-mad Eve Quinn. This type of portrayal is a new departure for Miss Borden, whose characterization is done with commendable restraint and is all the more effective on that account. She is, in fact, the up-to-date vamp par excellence."

In *Hello Sister* (1930), the first of Olive's two releases for 1930, George Fawcett plays Olive's wealthy grandfather, Fraser Newell. He makes a last-minute will that only allows his granddaughter Vee (Olive) to inherit his million-dollar fortune if she puts an end to her out-of-control behavior for at least six months. She must cease drinking, smoking, gambling, swearing, and partying to the wee hours of the morning. She must also become an active church member. If she doesn't obey his last wish, she will be cut off without a penny. Olive's ride in the steeple chase was reviewed by *The San Antonio Express* (June 29, 1930) as "one of the most exciting scenes ever filmed for the talking screen."

Pretending to be sinless, Vee organizes a stage production for a church bazaar that evokes the shade of an old apple tree from a previous era. Lloyd Hughes, appearing in an Edwardian overcoat, top hat, and a blatantly fake handlebar moustache, sings Russ Columbo's "(What Good Am I) Without You?"; Olive, as the fair maiden receiving his sentiments, totes a parasol and strikes a demure pose. The swain and his paramour proceed into a duet about a "moon above" and "nights of love" before several other couples in the same attire join them for a Gay Nineties–style revue. Each pair engages in a simultaneous kiss, but

Olive with her leading man, Jack Oakie, in a publicity still for *The Social Lion* (1930).

Olive on the cover of *Motion Picture Classic*, November 1929.

Circa 1930.

when they emerge from their embraces, the women end up wearing the moustaches (*Russ Columbo and the Crooner Mystique*, Joseph Lanza and Dennis Penna, Feral House, 2002).

Next up was *The Social Lion* (1930) with comedian Jack Oakie. Olive plays Gloria, a ritzy daughter of society who tries her best to make a sap out of Oakie but fails. Olive was the second female lead behind Mary Brian. Reviews were favorable, with many calling it "rollicking good fun with lots of laughs and a solid cast."

During the production of *The Social Lion*, the *Los Angeles Times* (April 27, 1930) reported that Olive wears a pansy ring as a good luck charm. It was made from her late father's tie pin. Aside from a brief newspaper biography mentioning Olive's father's death when she was an infant, this *Los Angeles Times* article is the only other reference to her father in the hundreds of newspaper articles searched. A couple of magazine articles in the mid-to-late twenties mentioned without elaboration that her father died when she was an infant.

Despite glowing reviews for her performance in *The Social Lion*, Olive would not appear in another film for close to two years. According to her co-star Mary Brian, Olive refused to mix with the rest of the cast and mostly stayed in her dressing room with her mother during the production.

For a number of reasons, she was completely miserable while filming *The Social Lion*. Her long-time romance with George O'Brien was over, as was her contract with Fox. Despite freelancing to various studios, with moderate success, Olive was less than enthusiastic about where her film career was going since the talkies began. So, she turned her back on Hollywood, moved east, and directed her attention toward the theatre.

CHAPTER 13

The Stage

In September of 1930, famed Hollywood gossip columnist, Louella O. Parsons announced Olive's move east in pursuit of a stage career: "Olive Borden, who went through so many months of misery after she left the Fox Company trying to get herself a job, is soon to leave for New York. Olive has signed to play the leading role in a play which A.H. Woods is producing. The rumor is that her salary is $1,500 [converts to approximately $19,000 in 2009] a week. Of course, I haven't seen the contracts and am only repeating gossip. Olive proved herself a sensible girl by economizing and getting out of debt after she broke with the Fox Company. That was another case of a player's making a decision without weighing the consequences" (*Los Angeles Examiner,* September 2, 1930).

Ironically, it took less than a month for Olive to return to California, and it wasn't surprising that Parsons knew all about it. "Most of our screen people return in one way or another. Olive Borden, who went East to appear on the stage, is back among us and will confine her efforts to picture making. Sensible girl" (*Los Angeles Examiner,* September 30, 1930).

Less than a week later, Louella announced Olive's upcoming appearance in yet another new play. "Olive Borden isn't back in town to stay. She is only here temporarily, having signed with Lee Shubert for the feminine lead in *On the Spot,* a play which was produced in London and made a hit and is now to be brought to New York. I have always thought Olive one of the prettiest girls on the screen, but she has never really had the right chance. Perhaps the stage will do for her what the screen has never been able to do, that is bring out her personality and her charm" (*Los Angeles Examiner,* October 4, 1930). There is no further information to be found for the play *On the Spot.*

Aside from drifting between film and stage work, Olive also drifted between several houses and apartments during her Hollywood years. A 1930 census record shows that Olive had been residing at the Romanesque Villa Apartments on 1301-1309 North Harper Avenue in Hollywood. Many Hollywood stars called the exclusive apartments home, including Marlene Dietrich, Bebe Daniels, Laura La Plante, Anita Stewart and Will Rogers' leading lady Marie Mosquini. Olive's personal maid, Lila Elinor, was listed as living at the same address. She died in July of 1978, at 79 years old.

On December 10, 1930, Parsons announced in her *Los Angeles Examiner* column that Olive was signed for the lead in the new Garnett Weston-Garrett Fort stage play *The Devil Is a Lady.* Frieda Inescort was also to be part of the cast.

By December 20, Olive had started work in a preliminary engagement of *The Devil Is a Lady* in Great Neck, Long Island, New York. The few plays that Olive was linked to rarely

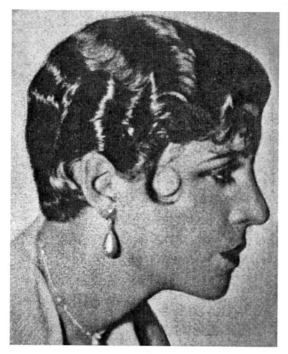

A profile shot of Olive's dramatic new hairstyle, circa 1930.

A photograph feature in *Photoplay* unveiled Olive's new short "do."

got past the rehearsal stages. One- and two-night revues proved popular but with such a limited engagement in each town, they were bound to fill theaters, and they did.

By early January, *The Devil Is a Lady* was in serious trouble. Monroe Lathrop of the *Los Angeles Evening Express* (January 9, 1930) said, "Two new plays by bright young men of Hollywood are set for the 'death watch' in New York next week. That frightful occasion upon which thumbs are turned up or down by the appraising critics." *The Devil Is a Lady* was one of them; there was a report that upon trial in a suburban theater, the audience found it in need of some major revisions.

Producer Jack White discussed his work on *The Devil Is a Lady* with author David N. Bruskin, for the book *The White Brothers: Jack, Jules & Sam White* (The Scarecrow Press, 1990). He remembered Frieda Inescort and Olive being a part of the production but he said "the male was insignificant, so I never could remember his name."

There was some speculation that the play *did* reach Broadway. One promotional booklet for a 1935 in-person appearance by Olive at a Midwest theatre promoted her as a "Film and Broadway Star." In hindsight, it was some obvious, harmless embellishment by a desperate theatre owner to garner a bigger crowd at a time when Olive's star power had faded. Jack White told the story of how he came to be involved with *The Devil Is a Lady* and confirmed that it never reached Broadway. "I met a friend of mine on a train who had what he thought was a good script for a show," he said. "I took half the deal; he lost as much as I did, $25,000 [converts to approximately $325,000 in 2009] each. It didn't turn out at all like it should have. It was a ghost story. Today, ghosts are popular. At that time, it didn't belong."

The play lasted seven weeks. It went on the Loew's Circuit and then they took it as far as uptown New York. They were going to open it on Broadway because they thought they had nothing to lose. "'I've got something to lose,' White said firmly. 'My reputation. It isn't a very good production, and I don't want it to open on Broadway. We don't owe you anything. We allowed you to collect all the box office income. I don't even know what the income that you took at the box office amounted to, but you do not open on Broadway.' And that was the end of my experience on Broadway."

The *Chicago Daily Tribune* (April 5, 1931) ran an article that mentioned Olive's vaudeville stint, but it was a pity piece, with a reflective tone on "what could have been" if only she made the right career choices. It read, "Olive Borden is touring the eastern vaudeville circuits in an act with Nick Lucas. Poor Olive has always been badly advised. With the most beautiful figure and face and with plenty of dramatic ability, she has somehow missed.... The business does not wait for poor guessers, it passes right along."

By November of 1931, Olive was still trying her luck in the legitimate theater, but the *Chicago Daily Tribune* (November 8, 1931) once again reported that "Olive Borden has been tried in three plays, none of which ever reached New York."

In 1930, the Internal Revenue Service cited Olive for $519.95 (converts to approximately $6,500 in 2009) in unpaid taxes for the year 1928. She was not alone. John Barrymore ($28.21), Ford Sterling ($1066.42), Alice Day ($306.58), William Collier, Jr. ($284.55) and Norman Kerry ($140.08) were also named. It wasn't the first time the IRS cited Olive for unpaid taxes. On January 28, 1928, she was asked to pay an additional $240.78 (converts to approximately $3,000 in 2009) for the 1926 financial year.

Aside from Olive's tax problems, the new decade meant the unraveling of a career that once held so much promise. Olive's post–1930 films were all shot away from Hollywood or overseas. Not the locations for an actress at the peak of her career. Her vaudeville stint was short-lived and mostly unsuccessful. And, personally she was about to enter a relationship that would take its toll and make newspaper headlines for reasons she would never imagine.

CHAPTER 14

"I Do" — Times Two!

Early in 1931, Olive had made a move to New York City. The loss of her Fox contract and her failed relationship with George O'Brien were haunting her every thought. She was also depressed at her diminishing star power. She needed a fresh start and she dove in feet first.

Soon after her relocation, Olive married the charming Theodore Spector, a stockbroker. Theodore applied for a marriage license on March 28, 1931, and justice of the peace Winfred C. Allen married the couple in Harrison, New York, the same day. Claudia Castle and Frederick Florin witnessed the ceremony. Several reports indicated that Olive was practically kidnapped from a dinner party by her husband-to-be. She was eating with fellow actresses Anna May Wong, Claire Windsor, Betty Blythe and Ruth Roland when a telephone caller said that her mother desperately needed to see her in the lobby. Olive rushed downstairs thinking there was some sort of an emergency but it was Theodore waiting for her, not her mother. He rushed her into a cab and off they raced to get hitched (*Charleston Gazette*, May 3, 1931).

On the marriage license, Theodore stated that this was his first marriage. He had conveniently forgotten about marrying his first wife, Pearl Spector, on March 20, 1919. And there was that small matter of divorce that wasn't taken care of either. Theodore was a bigamist!

At the time, Olive was twenty-four years old and she gave her real birth date of July 14, 1906. However, she didn't admit to residing in New York and gave her residential address as 708 Yarmouth Avenue in Norfolk, Virginia. Theodore, her thirty-one-year-old groom, gave his birthday as August 8, 1899. However, this date conflicts with his handwritten World War I draft papers (September 10, 1918) that claims he was born on August 28, 1899. The latter is the most likely date of birth. The number "2" seems to have been mistakenly omitted from the license by a typist. There are other obvious spelling errors on the license proving the inefficiency of the person responsible for the information transfer. The New Jersey county of Passaic is misspelled "Passaci," Sibbie's name is misspelled "Sibbri" and the address of one of the witnesses shows as 1050 *Part* Avenue, NYC, instead of 1050 *Park* Avenue, NYC.

Theodore's occupation on his draft papers is listed as showman. His occupation on the marriage license is broker. The latter was an occupation that he stuck with for a number of years. Strangely, Olive makes no mention of her acting profession and lists her occupation as — none!

There would be no happily-ever-after for Olive and Theodore — far from it. They separated before their first wedding anniversary because he wanted her to quit acting and become a traditional housewife. Olive said, "Ted wanted me to quit the stage, but I simply cannot do it. I have been in the profession quite a while, and I love it. We could not agree on the subject, so we decided the only thing to do was to separate" ("Olive Borden Quits Husband," *Oakland Tribune,* April 18, 1932).

But the amicable split ended with far more drama than anyone expected. The short-lived union was annulled on November 21, 1932, after a bigamy trial eventually proved that Theodore *was* legally married to another woman. His first wife described "Teddy" Spector as a "tall, good-looking brute who certainly had a fast line."

Mrs. Pearl Haworth Spector, a pretty, petite beauty parlor owner-operator in Buffalo, New York, was a young girl of fifteen when Spector proposed to her in 1919. The first Mrs. Spector said "Teddy" left her in 1920 with the hasty announcement, "I've got plenty of brains and I'm not going to waste them fussing around here!"

It would be twelve years before they'd see each other again, this time face to face with their attorneys present. Mrs. Spector confronted her estranged husband and asked the million-dollar question, "How is it that as brainy a man as you would marry a woman while he was still the husband of another?"

Teddy's dramatic reply was unexpected. "Well, I had to marry Miss Borden. She threatened to jump off a ten-story building if I didn't."

In New York, "Teddy" released a statement saying he had married Olive with a clear conscience as he was under the impression that his first wife had legally divorced him during his absence. He went on to say that the first Mrs. Spector had called him on the telephone to inform that he was a free man.

Mrs. Spector dismissed his statement as "baloney." She said that just a few days before he married Olive, he had

FROM THE GROOM

Full name...... **Theodore Spector**

Color...... **White**

Place of residence **105 Graham Ave.**
Paterson (street address) **N. J.**
(city, town or village).

Age... **31**...... Date of birth **Aug. 8, 1899**

Occupation...... **Broker**

Place of birth...... **Paterson, N.J.**

Name of groom's father......
Arthur Spector

Country of father's birth **England**

Maiden name of groom's mother
Anna Oreskes

Country of mother's birth...... **Hungary**

Number of proposed marriage **First**

I have not to my knowledge been infected with any venereal disease, or if I have been so infected within five years I have had a laboratory test within that period which shows that I am now free from infection from any such disease.

Former wife or wives

living or dead......

Is applicant a divorced person......

If so, when and where, and against whom divorce or divorces were granted......

I declare that no legal impediment exists as to my right to enter into the marriage state...... **No**

Theodore Spector's section of the marriage certificate. In highlighted text, he states that his marriage to Olive is his "first."

phoned her to specifically ask for a divorce and he told her he'd pay for it in full, if only she'd agree. She denied that she said, "If I can't have you, then nobody can," before hanging up the phone. "He's six feet tall, dark and very handsome. But now I'm through with him," Mrs. Spector confessed. Mrs. Spector filed a lawsuit in her home town of Buffalo, and on May 12, 1932, she traveled to White Plains in Westchester County, where Port Chester is situated, to testify before the grand jury in Spector's bigamy trial.

The district attorney said there wasn't enough evidence to prove that the same man, Theodore Spector, had married both women. Frustrated but not willing to give up without a fight, Mrs. Spector went home to gather more evidence. Two weeks later, a determined, scorned woman traveled back to White Plains and

FIGURES IN BUFFALO TRIANGULAR LOVE AFFAIR

OLIVE BORDEN

'TEDDY" SPECTOR   MRS. PEARL SPECTOR

An example of the typical newspaper coverage at the time of the 1932 bigamy trial. This grainy newspaper photograph is the only known published image of Olive's two-timing husband, Theodore Spector.

this time she had all of her paperwork in order. Subsequently, Mrs. Spector won her divorce in the Buffalo courts after her attorney, Mr. John E. Barry, testified that Theodore Spector had admitted to him that he did indeed marry Olive with full knowledge that he was still legally married to his client, claiming that he had been forced into the union by her threat of suicide.

Two-timing "Teddy" had told his new movie star bride that he had never been married. She was charmed by his smooth persona, just as Pearl had been a dozen years before. She had no reason to believe he was lying. The bigamy trial was nationwide news.

Olive's name was in the papers almost daily, not because of her flourishing movie career, but with headlines such as "Actress in Love Triangle" and "Two Beauties and a Broker." It was unwanted media attention and she was humiliated. Olive decided there was nothing else to do but to end their relationship — for good. On May 14, 1932, Olive sued "Teddy" for annulment and via her attorney, Frederick Boehm, announced that she intended to act on that decision, regardless of the outcome of the bigamy trial ("Beauties and Broker Figure in Bigamy Fight: Olive Borden Leaves Her Husband, Learning He's Married," *The Mansfield News,* Mansfield, Ohio, August 26, 1932).

During the hearing, Olive's ego was given a boost by the judge. "You are good looking, indeed," he told her. "You are one of the few actresses who appear to equal advantage, on and off the screen" ("Olive Borden: The Joy Girl of the Silent Screen — Part II," Michael Ankerich, *Classic Images,* No. 187, January 1991). Olive told the grand jury that she had been separated from her husband for several months and she was currently working in vaudeville (she began stage work for that year on April 18, 1932) because her screen contract barred her from being married.

When it was all said and done, "Teddy" went to trial with two wives and ended up with none. The grand jury freed both women of their marital ties. Pearl Spector was granted a divorce and Olive got her requested annulment. However, bigamy charges were dropped due to a lack of corroborative evidence and "Teddy" walked away a free man.

Following his relationship debacles, "Teddy" was arrested on May 8, 1934, on suspicion of shady stock dealings. He still gave his address as Paterson, New Jersey. After that bump in the road, he all but disappeared. He was known to go by several aliases, including Theodore Stewart and Teddy Stewart; however there are no death records matching any of his known names (*www.ancestry.com*).

"Olive never spoke of this marriage in my presence," said Ralph Graves, Jr., "but my father told me she called her marriage to Spector and the aftermath—'humiliating.'" The title of Olive's only film release for 1932 was the aptly named *The Divorce Racket*.

CHAPTER 15

A Fading Star...

In a poignant foreshadowing of the lack of thespian mourners at her own funeral, Olive and actor brothers, Owen and Tom Moore, were the *only* film people to attend the funeral service of Lya de Putti in December of 1931. Miss de Putti, a highly respected Hungarian-born stage and screen star, died of pneumonia when she was thirty-two years old, following an operation to remove a chicken bone from her esophagus.

Aside from Olive's sporadic stage work, which by no means supported her abundant spending, she had no films released in 1931. And, with only one release the following year (*The Divorce Racket*), Olive's movie career was at a standstill. She went from *eleven* releases between 1926 and 1927 to *one* release in 1932.

It was during the fall of 1933 that Olive returned east to make her last films, all shorts. At Warner's Vitaphone studio in Brooklyn, she appeared in *The Mild West* (1933) with Janet Reade and *Gobs of Fun* (1933) with Charles Judels. *Film Daily* (May 6, 1933) ran a notification of Olive's return: "After an absence from the American screen of several years, Olive Borden returns in a two-reel comedy which goes into production today at the Brooklyn Vitaphone Studio, with George Givot and Charles Judels playing the leading male roles." For Al Christie at the Astoria studio, Olive was in the cast of *The Inventors* (1934); in a telltale sign of things to come, Olive's role went uncredited.

A New York passenger list for the S. S. *Champlain*, sailing from Plymouth, England (leaving February 9, 1933), to New York City (arriving February 16, 1933), lists Olive as a married woman, born July 14, 1907 (she was born in 1906). Her birthplace is typewritten on the ship's manifest as Richmond, Virginia, but it's crossed out and Norfolk, Virginia, is handwritten above it. Her New York City address is 59 West 10th Street and her passport number is 4346. Olive's marriage to "Teddy" had been annulled a couple of months before her trip yet she still listed herself as a married woman. After she was abroad for three months, during which time she made the British International film *Leave It to Me* (1933), a photo of a smiling Olive arriving back in New York with her wire-haired terrier was printed in the various papers.

In an eleventh-hour attempt to revive her failing career, Olive traveled to the newly constructed Sun Haven Studios in St. Petersburg, Florida. The studio was being hyped as "Eastern Hollywood" and, following his split with MGM, comedian Buster Keaton announced his next six films would be made there. One of those films, *The Fisherman*, was to star Olive. None of the six films made it past the idea stage, although there have long been rumors that several scenes of *The Fisherman* were shot before the production was shut down.

Before long, it became painfully obvious that Sun Haven Studios was a place where washed-up actors went to take one last stab at reviving careers that were all but over. Location problems were ongoing and the tropical Florida heat and bugs proved unbearable. Financing fell through on the films and as a result "Eastern Hollywood" would become a mere footnote in the movie history books.

After completing three minor productions during the early 1930s, including Olive's last film, *Chloe, Love Is Calling You* (1934), Sun Haven Studios closed its doors. Olive began an affair with director Marshall Neilan, a notorious alcoholic. She increased her alcohol intake to keep up with him and as a result, their relationship was often tumultuous. When the couple split, Olive continued to drink, eventually becoming an alcoholic herself. *Chloe, Love Is Calling You* by today's standards is so racially offensive, it's hard to watch without cringing. It's the last film she ever made. Although far from her best work, as of 2009, it's one of the few films starring Olive that has been commercially released on DVD.

Author Bryan Senn gives *Chloe, Love Is Calling You* a scathing analysis in his book *Drums of Terror: Voodoo in the Cinema* (2003), saying,

> Such lines as "Don't you know no good come from mixin' white folks and black?!" and "You black as your blood, you is!" and "You think that because you got white blood, some white man would have you? Yeah, he'd have you all right — but he wouldn't marry you!," hammer home the "horror" of miscegenation. Such abhorrent attitude comes not only from the plot and dialogue but from the very appearance of the characters as well. When "Chloe" (Olive) and the audience are under the impression that she is part "Negro," actress Olive Borden appears frumpy, wearing unflattering makeup and a dowdy, sackcloth dress. After it's confirmed that she's all white, however, Ms. Borden's natural assets come visibly to the fore, enhanced by careful glamour makeup and revealing satin gowns. *Chloe, Love Is Calling You* offers the viewer a dreary one hour of dull talk and insulting racism. After finally viewing this "lost" film, one can only wish it had stayed that way.

With her film career behind her, a few sporadic personal and stage appearances during 1934 and 1935 was the only work that Olive was now getting. For years, Olive was used to making headlines because of her career; however, her name made the papers for a different reason when on February 27, 1935, Olive was named in a high-profile divorce proceeding. Along with fellow actress Gertrude Vanderbilt, she was named in the divorce of Walter W. Emerson, actor-writer, and his socially prominent wife, Mrs. Jane Scholtz Emerson. It was Mr. Emerson who sued his wife for divorce, naming Barton Sewell, wealthy Beverly Hills sportsman, as co-respondent. In retaliation, Mrs. Sewell hit back with tes-

FIRST 'CHLOE' SCENES SHOT

Actual Production of Film Featuring Olive Borden Under Way at Kennedy City Today

A Florida newspaper headline announcing that *Chloe, Love Is Calling You* (1934), starring Olive, has begun shooting. While film production in Florida was then considered the "next big thing," it had no impact on Hollywood productions. In fact, the much-hyped Sun Haven Studios, dubbed "Hollywood East," closed its doors after three forgettable, poor-quality films.

timony that her husband had "stepped out" with Olive and Gertrude on a trip he made east (*The San Antonio Light*, February 27, 1935). It seems the naming of names on Mrs. Emerson's behalf was a mere retaliation to her husband's accusations of *her* infidelities. A friend of Mr. Emerson testified that he did indeed see Olive on a trip to New York but only "because they were both in show business." He said it was on the same trip that he met Vanderbilt (*The Oshkosh NorthWestern*, February 27, 1935).

This back-and-forth blame game was settled without too much disruption to Olive's life. She also claimed the relationship was completely innocent; however, being mentioned in the papers as "the other woman" was embarrassing for her. And, given the fact that she had recently remarried, the scandal could not have happened at a worse time.

On November 2, 1934, Olive married John Moeller in Manhattan. To avoid publicity, and following the embarrassing bigamy trial and media circus during her first marriage to Theodore "Teddy" Spector, on the official marriage license she states her "full name" as — Mary Borden. Her place of residence is listed as 313 West 91st Street, New York, New York, her place of birth as Richmond, Virginia. Her father's name — Harry. Her mother's name (maiden) — Sybil Shields. She states her age is twenty-six — two years younger than she actually was at the time. Her occupation — none. Olive also states that her marriage to John Moeller is her first! While it was technically her *second* marriage, the Spector union *was* annulled which does legally make this her first. An annulment, in the eyes of the court, is as good as the marriage never existing to begin with.

Moeller was an electrician for the railroad and in 1942 he joined the Navy. On the marriage license he lists his occupation as "electrical engineer," his age as twenty-six, his place of residence, 30-11 92nd Place, Richmond Hill, Long Island, New York (see Appendix 2 for clarification). His mother's name was Elizabeth (born in Germany), his father's name was William. According to a 1930 census, William Moeller was also born in Germany and he immigrated to the United States with his family in 1880 at the age of twelve. He and his wife Elizabeth had eight children, three girls and five boys.

On the second page of the marriage license, the witnesses are listed as Cecelia Rice and T. J. Douglas (Douglas' name is stamped on the page). Philip A. Hines was the deputy city clerk who performed the ceremony. His residence is given as 845 West End Avenue.

The newlyweds lived with John's father in a modest three-room apartment on Long Island. Their marital home was the address given by John on the marriage certificate. For seven years Olive's main role was that of a dutiful housewife; ironically, it was the very role she refused to play for her first husband, "Teddy" Spector. The marriage lasted longer than expected, but by 1941, the relationship was beyond repair.

Olive was now facing the failure of her second marriage and once again her finances were in disarray; this time she had no choice but to file for bankruptcy. With no money and another failed relationship behind her, Olive (now thirty-five) realized that time was cruelly against her. Her dreams of becoming a mother were as washed-up as her career.

Despite Olive's career ending with *Chloe, Love Is Calling You*, it's interesting to note that four years after its release (September 19, 1938), gossip columnist Jimmie Fidler would connect Olive's name to one of the biggest films of all time. He started his "In Hollywood" column (*The Chronicle-Telegram*) with, "Too bad *Gone with the Wind* wasn't written ten years earlier — Olive Borden was the perfect 'Scarlett,' background and all."

On March 7, 1941, in John Chapman's "Looking at Hollywood" column (*Chicago Daily Tribune*), it was stated, "Lawyers are trying to find Olive Borden, one-time star who has been destitute. Her long-time bankruptcy proceeding has been settled and there's some money left over for her." Olive's name barely made the papers by the later 1930s, and when it did, it was due to her bankruptcy proceedings or an occasional "where are they now?" piece. *The Olean Times-Herald* (February 3, 1937) ran the story "Sennett's Bathing Beauties: Filmland's Forgotten Women"; the article made the observation that only two of the

MARRIAGE CERTIFICATE

TO CLERGYMEN AND MAGISTRATES

The license issued, including the abstract of facts, and certificate duly signed by the person who shall have solemnized the marriage therein authorized shall be returned by him to the office of the town or city clerk who issued the same within five days succeeding the date of the solemnizing of the marriage therein authorized and any person or persons who shall wilfully neglect to make such return within the time above required shall be deemed guilty of a misdemeanor and upon conviction thereof shall be punished by a fine of not less than twenty-five dollars or more than fifty dollars for each and every offense.

I, *Philip A. Hines* a DEPUTY CITY CLERK

residing at 845 WEST END AVE.

in the county of New York and State of New York, do hereby certify that

I did on this day of NOV 2 - 1934 in the year A. D. 1934

at MUNICIPAL BUILDING in the county of New York and State of New York, solemnize the

rites of matrimony between *John Moeller*

Richmond Hill in the county of New York and State of New York, and

of *New York* *Mary Borden*

in the county of New York and State of New York

in the presence of *Cecelia Rice* and T. J. DOUGLAS

as witness and the license therefor is hereto annexed.

Witness my hand at MUNICIPAL BUILDING in the county of New York

this day of NOV 2 - 1934 A. D. 1934.

In presence of

Cel Rice

(Signature of Witness)

Residence *1234 Ocean Ae*

T.J. Douglas

(Signature of Witness)

Residence

[signature]

(Signature of Person Performing Ceremony)

845 WEST END AVE.

(Address of Person Performing Ceremony)

The marriage license (November 2, 1934) of Olive Borden and John Moeller. Olive used her middle name, Mary, to avoid publicity. Her signature "Mary Borden" can be clearly seen on the document.

many bathing beauties were still viable in film: Carole Lombard (Jane Peters in her Sennett days) and Sally Eilers. Olive was called a "half-forgotten nymph," along with Maude Wayne, Roxie McGowan, Mary Thurman, Vera Stedman, and a few other names that used to mean something. By 1937, these young women (most of them no older than thirty) were finished with Hollywood, or rather, Hollywood was finished with them.

CHAPTER 16

The War, the Mission ... the End

By 1941, Olive's reality was no longer a dream existence — it was a nightmare! She had lived the all-too-typical clichéd "rags to riches and back to rags" tale. Olive and her mother traveled to Hollywood almost two decades before with an outside chance of making a living in the film business; with her good looks and a lot of spunk she worked herself to the top and had everything money could buy. Foolishly, she spent it quicker than she made it. Now, she was back to where she started, only this time she was thirty-five, depressed and a bona fide alcoholic. In Hollywood terms, she was a middle-aged has-been.

The hope, innocence and youthful exuberance that Olive brought to Hollywood in 1922 were gone. There were thousands of new young girls traveling to Hollywood each year, all hoping for their own shot at fame just as she once did. Olive now looked old enough to play their mothers. It was not the part she wanted to play. What's more, those parts were never offered. Olive was forgotten. After having it all, losing it all was a hard pill to swallow. For the remainder of her life it was booze that helped ease the pain of a failed career. Ultimately, it was booze that would also destroy her.

In November of 1942, Olive took a positive step toward sobriety and decided to enlist as a WAAC (Women's Auxiliary Army Corps); later renamed the Women's Army Corps (WAC). She was sent to the first WAAC training center to open in Fort Des Moines, Iowa. Before enlisting as a WAAC Olive had already been working in New York as a nurse's aide; much of her time was spent rolling bandages but for the first time in years she felt like she was being useful. In her own small way she was contributing to the war effort and her self-confidence had significantly improved. Her drinking didn't cease completely but she managed to keep it under control and was competent at her job.

At Fort Des Moines she took a job as a nurse's aide, ambulance driver and Army chauffeur. She was paid $12.50 per week (converts to approximately $160 in 2009). It was a far cry from the weekly $1500 (converts to approximately $19,000 in 2009) she was earning at the height of her Hollywood career. She once commented that "being a WAAC is harder work than being an actress."

An undated Iowa newspaper ran the headline, "Film Actress Olive Borden Succumbs to WAAC Lure," and accompanying the article was a headshot of a fuller-faced Olive in uniform. She explained her reasons for enlisting: "I didn't have any children dependent on me. I wanted to help where I could do the most good. I figured the WAACs would know where that was."

U.S. Army records show that Olive enlisted for service under her married name of Olive Moeller. Her official enlistment date was December 11, 1942. Her branch code was "Inactive Reserve" and her grade code was "Aviation Cadet." She is listed as having "two years of high school education," and despite being separated from John Moeller, she's still listed as "married." Her civil occupation is that of a "General Industry Clerk." There is no mention of her previous years as an actress; the likely reason she enlisted under her married name was to avoid any possible fanfare that her famous past may have brought her way.

Olive's days in the Army were more dangerous than first expected. She received an army citation for bravery for turning over an enemy ammunition truck and according to a report written by Dorothy Manners of *The Lowell Sun* (November 2, 1944), "She's just been released from the Walter Reed hospital with an honorable discharge — but says she isn't interested in a [Hollywood] career anymore..."

After her "medical disability" discharge, very possibly induced by her increasing dependence on alcohol, Olive did attempt a Hollywood comeback but it was useless and she knew it. "Since I've got out of the Army I've gone from job to job; something always goes wrong," she said (*Cut! Hollywood Murders, Accidents and Other Tragedies*, Global Book Publishing, 2005).

With her hopes for a comeback fading, Olive moved into the Sunshine Mission, a home for destitute women. The mission was in the Skid Row area of Los Angeles. Olive's mother, the one dominant force in her life, had been working at the mission as a housekeeper since 1944 and eventually became the superintendent. Sibbie got Olive a job as a housekeeper and she spent her days making beds, washing dishes and scrubbing bathroom floors.

One Thanksgiving Day, the first holiday Olive spent at the mission, she insisted on taking over the operation of the kitchen. She worked for hours, cleaning, dressing and cooking a dozen giant turkeys for the unfortunate, homeless and penniless. Unfor-

Olive (in uniform) joined the Women's Auxiliary Army Corps under her married name Olive Moeller on December 11, 1942. She was paid just $12.50 a week for her services. At her peak as an actress she was earning $1500 a week!

Olive on the job as a WAAC in the Army, circa 1943. By November of 1944, after serving two years, she was given an honorable discharge due to a "medical disability." According to an article in the *Evening Standard* (January 21, 1943), Olive was the "first celebrity to join the WAACS" and she was reportedly "cited for a Croix de Merite."

tunately, Olive was now one of them. There were fleeting times of enjoyment for her, mostly when she was working with the children. But it wasn't enough.

Sibbie was genuinely happy at the mission. In the words of the home's own publication, it was Sister Sibbie who, "having received the baptism of the Holy Spirit in our mission services, could not rest until we had interceded with prayer for her daughter, that she would also find Christ. God has marvelously answered prayer, and now this extraordinarily talented young woman has accepted Christ and has dedicated her life to fallen humanity and the Lord's work."

Being at the mission wasn't a happy time for Olive. Waves of depression would consume her. The menial work was a constant reminder of what a mess her life had become. A *Los Angeles Times* article (January 15, 1945) pictured a chubby-faced Olive holding a fluffy cat with a trophy nearby ... a former movie beauty, obviously way past her prime, pictured holding a champion feline now more famous than herself. "Miss Olive Borden, Former Film Actress, presented the silver cups to the winning felines in the 10th Annual Championship Cat Show at the Masonic Temple Auditorium in Hollywood," the article stated. Olive went from the heights of being a Hollywood movie star to judging Hollywood cat shows.

Olive disappeared from the mission shortly after she helped arrange an act in a pageant play. "I guess the pageant got her thinking about her old acting days," said mission brother Wilfred West ("Ex-Screen Star Olive Borden Dies in Los Angeles Mission," *The Amarillo Daily News*, October 3, 1947).

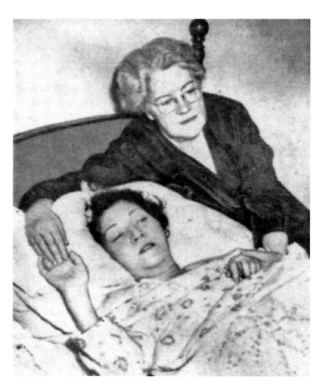

Late September, 1947: A rare photograph of Olive on her death bed at the Sunshine Mission. Her devoted mother, Sibbie, holds her hand. Olive died at 8 A.M. on October 1.

By the spring of 1947, Olive couldn't take it any more. Depressed, and without a word to her devoted mother, she left the mission under cover of night. A search for her whereabouts, lasting for several months, sent Sibbie into such a nervous state there were concerns for her own health. Not knowing if her daughter was alive or dead caused her unspeakable grief, but Sibbie didn't give up searching.

She eventually found Olive in a rundown hotel, empty alcohol bottles strewn about the room, and her darling Olive in desperate need of medical attention. Brought back to the mission, Olive was immediately seen by a doctor who diagnosed double pneumonia, heart and lung disease and severe stomach problems—the direct results of years of alcoholism.

Soon after her return, on the morning of October 1, 1947, Olive passed away. She was only forty-one years old. Ironically, it was forty years to the day after her father's burial in 1907. Sibbie was by her side, as she had always been in life — and now in death.

As for the ailments that led to her death. There are two ways cirrhosis can kill someone. Long-term drinking that eventually leads to cirrhosis in old age, or a worse kind, caused by concentrated binge drinking that affects the person in the prime of their life, especially women. The fact the Olive was destitute points to cheap, harsher liquor, poor diet and unsanitary living conditions. All of those factors combined would have severely depleted her immune system, leading to double pneumonia, then death (source: conversation with Dr. Levica Narine).

The only possessions that Olive had at the time of her death was a tattered autographed photo of herself and a scrapbook of clippings from her Hollywood years. While her few personal possessions were a reminder of happier days, the harsh reality of Olive's 1940s lifestyle and what she had become made the contents of that scrapbook a dossier of bittersweet memories. It seemed like a different life. A different person. Olive died a penniless alcoholic, a washed-up movie star. Her fans, friends and peers had buried her years before her actual death.

Newspaper reports suggested that Olive died of a "stomach ailment." She had suffered heart and liver problems for some time and the double pneumonia was too much for her frail body to take. Olive's death certificate stated that her immediate cause of death was cirrhosis of the liver. The physician who signed the death certificate stated that he last saw Olive alive the day before, on September 30, 1947. She died the following morning, October 1, 1947, at 8 A.M.

Based on other documentation, Olive's death certificate has three interesting contradictions. It stated that Olive was born in Richmond, Virginia, not Norfolk, Virginia, as it is so often reported. But the 1933 ship manifest listed Olive as a passenger on board and the typewritten information stated Olive's birthplace as Richmond, Virginia. Somebody (possibly Olive?) crossed out Richmond, Virginia, and wrote Norfolk above it. Further, both of Olive's marriage certificates states her place of birth was Richmond, Virginia.

The July 14 birth date was the com-

Star Of Silent Films Dies In Mission Home

Los Angeles, Oct. 1 (P)—In a women's mission in a squalid city area, Olive Borden, 40, once one of the highest paid charmers in motion pictures, died in penury today.

The great and near-great of the motion picture world with whom she once had associated had forgotten her, and, in straitened circumstances and failing health, she had lived and worked in the Sunshine Mission Home for Girls since 1945.

At the bedside of the once-beautiful actress when she succumbed to heart and lung ailments was her mother, Mrs. Sybil Borden, who operates the commissary at the mission.

She began her film career in the old Hal Roach comedies, and in 1925 was named Wampas baby star of the year.

A newspaper obituary announcing Olive's death. It mistakenly states her age as forty; she was actually forty-one when she died.

monly used date while Olive was alive and her delayed birth certificate (issued on November 20, 1942) and both marriage certificates confirms her birth date and year as July 14, 1906. There's certainly enough corresponding information to say that the July 20 birth date on her death certificate is incorrect. In fact, the date may well have been confused with her mother's birth date: Sibbie's birthday was July 20, 1884. However, the delayed birth certificate and her baptismal certificate concurs with her death certificate and states that she was born in Richmond, Virginia, *not* Norfolk, Virginia. There is conflicting information from several sources and documents in relation to both cities. It's one of the two, with a definite leaning toward Richmond.

The final mystery on Olive's death certificate was the answer to the question "How long had the deceased lived in this community?" The community in question was Los Angeles, California. The answer was *thirty* years. Olive was 41 years old when she died. Being a California resident for three decades would make her eleven years old when she and her mother moved west, not sixteen, as the story goes.

After her daughter's death, Sibbie was quoted as saying, "On the other side of town they call this Skid Row. But maybe it's just as well that it happened this way. Ollie died among people who really loved and idolized her. She was happy" (*Los Angeles Times*, October 5, 1947). Several fan magazines (*Photoplay, Motion Picture Classic* and *Movie Monthly*) even printed that Olive's last words to her mother were, "I have found the one thing that Hollywood couldn't give me — happiness."

Olive had lived and worked at the mission on and off since 1945. At the time of her daughter's death, Sibbie was the manager of the mission's commissary. Ironically, the day before Olive died, a reporter had tracked her down and she was quoted as saying, "The whole world has fallen in on me. But the doctors will make me well" ("Olive Borden Former Film Star Dies in Poverty," *The Coshocton Tribune*, October 2, 1947).

Given the fact that Olive ran away from the Sunshine Mission, it's hard to believe she ever found her inner peace there. She had sought solace in religion and shortly after living at the mission she became a born-again Christian. The women and children who used the mission as shelter would affectionately call Olive and Sibbie "Sister Ollie" and "Sister Sibbie." Everyone loved Olive. She'd spend hours helping the mothers bathe their babies and she'd read and play games with the older children. She often helped them with their homework before bed. The children were the only anchors that kept her there. They needed her. They relied on her. Deep down Olive knew she needed them and relied on them just as much. But when the night came and she retired to her room, thoughts of what might have been and of all things lost filled her head. A depth of sadness consumed her. For her, the only way to forget was to drink. Alcohol numbed her pain at night and the children and her chores kept her busy enough throughout the day so she had little time to reflect on her past then. But there was always a feeling of sadness within her. An emptiness. When she did smile, one sensed it was the best bit of acting she had done in years. "She was always smiling," said Ralph Graves, Jr. "Always happy, or so she wanted people to believe. My father said there was a lot of regret, a lot of 'what might have been,' with Aunt Olive. And that was back when her life and career still had hope and promise. She was always saying, 'if only this ... if only that...' I can only imagine how burdened, how depressed she felt towards the end of her life when things were so hopeless that she had nothing. She had everything. Everything! She went from having everything to the lowest point that anyone could go. It's very upsetting to know she ended up the way she did. If only..."

The year before Olive died, *The Los Angeles Times* (June 16, 1946) ran a story about the mission: "They welcome her, the children especially, with glad cries of 'Ollie!' whenever she enters. At the mission she keeps busy. Sometimes she poses in tableaus that illustrate sermons. At others you hear her voice on the mission telephone: 'This is the Sunshine Mission and God bless you.' You see her dressing some little ragged child or helping her mother."

This sugarcoated account of Olive's post-film life was an attempt to make the public believe that her work at the mission was her true calling. But Olive was far from happy there. It was a daily reminder of her life's many failures. Failed marriages. Failed career. Failed wealth. Failed dreams.

On the odd occasion when someone did recognize her as Olive Borden — Movie Star, it was the depth of humiliation that she felt when he or she looked at her with puzzlement along with the question that almost always came next: "Well, if you really are *her*, then why are you *here*?" (*Los Angeles Evening Herald Express*, undated, 1947).

Olive was now all but forgotten by her peers and the public who used to adore her. Her world consisted of her mother, the people at the mission (sometimes as many as one hundred new faces in one day) and her best friend of all — alcohol. Her life was contained within those mission walls. For a woman who once had beauty, fame, luxury, wealth and the admiration of millions, as Ralph Graves, Jr., commented earlier, the mission was the polar opposite to that lifestyle. A place of strict austerity, it was an awfully lonely, depressing and suffocating new world for Olive to be in. The mission was a saving grace for many women and children in need; women who never had the opportunities that Olive had in life were eternally grateful for its existence. But for Olive, her time at the mission was a prison sentence. She didn't belong there. To Olive, it became increasingly apparent that her only chance at peace, her only escape — was death.

When Sibbie was asked the year before Olive's death if she thought her daughter ever wished she were back in pictures, she thought for a moment and answered, "Yes. At times. She gets restless, of course. Sometimes, looking back, I think that I mothered her too much..."

Sibbie's half-hearted confession of guilt at being an over-protective mother did not last long. After a moment's pause she continued, "But it was Olive herself who made the fateful decision not to take a salary cut when, in 1927, Fox asked its leading players to do so, and so caused the eventual severance of her career at that studio" ("Star of 30's Adopts Missionary Career," *The Los Angeles Times,* June 16, 1946). Despite Sibbie's claim that Olive's refusal to take a Fox pay cut was solely her own choice, it's inconceivable to think that Sibbie, the meddling mother that she was, had no influence over Olive's eventual career-destroying decision to leave the studio without so much as a compromise. Ralph Graves, Jr., said, "I have no doubt that Olive's mother would have influenced her decision to leave the studio. She just wasn't the type *not* to give her opinion — about anything, let alone something as important as Olive's career."

Some twenty years before her death, in a 1927 interview for *Movieland* magazine, Olive spoke about what money meant to her. "I wanted money, a lot of it. Why? I don't know except that earning it pleases ego, spending it whets vanity. It adds to that absurd importance. With the inflated estimation of self, the more money you get, the more you want, to increase prestige. And it is handy to purchase places [houses] and such trinkets."

The *Los Angeles Times* (October 5, 1947) ran the headline, "Friends at Mission Pay Olive Borden Tribute." The article described a bright beam of sunshine shining light on a

They were inseparable in life, so it is only fitting that Olive and Sibbie Borden were eventually laid side by side in death. Their modest grave markers are in the Liberty Section at the star-studded Forest Lawn Memorial Park in Glendale, California.

cross of crimson carnations as the service began at the Sunshine Mission Chapel on 558 South Wall Street. People who came to know Olive at the rescue home were in attendance but there were no Hollywood stars. *Come to My House* assistant director Jack Boland (1892–1967) and her former leading man in the film, Cornelius Keefe (1900–1972), made appearances. Filmdom's representatives consisted mostly of studio grips, gaffers and carpenters. The pallbearers, recruited just before the service began, took the casket to the waiting hearse.

"I don't know why my father didn't go to her funeral," said Ralph Graves, Jr. "There was no falling out or anything. Aunt Olive just sort of disappeared after she left Hollywood. Even when she died, a lot of people commented, 'Oh, isn't that terrible,' but not many turned out to pay their last respects."

Pastor and founder of the Sunshine Mission, Mrs. Essie Binkley West, officiated at Olive's funeral. Although heartbroken, the homeless children living at the mission sang for

A 2009 photograph of Olive's grave at Forest Lawn Memorial Park in Glendale, California. She was buried on October 4, 1947. The Sunshine Mission paid for her funeral and burial costs.

"their Ollie" one last time. The mission paid for all funeral expenses and related costs.

Hollywood has always been a fickle town. Olive's story proves it, as do so many other sorry tales of stars, once at the top of their game, dying in poverty, forgotten about, washed-up. The *Joplin Globe* (October 12, 1947) was one of the few newspapers ballsy enough to blame Hollywood and the industry for Olive's early demise: "The death of silent screen star Olive Borden, in abject poverty, points out again one of the chief charges that can be levied against Hollywood.... She had been a top-notch star and a better than good actress. Surely the industry, if it had bothered to remember her existence, could have found enough work for her to give her a decent livelihood..."

It is hard to imagine that, as Sister West of the mission put it, "None of her friends knew of her plight. She was too proud to tell them" (*Long Beach Independent*, October 2, 1947). That statement also contradicts the stories about Olive finding her "true calling" at the mission and being happy there. If that were the case, she wouldn't care who knew. In fact, she might have even proudly told people from her past about her new life's calling.

Twelve years after Olive passed away, her beloved mother Sibbie was laid to rest beside her. She was seventy-five years old.

She didn't. What's worse, she died knowing that few people would care that she was dead. Olive's death was covered by almost every paper across the country. In many of them, news of her demise appeared as a couple of paragraphs amongst a whole page of other "worthier" items. The headline "Former Star Dies in Poverty" was the most consistent heading above the announcement of her death. Olive's obituary in the October 13, 1947, issue of *Time* magazine was a callous, unsympathetic couple of lines calling her a "briefly famed screen beauty of the 20's" and a "haggard, hard-drinking off-&-on guest" of the Sunshine Mission for three years. It was a disrespectful footnote that was undeserved, and a little shocking, given the usual reverential style of reporting from a publication as acclaimed as *Time*.

Olive was buried wearing her "lucky" pansy ring made out of her late father's tie pin; she held an orchid in her hand. She was laid to rest on October 4, 1947, in the Liberty Section at Forest Lawn Memorial Park in Glendale, California. Her mother finally confirmed that Olive's true birth year was 1906 because she wanted her gravestone to be correct. It reads:

Olive Borden
Beloved Daughter
1906 — 1947

Sibbie Borden was laid to rest next to her daughter twelve years later. She died in Los Angeles on November 20, 1959. Sibbie was no stranger to alcohol herself, but unlike Olive, her addiction didn't prevent her from reaching old age. She was seventy-five years old. Her gravestone reads:

Sibbie Borden
Beloved Mother
1884 — 1959

Over a decade after her death, Olive was one of the first eight actors to be chosen for a Hollywood Walk of Fame star. There were hundreds of nominees and Olive's name was

randomly drawn to receive the inaugural tribute.

The official groundbreaking ceremony was held on February 9, 1960. Olive's star is situated at 6801 Hollywood Boulevard. The other seven honorees were Joanne Woodward, Burt Lancaster, Ronald Colman, Edward Sedgwick, Ernest Torrence, Preston Foster and Louise Fazenda. Olive's devoted mother died less than three months before her daughter received the honor.

Olive's Hollywood Walk of Fame star is situated at 6801 Hollywood Boulevard.

CHAPTER 17

Epilogue

At sixteen years old, Olive Borden dreamed of becoming a movie star. But she wasn't living in Hollywood, or anywhere near it. She was a high school dropout living in Virginia with her widowed mother. Given her circumstances, it was a mighty big dream to have, but not all that uncommon for most girls her age. However, unlike most of those other girls, by the time Olive was nineteen, *her* dream was realized. Moreover, she was already a leading lady, one of Hollywood's youngest, and a popular one at that.

Olive Borden lived her Hollywood dream; it was short, but she still succeeded in what she set out to do. There were mistakes along the way, both personal and professional, and following her Fox walkout, her career, relationships, looks, riches and health all gradually slipped away. Alcohol made Olive's stark new reality a little easier to bear.

With that said, Olive Borden should not be an infamous Hollywood name because of her tragic, premature end. Rather, she should be praised, admired and remembered for what she achieved during her short life and career. Furthermore, the blame for her career nosedive, financial failures and alcoholism should not rest squarely on *her* shoulders. She was young. There was no one to guide her. She wasn't a trained actress who came to Hollywood via the theatre. She learned her craft as she moved from film to film, as did many of her peers. She wasn't a businesswoman; neither was her mother. As quickly as she made money, she foolishly spent it, with her mother's help. There was no firm hand or levelheaded intermediary to advise her on contract negotiations or to teach her how to invest her money for the future. She lived in the moment. She spent what she had when she had it. She did as she pleased and said it as she saw it. Kind to a fault, she was well liked by her contemporaries and her film crews because she was a down-to-earth, chatty, fun-loving, humorous girl. She was normal — normal in an industry that thrived on the abnormal. If there is blame to be laid for what became of Olive Borden, much of it rests within the Hollywood community and the industry itself for allowing her to sink to the depths of nothingness, broke and broken, monetarily and spiritually. No one stepped in to help her, and when she needed help, many of her peers *still* had the power, the positions and the finances to do so. They did nothing.

In a late 1970s interview for the Kevin Brownlow–David Gill *Hollywood* (1980) series, George Harris, one of her co-stars in *3 Bad Men* (1926), remembered Olive briefly as he pointed at her image in a film still from the epic picture. He said, "This is Olive Borden, who was a great girl. Poor girl, she finished up in the slums of Los Angeles as a wino." A perfect example of the unflattering tagline that Olive was too often left with after her demise.

Hollywood was a revolving door. You're in, you spin within the giddy heights of success for a few years and then you're spat out the other side! Done and forgotten. Alive or dead — it didn't matter. It's that quick. That harsh. And, sad to say, not all that uncommon. Seldom did the fame, fans, money, lovers or friendships last beyond the "use by" date that studio bosses invisibly stamped on the foreheads of the stars who consistently made them millions. It *was* a production line.

Olive Borden was fully prepared for the success that Hollywood threw at her. What she wasn't prepared for was the rejection.

That killed her.

Part Two

The Films

What Is a "Lost" Film?

A "lost" film is a moving picture that has no known prints in existence — anywhere. Over the years, many "lost" films have been found. No films are really considered "gone"; the hope is that somewhere, in a grotty old attic or basement full of "junk," the lone copy of a cinematic gem is gathering dust and waiting patiently to be "found."

Some of the "found" films have been restored and shown at film festivals, even released on DVD. Others have been housed at various institutions and film archives throughout the world; never restored, in a deteriorating condition and not likely to be restored before the film is beyond repair. Sometimes when the *only* copy of a film is housed in an archive or film institution, while technically it's no longer considered "lost," in most cases the likelihood of it being publicly available is doubtful. So, is the film still "lost"? No. Not technically. But if it can't be viewed and enjoyed by the masses, it's no longer "lost" to time, but it *is* still "lost" in a sense — at least to the public.

Martin Scorsese's Film Preservation Foundation estimates that as much as 80 percent of the films made between 1894 and 1930 are "lost" and there are several reasons for that staggering percentage. Until safety film was introduced in 1949, Hollywood used the highly combustible and unstable nitrate film. As a result, many studio archives had entire storage vaults of films destroyed by fires. If not housed in a temperature-controlled environment, nitrate film will deteriorate rapidly. Some projectionists were so afraid that a film would burst into flames while it was being shown, they kept a bucket of water beside their projectors — just in case! The US Navy shot a training film, specifically for projectionists, that included footage of a controlled ignition of a reel of nitrate film. It showed that even when the reel was fully submerged in water, it continued to burn. So, while the bucket of water beside the projector seemed like a good idea, in hindsight, it would have had little effect if a fire broke out.

Either directly or indirectly, the majority of silent films were destroyed by the very studios that made them. When the silent era ended (circa 1930), sound was the new, exciting and improved version of entertainment. Silent films were old hat. Who'd ever want to see a film again without spoken dialogue? And why take up much-needed space by having silent films (on unstable, highly combustible stock) sit on shelves gathering dust? There wasn't a TV, VHS or DVD market back then. The films were worthless. And so the majority were eventually destroyed. Many of the films were recycled for their silver content following their theatrical run.

A year before his December 28, 1981, death at ninety-six, Allan Dwan, director of Olive's *The Joy Girl* (1927), sat down with silent film accompanist and author Stuart Oderman. In his book *Talking to the Piano Player: Silent Film Stars, Writers and Directors Remember* (2005), Oderman shared Dwan's articulate memories of his career (that spanned over fifty years), and of course, the topic of film preservation, or lack thereof, came up:

"So many of those old films were *allowed* to rot," Dwan says. "I suppose we're to blame. It's our own fault. We never thought of saving those early efforts... [I]t's because of a lot of collectors that any of our work survived. Studios stored them, and then they made room for newer products. That so much has survived is a miracle. A lot of those early films *disintegrated* over time, or because of the advent of sound. Sound, at the end of the silent era, meant progress."

Dwan recalled that many of silent films' earliest rescuers were forward-thinking theatre projectionists who would go to great lengths to protect a film they considered worthy. Because of the unpredictable nitrate stock the films were produced on, the reels were often buried in the dirt floors of cellars and basements. It would keep the films cool and prevent the combustion that would almost always occur if they over-heated. There are likely many films that are considered "lost" today that are *still* buried, maybe even entombed underneath a concrete floor that was poured by unsuspecting new inhabitants of an old house with no knowledge of the sought-after treasures that lay in the dirt underneath.

The film business has always been just that—a business. It just wasn't good *business* to archive a silent film that had already been released, nurture the unstable nitrate stock in a controlled environment, and take up valuable space for a film that has no sound and no further outlets for financial gain.

But, that was *then*...

Only now do we realize what a great disservice the industry did to itself, and to the public, by destroying the majority of its early history. Lon Chaney's *London After Midnight* (1927) is a classic example. It has long been a highly sought-after "lost" film. The last known surviving print was destroyed in a 1965 MGM studio fire. Despite worldwide efforts (for over forty years) to find another copy, to this day, no other print has surfaced.

With the guidance of the original script, together with a collection of film stills, a photographic reconstruction of *London After Midnight* was presented on Turner Classic Movies in 2002, but the actual film remains an elusive treasure yet to be found. For this film, if it were ever found, because of its main star (Lon Chaney), along with the appeal and legend surrounding it, any archive lucky enough to get their hands on a print would rush to preserve it (if it's not beyond repair) and release it commercially on DVD. In the case of *London After Midnight, that* would be good "business."

This brings me to the somewhat controversial subject of film preservation.

My friend, fellow film historian-author William M. Drew, gave me an account of why he thinks a great many silent films of the actresses are now considered "lost" when in reality, many of the sole copies that remain are simply hoarded away for years, sometimes forever:

Most of the leading female stars of the 1920s are well represented by their surviving works, including the many actresses I've interviewed over the years. The problem, however, is that the field of dissemination outside the archives is selective and badly skewed in its preference for male stars. With perhaps the sole exceptions of Mary Pickford (who had both the foresight and the means to establish her own foundation), Nell Shipman (who also had her own company) and possibly Clara Bow (thanks to David Stenn's dedication), very few feminine stars of the American silent era have been revived in their own right.

That is to say, when the works of feminine silent stars are revived, they usually enjoy this exposure because of the famous men with whom they worked (D. W. Griffith, Cecil B. DeMille, King Vidor, John Ford, G. W. Pabst, Rudolph Valentino, John Gilbert, etc.). For example, it's thanks to her association with Sennett, Chaplin and Arbuckle that Mabel Normand is belatedly getting some renewed attention.

Unfortunately for Constance Talmadge, apart from her work in *Intolerance* (1916), she did not have the kind of directors and co-stars that attract this kind of continuing interest on the part of the revival establishment, so most of her comedies languish in the archives. With the films thus withheld from public view, the myth is then continually repeated, over and over again, that very few of these actresses' films exist, that most are lost. I have read that myth so often with respect to Olive Thomas, for example, that I am heartily sick of it. At least half of her films have survived. If they'd only make them all available again on DVD, no one would ever say that. And as I've found with respect to Pearl White, Ruth Roland and the other serial queens, the longtime neglect of their films by the establishment is simply scandalous.

Look at someone as illustrious as Gloria Swanson. What films of hers usually get the most attention? Her films with DeMille, von Stroheim, and the recently rediscovered *Beyond the Rocks* (1922) with Valentino. She did two delightful comedies with Allan Dwan —*Manhandled* (1924) and *Stage Struck* (1925). While there have been old Kodascope-derived copies of *Manhandled* available for years, no one has really tried to put out a sparkling or refurbished print of it to market for DVD and TCM release, and *Stage Struck* has never been available outside the archives. The fact that the Swanson-Dwan collaborations are far better films than *Beyond the Rocks* is immaterial since, alas, they don't have famous leading men like Valentino. And as for their director, Allan Dwan, unfortunately, as talented as he was, does not have the kind of "name" value of a King Vidor or a John Ford, so the powers-that-be aren't jumping at the opportunity to recycle his early films via DVD.

Hence, Olive Borden's *The Joy Girl* (1927) stays where it is in the Museum of Modern Art's vaults, while *Summer Bachelors* (1926), which Dwan made with Madge Bellamy, hasn't even been repatriated here from the Prague archive, which has a copy. Even though these comedies are all probably just as good as the two silents Vidor did with Marion Davies, Dwan never became the "celebrity" that Vidor was and hence there is no rush to put out more of his films. So, it seems if a top feminine star of the silent era does not have a renowned male co-star or director, the likelihood is her films will remain locked up in archival obscurity.

This sad situation is not paralleled in many other countries. In China, for example, by far the single most renowned individual in their silent film history is the legendary actress Ruan Lingyu whose films are often revived. Equally celebrated in Germany and Scandinavia is the Danish actress Asta Nielsen. The works of these actresses are revived, not so much because of their leading men or their directors, but because they are esteemed in their own right as artists.

That we in America have not been willing to accord comparable honors to our own silent film actresses is, I believe, a definite reflection of our entrenched male dominant culture, all the more vicious because we refuse to acknowledge it, instead displacing or projecting indignation over gender inequities onto Asian and Middle Eastern cultures.

With sound, this kind of selectivity (read discrimination) mercifully disappears, thanks to the fact that the Hollywood studios repackaged their films of the 1930s and 1940s en masse to a later generation without withholding large numbers of films deemed "unimportant" (meaning films with women stars) according to the priorities of archivists and established historians. Consequently, it has been possible to have the impressive revivals we're now seeing of pre–Code feminine stars.

While a number of Olive Borden films are considered "lost," it is more accurate to consider many of the others "unavailable." Quite a few of them (in many cases the only copies known to exist) sit on shelves (in varying conditions) in archives somewhere in the world, waiting to be saved. On a positive note, most have been transferred to safety film so they will not deteriorate further; however, the downside is that the surviving titles aren't deemed "historically significant" enough to spend money on restoring. And, if they're not restored, they will *never* be commercially released on DVD. So, while many of Olive Borden's films aren't technically considered "lost," those few scarce prints that remain extant aren't readily "available" either. Let's hope that one day that will change.

Lastly, there are about thirty "found" films within Olive's filmography that have never before been attributed to her. Some of them are commercially available on VHS and DVD, and notations are included with the relevant purchase information. Her pay scale for these films ranged from $12.50 to $75 per week (converts to approximately $160–$945 in 2009). Her visibility in the titles available can be gauged by what she was paid. For instance, $12.50 was the going rate for an extra used in a crowd scene, $75 was a fee worthy of being involved in a scene where she can be seen quite easily. Any payment in between and the "let's spot Olive" game begins; look carefully enough and you just might ... I guess that's all part of the fun.

Filmography

Arranged by earliest release date

• Hollywood in 1923

Number of film releases: 576.

At a cost of $21,000, Mack Sennett, Harry Chandler and the *Los Angeles Times* put up the HOLLYWOODLAND sign (later shortened to HOLLYWOOD) to publicize a real estate development. The letters were 30 feet wide and 50 feet tall, built of sheet metal panels attached to scaffolding frames. Each letter was studded with 20-watt light bulbs at eight-inch intervals. Albert Kothe lived in a hut behind one of the letter Ls and was employed full-time to change the bulbs as they burned out (*Guinness Film Facts and Feats*, Patrick Robertson, 1985).

Top male and female box office stars for the year according to a Quigley Publications poll of exhibitors:

Male: Thomas Meighan.

Female: Norma Talmadge.

Ponjola (1923)

Directors: Donald Crisp and James Young. Writers: Charles Logue (screenplay) and Cynthia Stockley (novel). Cinematographer: Paul Perry. Release Date: October 29, 1923 (USA). Duration in Reels: 7. Production Company: Sam E. Rork Productions. Distributor: Associated First National Pictures. Genre: Drama. Cast: Anna Q. Nilsson (Lady Flavia Desmond aka Countess Tyrecastle), James Kirkwood (Lundi Druro), Tully Marshall (Count Blauhimel), Joseph Kilgour (Conrad Lypiatt), Bernard Randall (Eric Luff), Ruth Clifford (Gay Lypiatt), Claire Du Brey (Luchia Luff), Claire McDowell (Mrs. Hope), Charles Ray, Edwin Sturgis, **Olive Borden (Extra — uncredited).**

Olive worked as an extra with streaked makeup and darkened eyes. The story was based in South Africa. *Ponjola* was also the name of a South African alcoholic drink. A print of *Ponjola* exists in a private collection.

During the course of 1923, Olive worked at Sennett Studios (six months) and Christie Studios (four months). However, none of these minor film roles are traceable.

• Hollywood in 1924

Number of releases: 579.

U.S. weekly cinema attendance: 46 million.

Average ticket price: 25 cents.

Top box office stars according to a *Film Daily* poll of exhibitors:

1. Harold Lloyd, 2. Gloria Swanson, 3. Tom Mix, 4. Thomas Meighan, 5. Norma Talmadge, 6. Corinne Griffith and Rudolph Valentino (tied), 7. Douglas Fairbanks, 8. Colleen Moore, Mary Pickford and Reginald Denny (tied).

The *New York Times* top ten best films:

1. *The Dramatic Life of Abraham Lincoln*, 2. *The Thief of Bagdad*, 3. *Beau Brummel*, 4. *Merton of the Movies*, 5. *The Sea Hawk*, 6. *He Who Gets Slapped*, 7. *The Marriage Circle*, 8. *In Hollywood with Potash and Perlmutter*, 9. *Peter Pan*, 10. *Isn't Life Wonderful?*

Clark Gable makes his film debut as an extra in the silent film *Forbidden Paradise*.

Neck and Neck (1924)

Director: Fred Hibbard. Producer: Jack White. Release Date: February 3, 1924 (USA). Duration in Reels: 2. Production Company: Jack White Corporation (as Mermaid Comedies). Distributor: Educational Film Exchanges. Genre: Comedy. Cast: Lige Conley (Hector), **Olive Borden**, Peggy O'Neil (Peggy), Cliff Bowes, Hank Mann.

"Hector (Lige Conley) was born on a Texas farm. The nearest he's been to a city is what he has seen on a postal card and he thinks Edison invented patent leather. While Hector does his stuff pitching hay, the villagers argue how fast an electric fan has to travel to cool off a tomato. One of the villagers is Peg (Peggy O'Neil), who wants a husband, but her face saves her from many a kiss.

"Without a husband life is nothing to Peg (Peggy O'Neil), so she decides to risk it in a final attempt to get a man for her own. She gives two horses the tip to run away with her, and they make a great job of it, but the villagers only remark, 'It's only Peg, joy-ridin' again.'

"Hector (Lige Conley) throws himself on the breeches, saves the girl's life and is rewarded by her father with a trip to the city, and a course in State College. The village rounders gather at the train to warn Hector (Lige Conley) against the city slickers, but Hector (Lige Conley) reckons he'll be safe.

"He arrives in town and falls among taxi-drivers. He gets to the college and gives the professor's understudy a card of introduction from Mayor Cyrus Wilkins, who allows that Heck (Lige Conley) is Asparagus Corner's brightest prospect for the White House.

"Love drives Peggy (Peg O'Neil) to risk exposing herself to an education, so she arrives at college to find Hector (Lige Conley) having a hard time getting city broke. He uses taxi-cabs for an obstacle race down Broadway.

"At the last moment before the big race, the muscle bound skull crew finds themselves one man short. Peg (Peggy O'Neil) recommends Hector (Lige Conley) for the place and as they have nothing better, they put him in.

"When Hector (Lige Conley), who is little but corn-fed, gets in action, the rest of the crew will have to look out or their oars will throw them out of the shell. Hector (Lige Conley) coasts over obstacles, crashes opposing boats and conquers the dangers of the deep, but he wins the race, and realizes that Peg (Peggy O'Neil), college-trained, will be his sun-kissed butterfly for life" [Educational Films Press Sheet].

Moving Picture World (January 2, 1924) wrote, "A decidedly unique interscholastic rowing race is the outstanding situation in this Mermaid comedy. The highly amusing but altogether impossible stunts pulled by the hero with his boat again illustrates the cleverness of Jack White in devising new materials and will furnish many laughs."

Olive plays a girl at the college in the second reel. Although she has little to do, this short has a significant place in her filmography because it's the very first time she is clearly seen onscreen.

Theater Promotion (released to theaters by Education Pictures via a press sheet):

"For unequalled speed and fast action, Jack White, producer of Mermaid Comedies, has no equal. Speed is a comedy essential in slapstick comedies. A picture falls flat when the laughs die out for a few moments, and it is hard to get them started again, but Jack White keeps up a steady barrage of laugh-making situations which breaks down the reserve of the audience, and laugh piles on laugh, so fast that the result is one continuous roar of hilarity.

"In *Neck and Neck*, White has preserved this high speed of comedy gags and situations. Lige Conley, called 'The Speed Boy of Comedy,' is as funny as ever; Peggy O'Neill is as homely as ever and twice as funny, and Hank Mann adds many hearty laughs to a comedy already full of them.

"You will find *Neck and Neck* right up to the standard: the Jack White-Mermaid standard: ideal entertainment for all of your audience and packed and jammed with the kind of stuff that makes 'em laugh, and brings them often to your theatre."

TAGLINES: "An army of laughs running neck and neck to a breakneck finish in the new Educational-Mermaid Comedy, *Neck and Neck*, with Lige Conley and a big Mermaid hit."

"Hector was a slow boy in a fast town: but he showed them all how to row to victory in the big boat race. See this clever, laugh-making Mermaid Comedy: it's a clever comedy riot."

"A big comedy cast in this Mermaid Comedy, and laughs enough to make you feel good for a week."

"If you're strong enough to laugh thirty minutes without stopping, don't miss seeing *Neck and Neck*, the new Mermaid Comedy with that speed boy, Lige Conley, in one of his funniest roles. It's guaranteed to make you laugh."

The Museum of Modern Art has a 35mm print of this short (preserved from nitrate stock) with Czech flash intertitles.

Peggy O'Neil's name was spelled various ways throughout her career; she was often billed as Peggy O'Neil, Peggy O'Neill, Peg O'Neil, etc.

Wide Open (1924)

Director-Writer: Fred Hibbard. Release Date: March 2, 1924 (USA). Production Company: Jack White Corporation. Distributor: Educational Film Exchanges. Genre: Comedy. Cast: Lige Conley (Mr. Hazzard), **Olive Borden** (Mrs. Newlywed),

Otto Fries, Peggy O'Neil (Mrs. Hazzard), George Ovey, Jack Lloyd.

"George Washington never told a lie, but George never played golf. Mr. and Mrs. Hazzard (Lige Conley and Peggy O'Neil) do the latter constantly, and the former only when talking to better golfers. The Hazzards have a neighbor with an auto who takes them to the links. When the neighbors begin honking the horn under the Hazzards' widow at 6 A.M., it annoys the other residents of the apartment building so much that they bombard the autoists with everything that isn't nailed down, and compel them to drive away.

"At the golf club, the expert is lecturing to the novices. He takes Mr. and Mrs. Hazzard out on the course. The 'pro' has told them always to hit the ball from where it lies, so Hazzard follows the ball down a precipice and has to be pulled up by a fellow club member on horseback.

"Our hero drives into the water hazzard and walks to the bottom of the lake to recover. Before the eighteenth hole is reached, night overtakes the devoted pair, and they miss the last [trolley] car home. They spend the night on a bench with a young married couple whose baby carriage is protected by all the modern safety equipment.

"The first [trolley] car arrives shortly after dawn. Mrs. Newlywed (Olive) has trouble getting the perambulator through the door, and it projects outside as the car flies along. The baby lands in the lap of a would-be passenger, and a drunk falls into the baby carriage. Mrs. Newlywed finds the changeling, and threatens hysterics until the child's temporary custodian restores it to her arms.

"A sudden stop throws the motorman out, and the [trolley] car runs away. Hazzard, trying to check it, falls off and joins the motorman in his chase after the fugitive [trolley] car. Panic reigns among the passengers. The [trolley] car chases a fat woman on a bicycle, and she has a narrow squeak, but escapes. Just before the passenger list becomes a list of the dead and injured, the motorman overtakes the [trolley] car and puts it under control, but Hazzard decides he'll change his membership to a golf club where they have bus service" [Educational Films Press Sheet].

Theater Promotion (released to theaters by Education Pictures via a press sheet):

"Hold on to your hats! Here it comes, wide open, and hitting on every cylinder: the new Mermaid Comedy, *Wide Open*: two reels of action, thrills and laughs!

"A side-splitting golf game and a run-away street car are the high spots in this rapid-fire Mermaid, and there's enough action in either of them to make a couple of ordinary comedies. Together, they make a comedy that's a real riot from title to trailer.

"In *Wide Open*, you've got a comedy that will be the big item on your program. It's the thing people will talk about when they leave, for it's crammed full of the kind of Mermaid action that leaves them gasping for breath after a half hour of thrills and roars of laughter. Lige Conley is starred. He is supported by Peg O'Neil, Otto Fries, Jack Lloyd and Olive Borden. The direction is Fred Hibbard."

TAGLINES: "Extra added attraction! Action, thrills and laughs in the funniest comedy in months.

"It's one of those mile-a-minute, fast action comedies with more laughs than there are marks in Germany."

"A triple geared, high pressure comedy with the action running at break-neck speed and the laughter throttle wide open..."

"The funniest golf game ever played and a runaway street car are just two of the high spots of humor..."

A print of *Wide Open* exists in a private collection.

Air Pockets (1924)

Director: Fred Hibbard. Producer: Jack White. Cinematographer: Francis Corby. Release Date: May 25, 1924 (USA). Duration in Reels: 2. Production Company: Jack White Corporation. Distributor: Educational Film Exchanges. Genre: Comedy. Cast: Lige Conley (Octavius Jones the Inventor), Earl Montgomery (Uranius Holmes the Detective), Sunshine Hart (Peg's Mother), **Olive Borden (Morgan's Daughter)**, Peggy O'Neil (Peg), Otto Fries (Sanford Morgan).

Air Pockets starts out with the intertitle, "Stanford Morgan — a financial genius — who's motto is, 'A hair in the head is worth two in the brush.'" Lige Conley plays an inventor (Octavius Jones) out to get financing for his latest creation. When he ends up in Morgan's house and barges in on his business meeting, he introduces himself as "Octavius Jones, the silent brains of the motor industry." Out of a wooden box, he proceeds to unfold an automobile. He introduces the car as the "folding flivver," the car that will save the universe from garages. Of course, everything falls to pieces, including the car, when a window is opened and the propeller from a biplane causes the collapsible car to, well, collapse!

Olive plays Morgan's daughter, the heiress who gets caught up in a spectacular aerial biplane chase. With the usual cartoon-like stunts, crashes and spills that go with a Conley short, including Lige on the end of a seesawing ladder atop a speeding car and riding a runaway horse carriage on two wheels, *Air Pockets* is nothing short of amazing. The unfortunate racial stereotyping is the only downside to the story; at the time, it was an acceptable form of humor that was often used in many films.

Lige Conley is one of the most underrated comedians of the silent era. Born Elijah Crommie on December 5, 1897, in St. Louis, Missouri, he appeared in over one hundred films between 1915 and the late 1930s. He started his career in the stock company at the Mack Sennett studio (using the name Lige Crommie) and then moved on to Hal Roach's studio. He appeared in many one-reelers with Harold Lloyd, Bebe Daniels and Snub Pollard. Credited as Lige Cromley during his time at Roach, he was often overshadowed by Lloyd and returned to Sennett for a second time, again billed as Lige Crommie.

Following his second stint with Sennett, he followed director Fred Hibbard (aka Fred Fishback) to Universal Pictures. He finally achieved the fame he deserved when he appeared in many fast-paced two-reelers for Educational Pictures. With curly dark hair and a cheeky grin, Conley had a striking resemblance to an out-of-character Charlie Chaplin. In fact, the studio marketed him as the "next Chaplin," but he never came close to equaling Chaplin's success or popularity.

Tragically, a 1937 laboratory fire destroyed most of Educational's silent comedy archive. As a result, few of Conley's films survive today. The handful of Conley films that remain are so brilliantly crafted and laugh-out-loud funny, they only serve to make one realize what a great loss it was when the rest of his work literally went up in smoke.

Conley's films were packed full of physical comedy, manic car, horse and train chases, clever scenarios and daring stunts. Ironically, he died on December 11, 1937, after he was struck and killed by a car in Hollywood after stopping to help a stranded stranger change a flat tire. He was only forty years old (http://en.wikipedia.org/wiki/Lige_Conley).

Prints of this short exist at Cineteca del Friuli, Gemona, Italy, the Academy Film Archive and the Library of Congress; 16mm reference print FAC4142. Grapevine Video released *Air Pockets* on DVD in 2003 as part of the *Films of Lige Conley* collection.

Don't Park There (1924)

Director: Fred Guiol. Producer: Hal Roach. Writer: Tay Garnett. Release Date: June 22, 1924. Duration in Reels: 2. Production Company: Hal Roach Studios Inc. Distributor: Pathé Exchange. Genre: Comedy. Cast: Will Rogers, Marie Mosquini, **Olive Borden (Extra — uncredited)**.

According to the Hal Roach Studios payroll ledgers, Olive received a one-time payment of $12.50 on March 19, 1924, for her work on the film. A print exists in a private collection.

Our Congressman (1924)

Director: Rob Wagner. Producer: Hal Roach. Production Dates: April: May 1924. Release Date: July 20, 1924. Duration in Reels: 2. Alternate Title: *Alfalfa Doolittle, Our Congressman* (USA). Production Company: Hal Roach Studios Inc. Distributor: Pathé Exchange. Genre: Comedy. Cast: Will Rogers (Alfalfa Doolittle), Molly Thompson (His Wife), Sammy Brooks, Chet Brandenburg, Beth Darlington, James Finlayson, William Gillespie, Madge Hunt, **Olive Borden (Extra — uncredited)**.

According to the Hal Roach Studios payroll ledgers, Olive received a one-time payment of $12.50 on May 3, 1924, for her work on the film. A print exists in a private collection.

Seeing Nellie Home (1924)

Director: Leo McCarey. Producer: Hal Roach. Production Dates: April 21: April 26, 1924. Release Date: July 27, 1924. Duration in Reels: 1. Running Time: 10 minutes. Production Company: Hal Roach Studios Inc. Distributor: Pathé Exchange. All Day Entertainment (VCI Entertainment: DVD — 2009). Genre: Comedy. Cast: Charley Chase, Ena Gregory, Martha Sleeper, **Olive Borden (Extra — uncredited)**.

According to the Hal Roach Studios payroll ledgers, Olive received a one-time payment of $25 on April 26, 1924, for her work on the film.

All Day Entertainment (in conjunction with VCI Entertainment) released a four-disc DVD set entitled *Becoming Charley Chase*; *Seeing Nellie Home* (1924), *Outdoor Pajamas* (1924), *The Poor Fish* (1924), *Should Husbands Be Watched?* (1925), *Bad Boy* (1925) and *Too Many Mammas* (1925) are included in the set. They're the only six surviving Chase shorts with Olive in the cast.

A Hard Boiled Tenderfoot (1924)

Director: J. A. Howe (as Jay A. Howe). Producer: Hal Roach. Release Date: August 10, 1924. Duration in Reels: 2. Production Company: Hal Roach Studios Inc. Distributor: Pathé Exchange. Genre: Comedy. Cast: Sidney D'Albrook, Laura Roessing, Frank Butler, **Olive Borden (Extra — uncredited)**.

Part of the Spat Family series focusing on the dysfunctional relationship of the fussy J. Tewksberry Spat, his combative wife and her loutish, know-it-all live-in brother.

Hal Roach grossed an average of $18,000 per Spat Family short. That's not particularly earth-shattering in comparison to his most popular series, the Our Gang comedies, which totaled close to $50,000 (*A History of the Hal Roach Studios*, Richard Lewis Ward, Southern Illinois University Press/Carbondale, 2005).

According to the Hal Roach Studios payroll ledgers, Olive received a one-time payment of $25 on April 24, 1924, for her work on the film. As of 2009, this short is presumed lost.

A Truthful Liar (1924)

Director: Hampton Del Ruth. Producer: Hal Roach. Cinematographer: Robert Doran. Production Dates: April — May 1924. Release Date: August 17, 1924. Duration in Reels: 2. Production Company: Hal Roach Studios Inc. Distributor: Pathé Exchange. Genre: Comedy. Cast: Will Rogers (Ambassador Alfalfa Doolittle), Molly Thompson (His Wife), Jack Ackroyd (Flunky), R.O. Pennell, Jack Cooper, **Olive Borden (Extra — uncredited)**.

According to the Hal Roach Studios payroll ledgers, Olive received a one-time payment of $12.50 on May 10, 1924, for her work on the film. A print exists in a private collection.

Sweet Daddy (1924)

Director: Leo McCarey. Producer: Hal Roach. Production Dates: June 13–June 18, 1924. Release Date: August 17, 1924. Duration in Reels: 1. Production Company: Hal Roach Studios Inc. Distributor: Pathé Exchange. Genre: Comedy. Cast: Charley Chase, Westcott Clarke, Jules Mendel, Earl Mohan, Martha Sleeper, **Olive Borden (Extra — uncredited)**.

According to the Hal Roach Studios payroll ledgers, Olive received two payments for her work on the film: June 14, 1924 ($12.50) and June 21, 1924 ($12.50). As of 2009, this short is presumed lost.

Why Men Work (1924)

Director: Leo McCarey. Producer: Hal Roach. Production Dates: July 2–July 7, 1924 (Retakes: July 8, 1924). Release Date — August 31, 1924 (USA). Duration in Reels: 1. Production Company: Hal Roach Studios Inc. Distributor: Pathé Exchange.

Genre: Comedy. Cast: Charley Chase, **Olive Borden,** William Gillespie, Katherine Grant, Earl Mohan.

According to the Hal Roach Studios payroll ledgers, Olive received two payments for her work on the film: June 7, 1924 ($25) and July 12, 1924 ($12.50).

The *Los Angeles Times* (August 6, 1924) wrote, "This one-reel comedy treats humorously the adventures of an amateur newsreel photographer when he attempts to take some pictures of a visiting governor. Charley Chase impersonates the cameraman, and most of the limited footage is devoted to his exploits behind the camera."

Moving Picture World (September 6, 1924) wrote, "...Charles Chase ... furnishes a lot of fun in this Pathé single-reeler. Chase is 'buffaloed' by a senior and rival photographer who so places his own camera that Chase photographs everything in sight except the objective point."

As of 2009, this short is presumed lost.

South o' the North Pole (1924)

Director: J. A. Howe (as Jay A. Howe). Producer: Hal Roach. Production Dates: March: April 1924. Release Date: September 7, 1924. Duration in Reels: 2. Production Company: Hal Roach Studios Inc. Distributor: Pathé Exchange. Genre: Comedy. Cast: Sidney D'Albrook, Laura Roessing, Frank Butler, **Olive Borden (Indian Squaw).**

Part of the Spat Family series.

According to the Hal Roach Studios payroll ledgers, Olive received five payments for her work as an Indian Squaw on the film: March 29, 1924 ($37.50), April 5, 1924 ($75), April 12, 1924 ($75.00), April 19, 1924 ($37.50) and April 26, 1924 ($25.00).

Taken from a 16mm transfer, the second reel of this short is featured on the three-disc DVD *Roach Volume Two: Odds, Ends, Spats & Doo-Dads: Plus Max and Mabel* by Looser Than Loose Publishing.

Outdoor Pajamas (1924)

Director: Leo McCarey. Producer: Hal Roach. Production Dates: June 23–July 15, 1924. Release Date: September 14, 1924. Duration in Reels: 1. Running Time: 10 minutes. Production Company: Hal Roach Studios Inc. Distributor: Pathé Exchange. DVD: Grapevine Video (2005), Looser Than Loose Publishing (2007: worldwide), All Day Entertainment (VCI Entertainment) (2009). Genre:

Comedy. Cast: Charley Chase, Martha Sleeper, Charles Bachman, Eddie Baker, Beth Darlington, Jack Gavin, Jules Mendel, George Rowe, Lyle Tayo, Leo Willis, **Olive Borden (Extra — uncredited).**

According to the Hal Roach Studios payroll ledgers, Olive received a one-time payment of $12.50 on June 28, 1924, for her work on the film.

All Day Entertainment (in conjunction with VCI Entertainment) released a four-disc DVD set entitled *Becoming Charley Chase*; *Seeing Nellie Home* (1924), *Outdoor Pajamas* (1924), *The Poor Fish* (1924), *Should Husbands Be Watched?* (1925), *Bad Boy* (1925) and *Too Many Mammas* (1925) are all included in the set. They're the only six surviving Chase shorts with Olive in the cast.

Should Landlords Live? (1924)

Directors: Nicholas T. Barrows and James D. Davis. Production Date: June 1924. Release Date: September 28, 1924 (USA). Production Company: Hal Roach Studios Inc. Distributor: Pathé Exchange. Genre: Comedy. Cast: Arthur Stone, **Olive Borden**, Helen Gilmore, Ena Gregory, Marie Mosquini, Robert Page, Martha Sleeper.

Arthur Stone provides two reels of laugh-filled nonsense in *Should Landlords Live?*, a title that has little to do with the story. A gawky "country hero" gets a job in an apartment house but his tribulations are not so much the results of association with the landlord as they are with the tenants. His greatest trouble comes when he encounters a vampish modiste, although a comedy janitor appears as a slapstick menace later in the picture.

Stone gets a considerable amount of laughs at the outset, when he is seen behind the counter of a combination grocery store and millinery emporium in a small town. He courts fame and wealth in the city, with disastrous results. Marie Mosquini, Ena Gregory and Olive are seen in the apartment house sequence and Martha Sleeper is seen in a bit part at the opening of the film.

According to the Hal Roach Studios payroll ledgers, Olive received a one-time payment of $25 on June 14, 1924, for her work on the film. As of 2009, the survival status of this short is unknown. There is a possibility this film exists in a private collection.

Lost Dog (1924)

Director: J. A. Howe (as Jay A. Howe). Producer: Hal Roach. Production Date: May 1924. Release

Date: October 5, 1924. Duration in Reels: 2. Production Company: Hal Roach Studios Inc. Distributor: Pathé Exchange. Genre: Comedy. Cast: Sidney D'Albrook, Laura Roessing, Frank Butler, **Olive Borden (Extra — uncredited).**

Part of the Spat Family series. According to the Hal Roach Studios payroll ledgers, Olive received four payments for her work on the film: May 3, 1924 ($62.50), May 10, 1924 ($62.50), May 17, 1924 ($62.50), and May 24, 1924 ($37.50). As of 2009, this short is presumed lost.

Too Many Mammas (1924)

Director: Leo McCarey. Producer: Hal Roach. Production Dates: July 18–July 23, 1924. Release Date: October 12, 1924 (USA). Duration in reels: 1. Alternate Title: *Too Many Mamas* (alternate spelling). Production Company: Hal Roach Studios Inc. Distributor: Pathé Exchange. DVD: All Day Entertainment (VCI Entertainment) (2009). Genre: Comedy. Cast: Charley Chase, **Olive Borden**, Beth Darlington, John T. Prince, Martha Sleeper, Noah Young.

According to the Hal Roach Studios payroll ledgers, Olive received two payments for her work on the film: July 19, 1924 ($25) and July 26, 1924 ($37.50).

Motion Picture News (October 11, 1924) wrote, "Here again Charlie Chase scores handsomely. *Too Many Mammas* is an especially good single reel comedy. In fact it is as breezy and amusing as the better two-reel comedies usually are."

The short involves a loyal office clerk whose employer impresses him into service as an "alibi" in order to take a blonde friend to a cabaret that evening. Charlie breaks a date with his own girl. Later, both the wife of the employer and the sweetheart of the clerk reach the cabaret and then a hilarious form of ingenious deception is employed. His crazy dance with the tough girl at the cabaret is a thoroughly amusing scene and his characterization throughout the reel is entertaining and memorable. Olive plays the boss' mistress.

The *Los Angeles Times* (October 8, 1924) wrote, "One can't expect a very coherent story in a one-reel comedy, but Hal Roach has a habit of packing a surprisingly large number of laughs into those which feature Charley Chase. His latest, called *Too Many Mammas*, is no exception."

In 2009, All Day Entertainment (in conjunction with VCI Entertainment) released a four-disc DVD set entitled *Becoming Charley*

Chase: *Seeing Nellie Home* (1924), *Outdoor Pajamas* (1924), *The Poor Fish* (1924), *Should Husbands Be Watched?* (1925), *Bad Boy* (1925) and *Too Many Mammas* (1925) are all included in the set. They're the only six surviving Chase shorts with Olive in the cast.

The Battling Orioles (1924)

Directors: Fred Guiol and Ted Wilde. Producer: Hal Roach. Writer: Hal Roach (story). Cinematographers: Floyd Jackman and George Stevens. Production Dates — October 22, 1923: February 8, 1924. Release Date: October 26, 1924. Duration in Reels: 5–6 (varies). Duration in Feet: 5,600. Production Company: Hal Roach Studios Inc. Distributor: Pathé Exchange. Home Video: Facets Multimedia Distribution (USA: VHS), Grapevine Video (USA: VHS), Movies Unlimited (USA: VHS). Genre: Comedy. Cast: Glenn Tryon, Blanche Mehaffey, John T. Prince, Noah Young, Sam Lufkin, Robert Page, Joe Cobb, Jackie Condon, Mickey Daniels, Ernest Morrison, **Olive Borden (Extra — uncredited)**.

According to the Hal Roach Studios payroll ledgers, Olive received a one-time payment of $12.50 on May 31, 1924, for her work on the film. A print exists in a private collection.

Sky Plumber (1924)

Director: James D. Davis. Producer: Hal Roach. Production Date: May 1924. Release Date — October 26, 1924. Duration in Reels: 2. Production Company: Hal Roach Studios Inc. Distributor: Pathé Exchange. Genre: Comedy. Cast: Arthur Stone, **Olive Borden (Extra — uncredited)**.

According to the Hal Roach Studios payroll ledgers, Olive received a one-time payment of $37.50 on May 24, 1924, for her work on the film. As of 2009, this short is presumed lost.

Hot Stuff (1924)

Director: J. A. Howe (as Jay A. Howe). Producer: Hal Roach. Production Dates: May: June 1924. Release Date: November 1, 1924. Duration in Reels: 2. Production Company: Hal Roach Studios Inc. Distributor: Pathé Exchange. Genre: Comedy. Cast: Sidney D'Albrook, Laura Roessing, Frank Butler, **Olive Borden (Extra — uncredited)**.

Part of the Spat Family series. According to the Hal Roach Studios payroll ledgers, Olive received four payments for her work on the film: May 31, 1924 ($37.50), June 7, 1924 ($50), June 14, 1924 ($37.50), June 21, 1924 ($37.50). As of 2009, this short is presumed lost.

All Wet (1924)

Director: Leo McCarey. Producer: Hal Roach. Cinematographer: Len Powers. Production Dates: September 10–September 15, 1924. Release Date: November 23, 1924. Duration in Reels: 1. Running Time: 12 minutes. Production Company: Hal Roach Studios Inc. Distributor: Pathé Exchange. Home Video: Grapevine Video (VHS), Videolibrary (VHS), Kino Video (*Slapstick Symposium: The Charley Chase Collection*, DVD, 2004). Genre: Comedy. Cast: Charley Chase, William Gillespie, "Tonnage" Martin Wolfkeil, Jack Gavin, Gale Henry; Janet Gaynor, Martha Sleeper, **Olive Borden (Extra — uncredited)**.

According to the Hal Roach Studios payroll ledgers, Olive received a one-time payment of $12.50 on September 6, 1924, for her work on the film.

Deaf, Dumb and Daffy (1924)

Director: J. A. Howe (as Jay A. Howe). Producer: Hal Roach. Production Dates: July-August 1924. Release Date: November 30, 1924. Duration in Reels: 2. Production Company: Hal Roach Studios Inc. Distributor: Pathé Exchange. Genre: Comedy. Cast: Sidney D'Albrook, Laura Roessing, Frank Butler, **Olive Borden (Extra — uncredited)**.

Part of the Spat Family series. According to the Hal Roach Studios payroll ledgers, Olive received two payments for her work on the film: August 2, 1924 ($75) and August 9, 1924 ($75). As of 2009, this short is presumed lost.

The Poor Fish (1924)

Director: Leo McCarey. Producer: Hal Roach. Production Dates: September 19–September 25, 1924. Release Date: December 7, 1924. Duration in Reels: 1. Running Time —10 minutes. Production Company: Hal Roach Studios Inc. Distributor: Pathé Exchange. DVD: All Day Entertainment (VCI Entertainment, 2009). Genre: Comedy. Cast: Charley Chase, William Gillespie, Katherine Grant, "Tonnage" Martin Wolfkiel, **Olive Borden (Extra — uncredited)**.

According to the Hal Roach Studios payroll ledgers, Olive received a one-time payment of $25 on September 20, 1924, for her work on the film. All Day Entertainment (in conjunction with VCI Entertainment) released a 2009 four-disc DVD set entitled, *Becoming Charley Chase*: *Seeing Nellie Home* (1924), *Outdoor Pajamas* (1924), *The Poor Fish* (1924), *Should Husbands Be Watched?* (1925), *Bad Boy* (1925) and *Too Many Mammas* (1925) are all included in the set.

They're the only six surviving Chase shorts with Olive in the cast.

Meet the Missus (1924)

Directors: Roy Clements and Fred Guiol. Producer: Hal Roach. Production Date: September 1924. Release Date: December 7, 1924. Duration in Reels: 2. Production Company: Hal Roach Studios Inc. Distributor: Pathé Exchange. Genre: Comedy. Cast: Glenn Tryon, Helen Gilmore, Al Hallett, Blanche Mehaffey, Noah Young, **Olive Borden (Extra — uncredited).**

According to the Hal Roach Studios payroll ledgers, Olive received a one-time payment of $12.50 on September 13, 1924 for her work on the film. A print exists in a private collection.

The White Sheep (1924)

Directors: Hal Roach, Roy Clements and Hampton Del Ruth. Producer: Hal Roach. Writer: Hal Roach (story). Cinematographers- Fred Jackman and George Stevens. Release Date: December 14, 1924. Duration in Reels: 5–6 (varies). Duration in Feet: 6,091. Production Company: Hal Roach Studios Inc. Distributor: Pathé Exchange. Genre: Comedy. Cast: Glenn Tryon, Blanche Mehaffey, Jack Gavin, Robert Kortman, Leo Willis, Richard Daniels, Chris Lynton, J. J. Clayton, Dick Gilbert, **Olive Borden (Extra — uncredited).**

According to the Hal Roach Studios payroll ledgers, Olive received a one-time payment of $25 on June 21, 1924, for her work on the film. After Roach and Pathé lost their star player Harold Lloyd, they were desperate to replace him and Glenn Tryon was earmarked to be the wholesome new All-American comedic hero to fill Lloyd's shoes. But Tryon's debut Roach features (*The Battling Orioles* and *The White Sheep*) were met with little success. Despite being more suited to shorts, which is where Roach conceded he should be, Tryon's future offerings were not hugely successful either. He stayed with Roach until 1927, but in no way, shape or form did he measure up to Lloyd (*Harold Lloyd: Master Comedian*, Jeffrey Vance and Suzanne Lloyd, Harry N. Abrams, 2002). A print of this film exists in a private collection.

The Royal Razz (1924)

Director: Leo McCarey. Producer: Hal Roach. Production Dates: October 1–October 7, 1924. Release Date: December 21, 1924 (USA). Production Company: Hal Roach Studios Inc. Distributor: Pathé Exchange. Genre: Comedy. Cast: Charley Chase, **Olive Borden,** Katherine Grant, Jules Mendel, Robert Page, Martha Sleeper.

According to the Hal Roach Studios payroll ledgers, Olive received a one-time payment of $12.50 on October 4, 1924, for her work on the film.

Chase is shown returning home in a trolley car, carrying a Christmas tree. The havoc it plays with the passengers can well be imagined and the seasonal prop is used to great effect. Arriving home, Chase endeavors to come down the chimney dressed as Santa Claus; he lands first in the furnace and then comes up through the vent in the floor. Director McCarey keeps the pace going and gets more laughs out of a scene where Chase calls a doctor who comes still dressed as Santa and the two get into a scrap, ending with Chase's wife hitting the wrong one!

Los Angeles Times (December 10, 1924) wrote, "*The Royal Razz* will doubtless prove acceptable for the Christmas season. It recites the trials and tribulations of playing Santa Claus, and that portion which shows Chase climbing down the chimney, getting lost, and emerging from the furnace instead of the fireplace is laughable..."

Chicago Daily Tribune (December 27, 1924) wrote, "*The Royal Razz* ... is getting a lot of laughs."

Moving Picture World (December 20, 1924) wrote, "This ... is one of the most amusing single-reelers of the series and in addition is particularly timely as it deals with the Christmas season fast approaching. It is chock full of pep and contains more laughs than many two-reelers."

Moving Picture News (December 20, 1924) wrote, "There is one situation which for comic effect stands out beyond all others — and there are many of fine quality. That is where Charlie, descending the chimney to make a spectacular entrance through the open grate in the living room, comes out via the furnace door in the cellar."

Supposedly, *The Royal Razz* was partially re-worked in 1926 and re-released as *There Ain't No Santa Claus*. A copy exists in a private collection. As of 2009 *The Royal Razz* is presumed lost.

Just a Good Guy (1924)

Director: Hampton Del Ruth. Producer-Writer: Hal Roach. Production Dates: July 1924. Release Date: December 21, 1924 (USA). Duration in

Reels: 2. Production Company: Hal Roach Studios Inc. Distributor: Pathé Exchange. Genre: Comedy. Cast: Arthur Stone (Wilmot), **Olive Borden**, Katherine Grant, Kewpie Morgan (Landlord), Fay Wray (Slippery Sue), Noah Young (Policeman).

According to the Hal Roach Studios payroll ledgers, Olive received three payments for her work on the film: July 5, 1924 ($75), July 12, 1924 ($62.50) and July 19, 1924 ($50). Oliver Hardy was often mistakenly credited for Kewpie Morgan's role in this short.

The UCLA Film and Television Archive (Los Angeles, California) has several prints of this two-reel short, at various lengths. The Hungarian National Film Archive has a print of *Just a Good Guy* in their archive. There is also a print in a private collection.

The Rubber-Neck (1924)

Directors: J. A. Howe (as Jay A. Howe) and Victor Potel. Producer: Hal Roach. Production Dates: June, July, September, 1924. (Studio was closed to production from August 10 to September 5, 1924.) Release Date: December 28, 1924. Duration in Reels: 2. Production Company: Hal Roach Studios Inc. Distributor: Pathé Exchange. Genre: Comedy. Cast: Sidney D'Albrook, Laura Roessing, Frank Butler, **Olive Borden (Extra — uncredited)**.

Part of the Spat Family series. According to the Hal Roach Studios payroll ledgers, Olive received three payments for her work on the film: June 28, 1924 ($62.50), July 26, 1924 ($37.50), September 6, 1924 ($75). As of 2009, this short is presumed lost.

• Hollywood in 1925

Number of releases: 578.

U.S. weekly cinema attendance: 46 million.

Tom Mix's salary — $20,000 per week.

Top male and female box office stars for the year according to a Quigley Publications poll of exhibitors:

Male: Rudolph Valentino.

Female: Norma Talmadge.

The New York Times Ten Best Films:

1. *The Big Parade,* 2. *The Last Laugh,* 3. *The Unholy Three,* 4. *The Gold Rush,* 5. *The Merry Widow,* 6. *The Dark Angel,* 7. *Don Q, Son of Zorro,* 8. *Ben-Hur,* 9. *Stella Dallas,* 10. *A Kiss for Cinderella.*

Laugh That Off (1925)

Director: J. A. Howe (as Jay A. Howe). Producer: Hal Roach. Release Date: January 25, 1925. Duration in Reels: 2. Production Company: Hal Roach Studios Inc. Distributor: Pathé Exchange. Genre: Comedy. Cast: Sidney D'Albrook, Laura Roessing, Frank Butler, **Olive Borden (Extra — uncredited)**.

Part of the Spat Family series. According to the Hal Roach Studios payroll ledgers, Olive received five payments for her work on the film: August 9, 1924 ($75), September 13, 1924 ($50), September 20, 1924 ($25), September 27, 1924 ($62.50), October 4, 1924 ($62.50). As of 2009, this short is presumed lost.

Note: Hal Roach payroll ledgers indicate that Olive was paid $25 on September 20, 1924, and $12.50 on September 27, 1924. These two payments were for her work in a short titled *Hard Working Loafers,* an Arthur Stone vehicle, with Olive in support. However, the short was never registered for copyright, a tell-tale sign that it was not completed.

Change the Needle (1925)

Director-Producer: Hal Roach. Production Dates: October: November 1924. Release Date: February 15, 1925. Duration in Reels: 2. Production Company: Hal Roach Studios Inc. Distributor: Pathé Exchange. Genre: Comedy. Cast: Arthur Stone, Bill Brokaw, James Finlayson, **Olive Borden (Extra — uncredited)**.

According to the Hal Roach Studios payroll ledgers, Olive received three payments for her work on the film: October 18, 1924 ($25), October 25, 1924 ($75), November 8, 1924 ($12.50). As of 2009 this short is presumed lost.

The Fox Hunt (1925)

Director: J. A. Howe (as Jay A. Howe). Producer: Hal Roach. Production Dates: October: November 1924. Release Date: February 22, 1925. Duration in Reels: 2. Production Company: Hal Roach Studios Inc. Distributor: Pathé Exchange. Genre: Comedy. Cast: Sidney D'Albrook, Laura Roessing, Frank Butler, **Olive Borden (Extra — uncredited)**.

Part of the Spat Family series. According to the Hal Roach Studios payroll ledgers, Olive received three payments for her work on the film: October 11, 1924 ($75), October 18, 1924 ($50), November 1, 1924 ($37.50). As of 2009, this short is presumed lost.

Dog Days (1925)

Director: Robert F. McGowan. Producer: Hal Roach. Writers: Hal Roach (story), H. M. Walker (titles). Cinematographer: Art Lloyd. Production Dates: October 29: November 5, 1924, and November 17 to 24, 1924. Release Date: March 8, 1925 (USA). Duration in Reels: 2. Runtime: 20 minutes. Filming Location: Motor Ave. and Woodbine St., Palms district, Los Angeles, California. Production Company: Hal Roach Studios Inc. Distributor: Pathé Exchange. Genre: Comedy. Cast: Peggy Ahearn, Wadell Carter, Joe Cobb (Joe), Jackie Condon, Mickey Daniels (Mickey), Johnny Downs, William Gillespie (Mary's Father), Allen "Farina" Hoskins, Eugene Jackson (Pineapple), Mary Kornman (Mary), Ernie Morrison, Sr. (Butler), Lyle Tayo (Mother), Dorothy Vernon (Mickey's Mother), **Olive Borden (Extra — uncredited).**

According to the Hal Roach Studios payroll ledgers, Olive received a one-time payment of $12.50 on November 22, 1924, for her work on the film. It was the average weekly salary of an extra. It was the thirty-sixth film in the hugely popular "Our Gang" series to be released. The opening title reads "Our Gang" Comedies: Hal Roach presents His Rascals in *Dog Days*. Forty prints were made for the film's original release. Much of the story centers on Mickey, his dog and Mary's birthday party.

Several incomplete versions have been released over the years. A 1987 VHS release from Video Yesteryear (*The Return of "Our Gang"*) contained a print with a 16:40 running time. When Video Classics (*Our Gang Silent Comedies Volume 6*) released the short on VHS, only 9:35 of footage was seen. The Picture Palace (*Our Gang Comedies VI*) released the same incomplete print. A complete print was found in 2008. Copyright was not renewed so *Dog Days* is now in the public domain.

Should Husbands Be Watched? (1925)

Director: Leo McCarey. Producer: Hal Roach. Cinematographer: Len Powers. Editing: Richard C. Currier. Production Dates: November 19–November 22, 1924. Additional scenes shot on December 5, 1924. Release Date: March 14, 1925 (USA). Running Time: 15 minutes. Duration in Reels: 1. Production Company: Hal Roach Studios Inc. Distributor: Pathé Exchange. DVD: Looser Than Loose Publishing (2007: worldwide), All Day Entertainment (VCI Entertainment, 2009). Genre: Comedy. Cast: Charley Chase (Jamison Jump),

Katherine Grant (Mrs. Jump), **Olive Borden (The New Maid)**, William Frawley (Beat Cop), Jack Gavin, Al Hallett.

Olive's role in *Should Husbands Be Watched?* (1925) is by far her most significant in her six surviving Chase shorts. Throughout this one-reeler, Olive plays the new maid to the *nouveau riche* Mr. and Mrs. Jump (Charley Chase and Katherine Grant); the short anticipates Chase's later two-reel marital farces, as Mrs. Jump begins to suspect her husband's (innocent, of course) relationship with Olive.

According to the Hal Roach Studios payroll ledgers, Olive received a one-time payment of $50 on November 22, 1924, for her work on the film.

Charley Chase (October 20, 1893 — June 20, 1940) was an American comedian, gag man, screenwriter and film director. Best known for his Hal Roach short comedies between 1924 and 1936, he was born in Baltimore, Maryland, and was sometimes credited under his birth name, Charles Joseph Parrott. His brother James Parrott (1898–1939) was also an actor and director. Despite Chase's lifelong battle with alcohol, which intensified after his brother's untimely death, he achieved a prolific filmography during his forty-six years. Chase's name belongs alongside such comedic greats as Charlie Chaplin, Roscoe "Fatty" Arbuckle, Buster Keaton, Harold Lloyd, Snub Pollard, Ford Sterling, Chester Conklin, Billy West, Laurel and Hardy and The Three Stooges. Be it acting, producing, directing or writing, he worked with many of Hollywood's greatest comedians and his name is associated, in some way, with over three hundred films.

This charming one-reel comedy tells the tale of a young couple whom after suddenly becoming affluent, find themselves engaging a maid (Olive). Unknowing in the ways and manners one puts on when one is served at table by a pretty, haughty young thing in a tiny white apron and cap, their first meal under the new regime is not a comfortable one and this is where the comedy unfolds. There is a climax with burglars about to send the husband off as the escort to the maid (Olive). His wife follows, and though she sees how hard the maid strives to vamp it up to Charley, he remains staunch in his affections for his wife and there is a happy ending (*Motion Picture News.* March 11, 1925).

"Looser Than Loose Publishing" released *Hal Roach: The Brothers Parrott* on DVD and

Olive shows off her legs, and her flexibility, in this somewhat unusual pose. "Ever since I have been in pictures, producers have been exploiting my figure. Personally I don't care for such photographs, but I have decided that as long as I am in this business I am going to do what I am told to do and not what I may happen to want to do," said Olive.

Should Husbands Be Watched? is featured on disc three. All Day Entertainment (in conjunction with VCI Entertainment) released a four-disc DVD set entitled *Becoming Charley Chase*; this short plus *Seeing Nellie Home* (1924), *Outdoor Pajamas* (1924), *The Poor Fish* (1924), *Bad Boy* (1925) and *Too Many Mammas* (1925) are included in the set. They're the only six surviving Chase shorts with Olive in the cast. A copy of the short also exists with Lobster Films, Paris.

The Dressmaker from Paris (1925)

Director: Paul Bern. Producer: Cecil B. DeMille and Paul Bern. Writers: Howard Hawks (story), Adelaide Heilbron (story and screenplay). Costume Design: Travis Banton. Release Date: March 17, 1925 (New York City: premiere), March 30, 1925 (nationwide). Running Time: 80 minutes (approximately). Genre: Drama-Romance. Production Company: Famous Players–Lasky Corporation. Distributor: Paramount Pictures. Cast: Leatrice Joy (Fifi), Ernest Torrence (Angus McGregor), Allan Forrest (Billy Brent), Mildred Harris (Joan McGregor), Lawrence Gray (Allan Stone), Charles Crockett (Mayor), Rosemary Cooper (Mayor's Daughter), Spec O'Donnell (Jim), **Olive Borden,** Sally Rand, Eugenia Gilbert, Etta Lee, Jocelyn Lee, Sally Long, Cecile Evans, Clara Morris, Christina Montt, Adalyn Mayer, Thais Valdemar, Yola D'Avril, Mabel Coleman, Dorothy Seastrom (Fashion Models).

Olive appeared in the fashion parade scene. Her gown was black with silver brocade and cuffs with strips of ermine. Heavy silken cords hang from the left hip. The cords and the lining of the dress were a stunning burnt orange.

An ad in the Logansport, Indiana, *Pharos-*

Tribune (Saturday, May 23, 1925) called the fashion models in the picture "The Fourteen Most Beautiful Women in the World Today":

1. Eugenia Gilbert: The Girl of the Sunkissed West. 2. Etta Lee: Princess of the Orient. 3. Jocelyn Lee: Ziegfeld's Queen of Beauty. 4. Sally Long: D. W. Griffith's Most Beautiful Discovery. 5. Cecile Evans: The Girl with the Coles Philips Ankles. 6. Clara Morris: Neysa McMeins Regal Red Head. 7. Olive Borden: WAMPAS Baby Star for 1925. 8. Christina Montt: Latin-America's Favorite Daughter. 9. Sally Rand: Named by Cecil B. DeMille as the Most Beautiful Girl in America. 10. Adalyn Mayer: The Cinderella Girl of 1925. 11. Thais Valdemar: The Fairest of Europe's Beauty. 12. Yola D'Avril: The Famous Model of Jean Patou. 13. Mabel Coleman: The Gibson Girl of Today. 14. Dorothy Seastrom: Venus of the Snows — and they're all beauties!

TAGLINE: "Here is the perfect entertainment of 1925! A gorgeous romance and fashion spectacle. With the world's beauties and the latest styles from Paris."

This was Leatrice Joy's last film for Paramount. As of 2009, it is presumed lost.

Excuse My Glove (1925)

Director: J. A. Howe (as Jay A. Howe). Producer: Hal Roach. Production Date: November 1924. Release Date: March 22, 1925. Duration in Reels: 2. Production Company: Hal Roach Studios Inc. Distributor: Pathé Exchange. Genre: Comedy. Cast: Sidney D'Albrook, Laura Roessing, Frank Butler, **Olive Borden (Extra — uncredited).**

Part of the Spat Family series. According to the Hal Roach Studios payroll ledgers, Olive received four payments for her work on the film: November 8, 1924 ($62.50), November 15, 1924 ($75), November 22, 1924 ($12.50), November 29, 1924 ($75). As of 2009, this short is presumed lost.

Bad Boy (1925)

Director: Leo McCarey. Producer: Hal Roach. Production Dates: January 16–January 26, 1925. Release Date: April 12, 1925 (USA). Alternate Title: *Big Bill Brodie* (working title). Running Time: 18 minutes. Duration in Reels: 2. Production Company: Hal Roach Studios Inc. Distributor: Pathé Exchange. Milestone Films (2005) for Turner Classic Movies (TCM). All Day Entertainment (VCI Entertainment: DVD: 2009). Genre: Comedy.

Cast: Charley Chase (Jimmy Jump), Martha Sleeper (Jimmy's Girlfriend), Evelyn Burns (Jimmy's Mother), Hardee Kirkland (Jimmy's Father), Noah Young (Dance Hall Troublemaker), Eddie Borden (Dance Hall Owner), **Olive Borden (Bit Part: uncredited, unconfirmed)**, Jack Gavin, Leo Willis.

In Charley Chase's second two-reeler, Olive is uncredited in a bit part. She is unseen in the short so it is still considered an "undetermined" role.

Charley Chase plays "Jimmy Jump," a spoiled mama's boy with a desperate father (Hardee Kirkland) who valiantly attempts to transform him into a real man by introducing him to the rough and tumble iron business where most of the hard "work" is done with the worker's fists. Poor Jimmy does his best to fit in and be "one of the boys."

When Jimmy returns home from work one day, his mother (Evelyn Burns) frantically asks him to help "entertain" the guests at her lawn party. He reluctantly agrees. As he next steps into frame, dressed in a whimsical, nymph-like outfit, holding a trumpet, we soon understand his reluctance. But Jimmy is all about pleasing his mother and off he skips to entertain the guests, as per his mother's wishes.

When his girlfriend (Martha Sleeper) sees him dressed as a garden nymph and dancing effeminately at his mother's lawn party, she huffs and puffs, finally calling him a "leaping tuna!" before storming off, furious at him for making such a fool of himself. Jimmy is then forced into finding his inner tough guy by dressing as an Irish rowdy in an attempt to fit in with the tough clientele at a rather unpleasant dance hall where she's seeking refuge. His charade works for a while, but when a picture of him in his nymph get-up is printed in the newspaper, his disguise is discovered and the rowdy patrons turn on him. Jimmy has no choice but to use his wits to defend himself, which he does, cleverly and amusingly so. His girlfriend of course takes him back with open arms.

The dance that Chase performs with Sleeper at the dance hall is the highlight of the short and one of the best examples of Chase's dancing talent preserved on film. (*Smile When the Raindrops Fall: The Story of Charley Chase*, Brian Anthony and Andy Edmonds, The Scarecrow Press, 1998).

As of 2009, several prints of this short exist in archives worldwide: The Museum of Modern Art, the International Museum of Photography and Film at George Eastman House, Rochester, New York (16mm: unpreserved), UCLA, National Film and Sound Archive, Australia, and the Filmoteca Espanola, Madrid. The short was released by Milestone Films in 2005 for the Turner Classic Movies channel as part of the *Cut to the Chase: The Charley Chase Classic Comedy Collection.* It has also aired on TCM on several occasions. It runs 18:39 and the score is by Dave Knudtson. All Day Entertainment (in conjunction with VCI Entertainment) released a four-disc DVD set entitled *Becoming Charley Chase—Seeing Nellie Home* (1924), *Outdoor Pajamas* (1924), *The Poor Fish* (1924), *Should Husbands Be Watched?* (1925), *Bad Boy* and *Too Many Mammas* (1925) are all included in the set. They're the only six surviving Chase shorts with Olive in the cast.

Black Hand Blues (1925)

Director: J. A. Howe (as Jay A. Howe). Producer: Hal Roach. Production Dates: November: Decem-

ber 1924. Release Date: April 19, 1925. Duration in Reels: 2. Production Company: Hal Roach Studios Inc. Distributor: Pathé Exchange. Genre: Comedy. Cast: Sidney D'Albrook, Laura Roessing, Frank Butler, **Olive Borden (Extra — uncredited).**

Part of the Spat Family series. According to the Hal Roach Studios payroll ledgers, Olive received four payments for her work on the film: December 6, 1924 ($75), December 13, 1924 ($75), December 20, 1924 ($62.50), December 27, 1924 ($75). As of 2009, this short is presumed lost.

Tell It to a Policeman (1925)

Director: Fred Guiol. Producer: Hal Roach. Production Dates: October: November 1924. Release Date: May 24, 1925 (USA). Duration in Reels: 1. Production Company: Hal Roach Studios Inc. Distributor: Pathé Exchange. Genre: Comedy. Cast: Glenn Tryon, **Olive Borden,** James Finlayson, Jack Gavin, Blanche Mehaffey.

Olive in a candid moment, playing up to the camera on a sunny afternoon.

According to the Hal Roach Studios payroll ledgers, Olive received a one-time payment of $37.50 on November 1, 1924, for her work on the film. A print is housed at the UCLA Film and Television Archive (Los Angeles, California). Another print exists at Cinemateca do Museu de Arte Moderna, Rio de Janeiro. There is also a print in a private collection.

Good Morning, Nurse! (1925)

Director: Lloyd Bacon. Producer: Mack Sennett. Writers: Frank Capra (scenario and story), Jefferson Moffitt (story), Felix Adler and A. H. Giebler (intertitles). Cinematographers: William Williams and Lee Davis. Release Date: May 31, 1925 (USA). Duration in reels: 2. Working Title: *Pills and Spills*. Production Company: Mack Sennett Comedies. Distributor: Pathé Exchange. Genre: Comedy. Cast: Ralph Graves, Irving Bacon, **Olive Borden**, Patrick Kelly, Natalie Kingston, Marvin Loback, William McCall, Eli Stanton, Eva Thatcher.

As of 2009, this short is presumed lost.

Riders of the Kitchen Range (1925)

Directors: Tay Garnett and George Jeske. Producer-Writer: Hal Roach. Production Dates: May 1924. Release Date: June 7, 1925. Duration in Reels: 1. Running Time: 10 minutes. Production Company: Hal Roach Studios Inc. Genre: Comedy. Cast: Earl Mohan, Billy Engle, Ena Gregory, Delloris Johnson, **Olive Borden (Extra — uncredited)**.

According to the Hal Roach Studios payroll ledgers, Olive received a one-time payment of $12.50 on May 17, 1924, for her work on the film. It was the average weekly salary of an extra.

There is an unusually lengthy space of time (about a year) between the time this film was made and the date it was released, as is the case with a few other Roach shorts too. Typically, these shorts were churned out very quickly and released within a couple of months of completion. It was a production line. However, things changed in March of 1923 when Pathé Exchange, Roach's distributor, signed a deal with his main rival, Mack Sennett. Roach was furious because it gave Pathé more shorts than they could possibly sell. As a result, many films were shelved and released at a much later date.

As of 2009, this short is presumed lost.

The Royal Four-Flush (1925)

Director: J. A. Howe (as Jay A. Howe). Producer-Writer: Hal Roach. Production Dates: December 1924: January 1925. Release Date: June 14, 1925. Duration in Reels: 2. Production Company: Hal Roach Studios Inc. Distributor: Pathé Exchange. Genre: Comedy. Cast: Sidney D'Albrook, Laura Roessing, Frank Butler, **Olive Borden (Extra — uncredited)**.

Part of the Spat Family series. According to the Hal Roach Studios payroll ledgers, Olive received a one-time payment of $75 on January 3, 1925 for her work on the film. There was also a $75 payment made on January 17, 1924, not attributed to any production. A notation of "Last Week" is written on the line alongside the $75. This was Olive's last paycheck from Roach Studios. As of 2009, this short is presumed lost.

Hal Roach (January 14, 1892–November 2, 1992) died two months shy of his 101st birthday.

Grounds for Divorce (1925)

Director: Paul Bern. Producers: Adolph Zukor and Jesse L. Lasky. Writers: Guy Bolton (adaptation), Violet Clark (writer), Ernest Vajda (novel). Cinematographer: Bert Glennon. Release Dates: June 28, 1925 (New York City, New York), July 27, 1925 (nationwide). Running Time: 60 minutes. Duration in Reels: 6. Duration in Feet: 5,692. Genre: Romance-Comedy. Production Company: Famous Players–Lasky Corporation. Distributor: Paramount Pictures. Cast: Florence Vidor (Alice Sorbier), Matt Moore (Maurice Sorbier), Harry Myers (Count Zappata), Louise Fazenda (Marianne), George Beranger (Guido), Gustav von Seyffertitz (Labell), Edna Mae Cooper (Marie), **Olive Borden (uncredited)**.

As of 2009, this film is presumed lost.

Note: *The Kingsport Times* reported that Paul Bern had given Olive her first chance at fame when he cast her as one of the fourteen fashion models in *The Dressmaker from Paris* (1925). The same article added that he also cast her in *this* film, released just a few months later ("News Notes from Movieland," *The Kingsport Times,* Kingsport Tennessee, May 17, 1925).

The Happy Warrior (1925)

Director: J. Stuart Blackton. Producer: Albert E. Smith. Writers: Marian Constance Blackton and A. S. M. Hutchinson (based upon his novel). Cinematographer: Paul H. Allen. Release Date: July 5, 1925 (USA). Running Time: 80 minutes. Duration in Reels: 8. Duration in Feet: 7,865. Production

Company–Distributor: Vitagraph Company of America. Genre: Drama. Cast: Malcolm McGregor (Ralph), Alice Calhoun (Dora), Mary Alden (Aunt Maggie), Anders Randolf (Stingo Hannaford: Circus Master), **Olive Borden (Ima: Gypsy Maid)**, Gardner James (Rolio), Otto Matieson (Egbert), Wilfrid North (Mr. Letham), Eulalie Jensen (Mrs. Letham), Andree Tourneur (Audrey), Jack Herrick (Foxy Pinsent), Philippe De Lacy (Ralph: at eight years of age), Robert Gordon (Rolio: at ten years of age), Leon Holmes (Frecklefaced Boy).

The *Chicago Daily Tribune* (July 27, 1925) wrote, "There's plenty of melodrama in the picture and some awfully good scenes of circus life... Olive Borden is especially appealing as a wistful, elfin gypsy maid and Anders Randolf makes a splendid impression in the part of the circus master."

"Olive Borden, whose name does not appear among the featured players, runs off at a gallop with the other acting honors by making a singularity appealing figure of Ima, to whom a relatively small role is assigned in the photoplay" (*New York Times*, July 7, 1925).

As of 2009, this film is presumed lost.

The Overland Limited (1925)

Director: Frank O'Neill. Producer: Sam Sax. Writer: James J. Tynan (story). Cinematographer: Jack MacKenzie. Release Date: July 14, 1925 (New York City), July 26, 1925 (nationwide). Duration in Reels: 6. Duration in Feet — 6,389. Production Company: Gotham Pictures. Distributors: Lumas Film Corporation and States Rights Independent Exchanges. Genre: Drama. Cast: Malcolm McGregor (David Barton), **Olive Borden (Ruth Dent)**, Alice Lake (Violet Colton), Ethel Wales (Mrs. Barton), Ralph Lewis (Big Ed Barton), John Miljan (Brice Miller), Roscoe Karns (Pat Madden), Emmett King (Carson North), Charles Hill Mailes (Schuyler Dent), Charles West (Bitterroot Jackson), Charles A. Post ("One Round" Farrell), Evelyn Jennings (Agnes Jennings).

Malcolm McGregor plays David Barton, a young, innovative railroad engineer who designs and erects a railroad bridge that saves a company millions of dollars. Olive plays his sweetheart, Ruth. Ralph Lewis plays Big Ed Barton, engineer of the Overland Limited, who saves a trainload of passengers from imminent death. Alice Lake plays Violet, a small town vamp. The crashing climax to the picture comes when the giant locomotive breaks through the steel girders and plunges into the river.

TAGLINE: "Like a steel comet, the mighty locomotive was hurled into the foaming waters below! The crashing climax of the greatest railroad photo-play ever made."

A print of this film exists in the Library of Congress.

All Wool (1925)

Director: Tay Garnett. Producer: Hal Roach. Production Date: April 1924. Release Date: October 25, 1925. Duration in Reels: 1. Running Time: 10 minutes. Production Company: Hal Roach Studios Inc. Distributor: Pathé Exchange (1925: theatrical). DVD: Looser Than Loose Publishing (2008). Genre: Comedy. Cast: Earl Mohan, Billy Engle, Sammy Brooks, Katherine Grant, George Rowe, **Olive Borden (Extra — uncredited)**.

The plot involves inept plumbers who exchange their pipe wrenches for knitting needles and tape measures. According to the Hal Roach Studios payroll ledgers, Olive received a one-time payment of $25 on April 19, 1924, for her work on the film.

A complete print taken from a new 16mm transfer was released on a three-disc DVD by Looser Than Loose Publishing (*Roach Volume 2: Odds, Ends, Spats and Doo-Dads: Plus Max and Mabel*). Olive has been cut from the final print.

• Hollywood in 1926

Number of releases: 740.

U.S. weekly cinema attendance: 50 million.

First feature film with sound (no dialogue): *Don Juan*.

Number of times John Barrymore kisses Mary Astor and Estelle Taylor in *Don Juan* (according to Warners' publicity department): 127.

August 30 (Monday, 11 A.M.) — There is mass hysteria at 31-year-old Rudolph Valentino's funeral. One hundred thousand people line the streets of New York City to pay their last respects. His body is transported to California by train and a second funeral is held on Tuesday morning, September 7, at 10 A.M. on the West Coast. Olive attended the second funeral service with her beau, George O'Brien, who served as one of the ushers (www.rudolph-valentino.com).

Top male and female box office stars for

the year according to a Quigley Publications poll of exhibitors:

Male: Tom Mix.

Female: Colleen Moore.

The *New York Times* Ten Best Films:

1. *Variety*, 2. *Beau Geste*, 3. *What Price Glory*, 4. *Potemkin*, 5. *The Grand Duchess and the Waiter*, 6. *The Black Pirate*, 7. *Old Ironsides*, 8. *Moana*, 9. *La Boheme*, 10. *So This Is Paris*.

The Yankee Señor (1926)

Director: Emmett J. Flynn. Producer: William Fox. Writers: Katherine Fullerton Gerould (novel *Conquistador*), Eve Unsell (writer). Cinematographer: Daniel Clark. Release Date: January 10, 1926 (USA). Duration in Reels: 5. Alternate Title: *The Conquering Blood* (USA). Production Company: Fox Film Corporation. Distributor: Fox Film Corporation. Genre: Western. Cast: Tom Mix (Paul Wharton), **Olive Borden (Manuelita)**, Tom Kennedy (Luke Martin), Francis McDonald (Juan Gutierrez), Margaret Livingston (Flora), Alec B.

A signed glamour portrait of Olive in her prime.

Francis (Don Fernando), Kathryn Carver (Doris Mayne), Martha Mattox (Aunt Abigail), Raymond Wells (Ranch Foreman), Tony the Horse (Tony).

"While there is not a great deal of plot, there is plenty of action ... [as well as] scenes of beauty, during the fiesta, where Tom is soon cavorting about with a Spanish dancer. These scenes are done in color, and Margaret Livingston plays the dancer most effectively. Olive Borden, a most attractive southern girl, plays the feminine lead" (*The Hamilton Daily News*, Hamilton, Ohio, August 14, 1926).

Reviewer Chester B. Bahn, dramatic critic of the *Syracuse Herald* wasn't sure Tom's character should get Olive in the end: "Olive Borden as Manuelita slowly places her arms around Tom's neck, and raises her lips to his. And the best that Tom can do is give her an osculatory salute that is little more than a peck, while his arms hang like two strings of sausages at his side."

Other stars signed to Fox during Olive's reign as their "studio darling" were Madge Bellamy, John Bowers, Louise Brooks, June Collyer, Dolores Del Rio, William Farnum, Charles Farrell, Janet Gaynor, Neil Hamilton, Buck Jones, Edmund Lowe, Victor McLaglen, Tom Mix, and Olive's beau George O'Brien.

As of 2009, this film is presumed lost.

My Own Pal (1926)

Director: John G. Blystone. Producer: William Fox. Writers: Lillie Hayward (writer), Gerald Beaumont (story). Cinematographer: Daniel Clark. Release Date: February 26, 1926 (USA). Duration in Reels: 5. Production Company–Distributor: Fox Film Corporation. Genre: Western. Cast: Tom Mix (Tom O'Hara), **Olive Borden (Alice Deering)**, Tom Santschi (August Deering), Virginia Marshall (Jill), Bardson Bard (Baxter Barton), William Colvin (Jud McIntire), Virginia Warwick (Molly), Jay Hunt (Clown), Hedda Nova (Mrs. Jud McIntire), Tom McGuire (Pat McQuire), Helen Lynch (Trixie Tremaine), Jack Rollens (Slippery Sam).

This was Olive's second Tom Mix feature. Her first was *The Yankee Señor* (1926). Several New York papers reviewed the film; however, none of them mentioned Olive's performance. The *New York Post* thought the only performance worth a mention was an uncredited canine!

American: "Altogether, *My Own Pal* is an average Tom Mix picture, which means something different to everyone. To countless little boys, anyway, and even some grown ups, it means just the sort of unpretentious, unsophisticated entertainment they enjoy."

Daily Mirror: "This is the three R's kind of entertainment: romping, rollicking, romantic. It doesn't disappoint either. Tom [Mix] rides his gorgeous horse Tony like a streak."

Evening Journal— "Tony, Tom's justly famous horse, gives the star a chance to still show he can ride, even though he rounds up a diamond smuggler by throwing a lariat from his motorcycle."

Graphic: "If last night's enthusiastic audience is any criterion this Mix picture is the best of them all. Tom has put aside the Spanish stuff he affected in his last coupla operas and this time we see him as 'one of the finest': an Irish motorcycle cop who cleans up the underworld in a few reels."

Herald Tribune: "It is the most naïve picture we have encountered since 1914, and now we're going to be perfectly frank and tell the truth till it hurts: we thoroughly enjoyed *My Own Pal.*"

Morning Telegraph: "It seems to us one of [Mix's] best; for it contains all the ingredients that have built up Mix's tremendous following; compounded with more skill than used to be employed in his early days as a star, and making for genuine entertainment, if you care for that kind at all."

New York Post: "The best acting of the piece is contributed by a very human little dog, pet of the cocksure child. Although the little dog's name is not mentioned on the program, we are moved to give it a pat on the head for an intelligent performance amid none too inspiring surroundings."

New York Telegram: "Any sympathy that we might have entertained for the naïve quality of this highly improbable story was promptly nipped in the bud by an attack of intense aggravation induced by the presence of one of those fatiguing screen children whose airs and affectations have no more in common with the genuine article than a bull in a china shop."

New York Times: "Mr. Mix is seen in the best cut policeman's uniform that has ever been tailored. He is kept busy for most of the latter chapters dodging villains and being falsely accused. He tosses scoundrels in water, lassoes four men and see that they are dragged by a flivver into the river."

Chicago Daily Tribune, March 21, 1926 — "Olive Borden — one of the WAMPAS girls — shows promise, though she is rather camera shy.

Supporting cast is good and direction O.K. Scenery and photography — splendid!"

The Lima News and Times Democrat, April 15, 1926 — "Olive Borden, the beautiful actress who has been seen in delightful roles in many major films, plays opposite Mix and further adds to her glories on the silver screen."

On October 12, 1940, while driving his 1937 Cord Sportsman through the Arizona desert, Tom Mix took a turn too fast and an unrestrained aluminum suitcase in the back seat flung forward and struck him in the head. The impact shattered his skull and broke his neck. His car plunged into a ravine. He was killed instantly. In a morbid attempt to honor his memory, the ravine was later named "The Tom Mix Wash." A plaque at the location reads: "TOM MIX January 6, 1880–October 12, 1940. Whose spirit left his body on this spot and whose characterization and portrayals in life served to better fix memories of the old west in the minds of living men" (www.imdb.com).

Between 1910 and 1935 he made over three hundred films. His horse, Tony the Wonder Horse, starred in one hundred eighty-one of those films and was just as popular as Mix, especially with children. Tony received thousands of letters a week from children all over the world. Tom and Tony earned millions of dollars from their films and personal appearances across America, Europe. Canada and Mexico. When Tony injured his hip at age 22, he was retired to the Tom Mix Ranch and replaced with Tony Jr., who carried Mix through the remainder of his career. Tony (the original) was named as Mix's survivor in obituaries around the world, provided for in Mix's will and entrusted to a lawyer friend who cared for him until 1942. Two years (to the day!) after the death of his cowboy master, Tony, forty-two years, became too weak and sick to eat or stand, and was humanely put to sleep by a veterinarian in his stall at the Mix Ranch.

Alongside the hand- and footprints of many of Hollywood's greatest stars, including Tom Mix's cowboy boot prints and handprints, Tony's "hoofprints" are embedded in the cement sidewalk outside Grauman's Theater in Hollywood, California (www.findagrave.com).

As of 2009, this film is presumed lost.

Yellow Fingers (1926)

Director: Emmett J. Flynn. Producer: William Fox. Writer: Eve Unsell. Cinematographers: Paul Ivano

Olive adorned in expensive jewelry, just the way she liked to be seen — on screen and off.

and Ernest Palmer. Release Date: March 21, 1926 (USA). Duration in Reels: 6. Duration in Feet: 5,594. Production Company–Distributor: Fox Film Corporation. Genre: Drama. Cast: **Olive Borden (Saina)**, Ralph Ince (Brute Shane), Claire Adams (Nona Deering), Edward Peil, Sr. (Kwong Li), Otto Matieson (Kario), Nigel De Brulier (Rajah Jagore), Armand Kaliz (De Vries), Josephine Crowell (Mrs. Van Kronk), May Foster (Toinette), John Wallace (Pegleg LaForge), Charles Newton (Higgins).

Based on Gene Wright's best-selling novel, *Yellow Fingers* was shot on picturesque Catalina Island, off the coast of southern California. It took three weeks for studio mechanics to construct an entire Malay village. The *Trinidad* was chartered to sail the Pacific while ocean shots were filmed.

The Davenport Democrat and Leader (June 13, 1926) wrote, "*Yellow Fingers* presents Olive Borden, recently signed by Fox films to a long term contract, in a fiery role especially fitted to her rich dramatic talent."

Film Daily (April 4, 1926) wrote, "Story of orient rich in colorful atmosphere. Strong love interest and action make this a 'natural' for the box office... Olive Borden as a fiery half-caste girl gives a fine portrayal in a difficult role... Other characters are well chosen in colorful parts."

Box office angle: "Oriental story, gorgeous

natural settings, tempestuous love interest, adventure: here is audience appeal that will go over nicely with the average audience."

Exploitation: "Title is sure-fire exploitation. Play up Olive Borden, whose work is fine. Also Ralph Ince. Bill as story of white girl saved from clutches of an Oriental."

Hamilton Evening Journal (June 25, 1926) wrote, "...Miss Borden possesses unusual dramatic talent, a decidedly fiery temperament and a wistful type of beauty which will undoubtedly carry her far in her screen career. *Yellow Fingers* is unusually good screen entertainment."

On May 27, 1926, some time after *Yellow Fingers* was released, Olive sent Charles Mank, Jr., a letter in which she mentions sending several photos to him under separate cover and she offers him a "trinket"—a little pair of slippers that she wore in *Yellow Fingers* that she thinks he might like as a "souvenir." She goes on to say that she will send them but if he "doesn't like them" to let her know and she will send whatever else he suggests. She ends the letter thanking him for "every boost that your club gives me."

In a letter dated June 11, 1926, Olive followed through on her promise and sent Charles her screen-worn slippers from *Yellow Fingers*. She told him she decided not to have them cleaned since she thought whoever won them would rather have them just as they appeared in the film, with "the makeup right on them." She then tells him if he thinks the slippers are an insufficient token, to let her know at once and she will be glad to furnish something else. She signed it, "with kindest regards, and every wish for success of the club, I am, Very Sincerely Yours, Olive Borden."

Charles "Chaw" Mank, Jr., (1902–1985) started corresponding with just about every movie star working in Hollywood. He was said to receive upwards of 10,000 letters from Hollywood's greatest names, per year! Beginning in the 1920s and for much of his life, he collected typed and handwritten letters, signed photos, trinkets and gifts from such noted actors as Rudolph Valentino, Clark Gable, Harry Langdon, Bette Davis, Humphrey Bogart, Tom Mix, Judy Garland, and Clara Bow, just to name a few. By 1927, he started his popular newsletter *The Movie Fans' News.*

In another letter to Mank (July 21, 1927), Olive begins by telling him that she received his letter upon her return from Canada where she has been filming exterior scenes for *The Country Beyond.* She says she thinks it will turn out to be a "very good picture." Olive once again offers him a "prize for a contest" he is running; she says anything that "he suggests" she'll send along. She thanks him for his efforts at boosting her career and asks if there is anything he needs her to do. She ends by telling him she is "delighted" to be featured in an upcoming issue of his magazine and that she is anxious to see the first issue.

On September 3, 1927, she writes another letter, again saying that she and her mother have "just returned from Canada" and they enjoyed a very lovely trip. She tells him that Canada is a "very beautiful country," that she has been "very busy" making her new picture *Pajamas* and that she is pleased that he enjoys her pictures. She advises him that she is sending him "a few prizes for the contest," along with a recent photograph of herself.

Aside from his prolific correspondence with Hollywood stars, Mank was a radio presenter, band leader, songwriter, author, silent film organist, newspaper columnist, record producer and "World Champion Movie Fan." Following his cancer-related death on April 14, 1985, his vast collection of Hollywood memorabilia was sold at auction houses all over the world. One has to wonder if Olive's little pair of slippers from *Yellow Fingers* was included.

A print of this film exists in the Narodni Film Archive in Prague.

3 Bad Men aka Three Bad Men (1926)

Director: John Ford. Producers: John Ford and William Fox. Writers: Herman Whitaker (novel *Over the Border*), John Stone (writer, adaptation, screenplay, titles and scenarios), Malcolm Stuart Boylan and Ralph Spence (titles and scenario). Cinematographer: George Schneiderman. Release Date: August 13, 1926 (special trade showing), August 28, 1926 (nationwide). Runtime: 92 minutes.

A rare issue of *Movie Fan News* dedicated to Olive and issued in September–October 1926 by famed film fan Charles "Chaw" Mank, Jr.

Duration in Reels: 9. Duration in Feet: 8, 710. Alternate Titles, *Three Bad Men* (USA: alternate spelling), *The World of Promise* (working title). Production Company–Distributor: Fox Film Corporation. Production Budget — $650,000. Genre: Western. Filming Locations: Jackson Hole, Wyoming, and Mojave Desert, California. Cast: George O'Brien (Dan O'Malley), **Olive Borden (Lee Carlton),** Lou Tellegen (Sheriff Layne Hunter), Tom Santschi ("Bull" Stanley), J. Farrell MacDonald (Mike Costigan), Frank Campeau ("Spade" Allen), Priscilla Bonner (Millie Stanley), Otis Harlan (Editor Zach Little), Phyllis Haver (Lily), George Harris (Joe Minsk), Alec B. Francis (Rev. Calvin Benson), Jay Hunt (Nat Lucas), Grace Gordon (Millie's Pal), George Irving (Gen. Neville), Bud Osborne (Hunter's Henchman), Vester Pegg (Henchman shooting Lucas), Walter Perry (Pat Monahan).

The Fresno Bee (November 7, 1926), wrote, "Seldom before had such a host of great screen favorites been cast in a single picture. More than a dozen internationally known stars with a supporting cast of thousands were all selected because they were ideally suited for the parts they were to play. For a full year the company worked under the blazing sun of the Nevada desert and in the frigid hills of the Shoshone and Teton ranges."

Film Daily (Sunday October 17, 1926) wrote, "Western spectacle. It's got everything fans want. Love interest, hard riding and plenty of action... Appealing Olive Borden and George O'Brien handle the love theme very nicely. Santschi, MacDonald and Campeau are delightful as the three bandits who reform so that they can carry out to the letter the faith reposed in them by Olive."

Box office angle: "Every angle means money. It's made in a lavish manner and is designed to make box-offices swell. It will."

Exploitation: "Tie-up with schools on the historical angle. The picture is founded on a true incident. The three bad men combination give you a keynote for advertising. It's out of the ordinary and should be taken advantage of."

Title card quote — "Mike Costigan and 'Spade' Allen weren't exactly thieves — but they had a habit of finding horses that nobody had lost."

This was John Ford's last silent Western. The film went back to the editing room and was cut down by almost twenty minutes after its premiere. Ford was said to be so disgusted with the radical changes that he wanted his name taken from the credits. Olive said *3 Bad Men* was her "favorite picture" (*St. Petersburg Times*, May 19, 1933).

Tim Lussier (http://www.silentsaregolden.com/) wrote, "...Olive Borden is not only charming, but beautiful as well. It is no wonder she wins the hearts of the three bad men. Her scenes with O'Brien are a pure delight." According to *Photoplay* (October, 1926), "This is real good entertainment: the kind the whole family can enjoy. A gripping and forceful story, the marvelous scenic effects, the romantic and tragic conditions of the great west, and the beautiful photography combine to make this one of the best pictures of the month."

While *3 Bad Men* is a superb picturization of the West in the 1870s, complete with director Ford's masterful touches. *Picture Play* (November 1926) claimed its emotional appeal is "almost nil" because of a slowly moving plot. The magazine continued, "Yet, because of the magnificence of the scenery, the beauty of the grouping and lighting, this is not as serious a drawback as it might have been under direction less inspired."

TAGLINES: "The latest, greatest and most elaborate of all epic pictures of the West! Destined to make moving picture history throughout the world. One year in the making — and what's more, it's worth it!"

"A drama of 3 BAD MEN and a girl in the world of promise where might was might and the 'quickness of the draw' was the law of the land."

"Terrors of the west, wreakers of havoc, border killers, they formed a protecting trio for this dainty bit of femininity — And they rode into eternity with a smile."

"The greatest thrill the screen has ever seen — the mightiest race for gold in the history of the world — that's what you'll see in *3 Bad Men*."

"Greatest Western Epic Ever Filmed!"

"The Greatest Picture since *The Covered Wagon*."

"They're Here to Create a Sensation! In the Mightiest of All Great Dramas of the Early West."

"The romance of a girl in the land of promise."

"It's one of the screen's masterpieces that will be re-issued from time to time for years to come."

"Into a land of terror — a land of gold-maddened men and frenzied women rode a slip of a girl — and 3 BAD MEN. They were border terrors — killers who settled disputes with the shooting iron, but they formed a protecting trio for this transplanted desert flower and they rode into eternity with a smile that she might realize the secret of her dreams."

"Here is a real story of two young pioneers, the orphaned Lee Carlton, played by Olive Borden, and footloose Dan O'Malley, played by George O'Brien. And guiding and watching over them like the fates themselves are the *3 Bad Men*, the bully, the card sharp and the rustler" (*Appleton Post-Crescent*, Monday Evening, June 27, 1927).

Ford's previous silent Western *The Iron Horse* (1924) grossed over $2 million worldwide — ten times its budget of $280,000. Despite being critically considered a better film, *3 Bad Men* failed to recoup its $650,000 production cost at the box office.

A signed photograph of Olive in her prime.

As of 2009, John Ford still holds the record as the only director to win four Best Director Academy Awards: *The Informer* (1935), *The Grapes of Wrath* (1940), *How Green Was My Valley* (1941) and *The Quiet Man* (1952). Ironically, none of the films were Westerns. Ford's contemporaries Frank Capra and William Wyler won the Best Director Academy Award three times.

This film was long thought to be lost to time; however, it was found, restored, and is now available on DVD in a double feature with another Ford film, *Hangman's House* (1928). The double feature is part of the "The Ford at Fox Collection" released by 20th Century–Fox in 2007. Ford chose Olive to be his leading lady in *Hangman's House*; however, as pre-production began she was just about to end her association with Fox.

The UCLA Film and Television Archive (Los Angeles, California) has two prints.

Fig Leaves (1926)

Director: Howard Hawks. Producer: William Fox. Writers: Howard Hawks (story), Louis D. Lighton, Hope Loring. Cinematographer: Joseph H. August. Costumes: Adrian. Production Date: March 1926. Release Date: August 22, 1926 (USA). Duration in Reels: 7. Duration in Feet: 6,498. Production Company–Distributor: Fox Film Corporation. Genre: Comedy-Romance. Cast: George O'Brien (Adam Smith), **Olive Borden (Eve Smith),** Phyllis Haver (Alice Atkins), George Beranger (Josef Andre), William Austin (Andre's Assistant), Heinie Conklin (Eddie McSwiggen), Eulalie Jensen (Madame Griswald).

In this extraordinarily beautiful story loosely based on the idea of Adam and Eve in a modern (1920s) world, Olive appears in a spectacular fashion revue and wears some of the most elaborate gowns ever seen in a motion picture production. In addition, there are many scenes in the Garden of Eden. These, as well as many of the fashion sequences, were filmed in stunning Technicolor.

Fig Leaves and *3 Bad Men* (1926) were released in U.S. theaters within one week of each other. Both films starred real-life lovers George O'Brien and Olive Borden in the lead roles. A 1926 article (unknown publication) titled, "Thoroughness Is Reason for Stars Success" gave valuable insight into the preparation for their roles in *Fig Leaves*:

"A reason for the success achieved by [O'Brien and Borden] on the screen is the thoroughness of their preparations for roles and their unflagging in-

A beautiful photograph of Olive taken December 7, 1926.

terest in every bit of 'business' called for in the script. Before starting work on *Fig Leaves*, O'Brien was given three weeks vacation. He spent three days with his family in San Francisco, where his father, Dan O'Brien, is the police chief. Then he quietly went to work for two weeks in his uncle's plumbing shop — for he's a plumber in the picture. Miss Borden, who is Eve Smith, the wife, in *Fig Leaves*, values her mother's opinion in great degree. She had but one question to ask her as she came out from the glare of the studio lights upon completion of a scene — an old question dating back to her childhood in Virginia. 'How was it, pardner? Am I doing this right?'"

(Olive and her mother often used the affectionate term "pardner" with each other.)

Director Howard Hawks suggested to the studio that he make a movie about Adam (George O'Brien) and Eve (Olive Borden) waking up in the Garden of Eden and call it *Fig Leaves*. "It made back its cost in one theater. From then on the studio asked me what *I* wanted to do," he said (*Major Film Directors of the American and British Cinema*, Gene D. Philips, Lehigh University Press, 1999).

Olive's costumes for *Fig Leaves* cost $50,000. After seeing Olive's skimpy costumes for the Garden of Eden scenes, Olive said her mother told her, "They'll keep you unclothed until you're forty!" (*Motion Picture Magazine*, June 1926).

TAGLINES: "Even in the Garden of Eden, Eve fed Adam — apple-sauce. The girl of today is no different from Eve. What an apple did to Adam a peach does to mere man today. A satire of fickle women in 13 ribs. A rib-tickling exposé of modern reckless women. The story of a modern Eve and clothesmania. *Fig Leaves* — an exposé of reckless wives gone clothes-mad."

"Clean as a whistle and topnotch from every production angle" (*Motion Picture News*, 1926).

"An ambitious production — it vies with the most lavish" (*Harrison's Reports*, 1926).

"From all sides it looks like a conspicuous winner" (*Variety*, 1926).

"It has arrived in several ways, not the least important of which is the Box-Office!" (*Film Daily*, 1926).

"This picture contains more feminine beauty than Ziegfeld has been able to assemble since he started glorifying the American girl" (*Motion Pictures Today*, 1926).

"A fine all-around box-office entertainment" (*Moving Picture World*, 1926).

Fox Studios released this pretty portrait shot to promote one of her most successful films, *Fig Leaves* (1926).

"The season's sensation! Very few theatres have been large enough to hold the crowds that wanted to see *Fig Leaves*!" (*Appleton-Crescent*, 1926).

Olive said her role of Eve in *Fig Leaves* was her favorite part ("St. Petersburg Will Become Important Picture Center in Opinion of Screen Star," *Evening Independent*, June 3, 1933). A print of this film exists at the Museum of Modern Art, Centre National de la Cinematographie, Paris, and Cinematheque Royale, Brussels, Weisbaden. Author has a DVD copy taken from a privately owned print.

By the end of his film career, George O'Brien (1899–1985) was a veteran of over eighty films. He was also the veteran of *four* wars: He served in the Navy in World War I, World War II, Korea *and* Vietnam. Highly decorated, he retired in 1962 with the rank of captain, having four times been recommended for the rank of admiral (www.imdb.com).

The Country Beyond (1926)

Director: Irving Cummings. Producer: William Fox. Writers: H. H. Caldwell, Katherine Hilliker (titles), Irving Cummings (writer), James Oliver Curwood, Ernest Maas (story). Cinematographer: Conrad Wells (a.k.a. Abe Fried). Release Date: October 17, 1926 (USA). Duration in Reels: 6. Duration in Feet: 5,363. Production Company–Distributor: Fox Film Corporation. Genre: Drama. Cast: **Olive Borden (Valencia)**, Ralph Graves (Roger McKay), Gertrude Astor (Mrs. Andrews), J. Farrell

MacDonald (Sergeant Cassidy), Evelyn Selbie (Martha), Fred Kohler (Joe), Lawford Davidson (Henry Harland), Alfred Fisher (Father John), Lottie Williams (Valencia's Maid).

The Country Beyond was filmed on location at Jasper National Park, Alberta, Canada. *Film Daily* (October 24, 1926) called Olive "a very sexy woodland nymph who captures the hearts of three of the five men in the cast." Not surprisingly, Ralph Graves succumbs completely to her charm. J. Farrell MacDonald, as the mounty, has "always loved her," and Lawford Davidson, the show producer, sees a brand new star on Broadway when he discovers Olive. Fred Kohler and Evelyn Selbie hold their own in meaty character roles.

"A great story of Broadway and the Northwest. The picture is most beautifully mounted and is exceptionally interesting" (*The Sheboygan Press*, November 24, 1926).

TAGLINE: "A soul gripping romance of love and adventure — From the cloud piercing peaks of the Northwest to the skyscrapers of New York."

The Museum of Modern Art and the Library of Congress both have the trailer in their

Olive on the cover of *Movie Monthly*, May 1926.

archives. As of 2009, the film itself is considered "lost."

• Hollywood in 1927

Number of releases: 743.

U.S. weekly cinema attendance: 57 million.

August 12, 1927: *Wings* opened at the Criterion Theatre in New York City with an unheard of roadshow admission price of $2 per ticket! *Wings* would go on to win the very first Academy Award for Best Picture. It was the only non-speaking film to ever win an Academy Award in that category.

Nineteen twenty-seven was one of the most exciting years in the history of Hollywood filmmaking. Aside from the silent World War I drama *Wings*, Buster Keaton starred in his Civil War masterpiece *The General*, Tod Browning teamed Joan Crawford and Lon Chaney for *The Unknown*, there was Fritz Lang's futuristic sensation *Metropolis*, and Janet Gaynor and George O'Brien lit up the screen in Murnau's, *Sunrise*. There was *Seventh Heaven*, also starring Janet Gaynor and De-Mille's Biblical epic *The King of Kings*; Edmund Goulding directed Greta Garbo and John Gilbert in *Love*; and of course, there was the film that changed everything — the first feature-length talkie, *The Jazz Singer*. The groundbreaking Al Jolson feature that incorporated musical sequences and some brief dialogue would transform the face of cinema: forever.

Top male and female box office stars for the year according to a Quigley Publications poll of exhibitors:

Male: Tom Mix.

Female: Colleen Moore.

Barbara Stanwyck makes her film debut as a fan dancer in *Broadway Nights*. As of 2009 it's a lost film. It was her only silent role.

The Monkey Talks (1927)

Director: Raoul Walsh. Producer: William Fox. Writers: Rene Fauchois (novel *Le singe qui parle*, Paris, 1925), Gordon Rigby. Cinematographer: L. William O'Connell. Release Date: February 20,

1927 (USA). Running Time: 60 minutes. Duration in Reels: 6. Duration in Feet: 5,500. Production Company–Distributor: Fox Film Corporation. Genre: Drama. Cast: **Olive Borden (Olivette),** Jacques Lerner (Jocko), Don Alvarado (Sam Wick), Malcolm Waite (Bergerin), Raymond Hitchcock (Lorenzo), Ted McNamara (Firmin), Jane Winton (Masisie), August Tollaire (Mata).

A February 27, 1927, review in *Film Daily* said the film was a "sensational novelty." It was complimented for being a splendidly made picture that contained a story that had some excellent, dramatic moments, "although it may be a bit grim for some." Jacques Lerner excelled in the difficult role of the monkey and was praised for his touching and authentic performance the world over. *Film Daily* described Olive as "a lovely tight rope walker." Her co-stars were praised for their solid performances too: "Don Alvarado, an imposing and handsome hero. Raymond Hitchcock, very good."

A March 1, 1927, *Los Angeles Times* review stated, "In the role of the little acrobat, Olive Borden was charming. Her performance was graced with a rare piquancy that completely won her audiences."

"Olive Borden's ingénue is largely gorgeous, although there are moments

A fresh-faced Olive relaxing in the garden at the height of her career. She is wearing her treasured pansy ring that was made out of one of her late father's tie pins.

when her eyes widened in horror or her lips pursed in disapproval she's the spitting image of Shelley Duvall's Olive Oyl. But, Borden does get to display her figure and quite-lovely legs via a selection of skimpy, form-fitting costumes and such, worn throughout the film (*Up From the Vault: Rare Thrillers of the 1920's and 1930's,* John T. Soister, McFarland & Company, 2004).

"...Jacques Lerner, who holds the distinction of being the world's most celebrated portrayer of animals, journeyed from Paris to create for the screen the role of Jocko, the talking monkey. Mr. Lerner originated the role in the stage play and won such outstanding success that Fox Films signed him for the same role in the film" (*Appleton Post-Crescent,* April 6, 1927).

The Hippodrome in New York City was the first theatre to run *The Monkey Talks.* The stage play was immensely popular, but without sound to carry it, the silent film version was less effective because it lacked the haunting voice of Lerner. His performance as Jocko still garnered positive reviews and most of the critics' praise was reserved for him. The *Los Angeles Times* (April 10, 1927) stated that he "easily steals the picture from Olive Borden, who is featured above him. She is unusually annoying in this picture because of her incessant prancing, mincing and arching of her insteps. The novelty of the film will carry it where its emotional appeal is minus." Olive trained under the direction of a slack wire expert for two weeks to get her balance just right for the dramatic close-up scenes in the story (*Syracuse Herald,* January 2, 1927).

TAGLINES: "One of the most novel and absorbing stories ever filmed — Gripping with suspense — Sparkling with humor — Pulsing with excitement — And brimming with romance! A real treat."

"Never Such a Mystery as the Monkey Who Talked and Set the Crowds Gasping Beneath the Big Top. All the Glamour and Mysteries Behind the Scenes of a Great Circus. Something New — Something Different — It Will Thrill, Amaze and Delight You."

As of 2009, the International Museum of Photography and Film at George Eastman House in Rochester, New York, holds an extensively decomposed 35mm nitrate print. It's complete and preserved but not digitally restored. All six reels exist but much of the early part of the film is unwatchable.

The Secret Studio (1927)

Director: Victor Schertzinger. Producer: William Fox. Writer: James Kevin McGuinness. Cinematographer: Glen MacWilliams. Release Date: June 14, 1927 (New York City), June 19, 1927 (nationwide). Running Time: 60 minutes. Duration in Reels: 6. Duration in Feet: 5,870. Production Company–Distributor: Fox Film Corporation.

Olive draped in pearls.

Genre: Drama-Romance. Cast: **Olive Borden (Rosemary Merton)**, John Holland (Sloan Whitney), Noreen Phillips (Elsie Merton), Ben Bard (Larry Kane), Kate Bruce (Ma Merton), Joseph Cawthorn (Pa Merton), Margaret Livingston (Nina Clark), Walter McGrail (Mr. Kyler), Lila Leslie (Mrs. Kyler), Ned Sparks (The Plumber).

Louella O. Parsons of the *Los Angeles Examiner* (April 30, 1927) wrote,

"What a blessed thing the movies are for these stage players who have served many years of their lives before the footlights. Joseph Cawthorn, whom there was no more popular musical comedy star in the days when he appeared with Julia Sanderson, has been completely won over by California. He was cavorting about on the set of *The Secret Studio* at the Fox Company, acting like a two-year-old. He has been engaged to play a part in this picture, opposite Olive Borden. This is Mr. Cawthorn's first experience, and if he likes the movies as well as May Robson we will probably have him out in California for life."

Indeed, he did just that. After his thirty-year Broadway career began to wind down, Cawthorn (March 29, 1868–January 21, 1949) turned his attention to Hollywood. He reinvented himself and became known as one of the great character actors of his time.

The Secret Studio was adapted from a popular newspaper serial ("Rosemary") written by Hazel Livingston. *The Secret Studio* was made once and then remade — entirely. A new cast, a new director: a new film! Olive and Margaret Livingston were the only members of the former cast to remain the second time around. Olive plays the role of Rosemary, a modern, thrill-seeking flapper. She described her character as "the type of girl who is basically sound and who, when she falls in love, falls head over heels and for good. In fact, it requires only her love for Sloan Whitney to bring out all the essential womanliness and the finer qualities of her nature" (*The Charleston Daily Mail,* July 24, 1927).

The *Los Angeles Times* (March 13, 1927) wrote, "Olive's work in *The Secret Studio* should materially enhance her popularity."

The *New York Times* (June 15, 1927) wrote, "Miss Borden does very well with her part, but now and again she appears to be lacking spontaneity."

Film Daily (June 26, 1927) wrote, "Romance and thrills in the life of an artist's model."

As of 2009, this film is presumed lost.

The Joy Girl (1927)

Director: Allan Dwan. Producer: William Fox. Writers: Frances Agnew (writer), Malcolm Stuart Boylan (titles), Adele Comandini (adaptation), May Edginton (story). Cinematographers: William Miller, George Webber. Release Date: September 3, 1927 (New York City), September 18, 1927 (nationwide). Running Time: 70 minutes. Duration in Reels: 6–7 (premiered at 7 reels and was cut to 6 for general release). Duration in Feet: 5,877 or 6,162. Production Company–Distributor: Fox Film Corporation. Genre: Comedy. Cast: **Olive Borden (Jewel Courage)**, Neil Hamilton (John Jeffrey Fleet), Marie Dressler (Mrs. Heath), Mary Alden (Mrs. Courage), William Norris (Herbert Courage), Helen Chandler (Flora), Jerry Miley (Vicary), Frank Walsh (Hugh Sandman), Clarence Elmer (Valet), Peggy Kelly (Isolde), Jimmy Grainger, Jr. (Chauffeur).

A September 11, 1927, review in *Film Daily* said, "Olive Borden is a snappy little flapper, bound to please them. Photographs like a million. Neil Hamilton, always a bit too dignified, but he's handsome enough to make them forget that. Marie Dressler good in an inning or two."

"Although a complicated love story stands out prominently as one of the features of *The Joy Girl*, the work of Olive Borden, brunette beauty, and the elaborate display of beautiful gowns and frocks, really add the necessary touch to make the production a real success" (*The Zanesville Signal,* January 4, 1928).

The Joy Girl was filmed on location in Palm Beach, Florida. It was based on the short story of the same name written by May Edington and published in *The Saturday Evening Post* (November 13: December 18, 1926). Olive was forever known as "The Joy Girl" after this movie was released.

TAGLINES: "The Story of a Snappy, Beautiful Flapper Who Wanted to Marry a Millionaire."

"He was a Millionaire Disguised As a Chauffeur Looking for a Wife!"

The Museum of Modern Art has a copy of this film, including its much-talked-about Technicolor reel.

Pajamas (1927)

Director: John G. Blystone. Producer: William Fox. Writers: Malcolm Stuart Boylan (titles), William M. Conselman (screenplay and story). Cinematographer: Glen MacWilliams. Release Date: October 23, 1927 (USA). Running Time: 60 minutes. Duration in Reels: 6. Duration in Feet: 5,876. Production Company–Distributor: Fox Film Corporation. Genre: Comedy-Romance. Cast: **Olive Borden (Angela Wade),** Lawrence Gray (John Weston), Jack J. Clark (Daniel Wade), Jerry Miley (Russell Forrest),

Film Daily (November 13, 1927) wrote, "...Some gorgeous views of the Canadian Rockies are compensation or a slow, uneventful story. Olive Borden flirts with pneumonia most of the time in a scanty pajama suit that seems inadequate considering the snow covered mountain background. Role offers her little."

"Taking a dislike to John Weston (Lawrence

A beautiful portrait shot of Olive at her peak.

Gray), a breezy young Canadian who has come to close a business deal with her father, Angela Wade (Olive) replaces her father's pilot in his private airplane and manages to crash in the Canadian wilds... An amusing outworking of a familiar plot" (*Moving Picture World*, December 10, 1927).

"The story is an impossible and tiresome one of the spoiled society girl who is tamed by a real he-man. Olive Borden neither emotes nor registers any degree of beauty" (*Syracuse Herald*, January 27, 1928).

Pajamas was filmed on location in the Canadian Rockies. As the title suggests, Olive's wardrobe mainly consisted of pajamas. Throughout the course of production she discovered how comfortable they were, and ditched her nightgowns and wore pajamas to bed for the rest of her life. George O'Brien was replaced with Lawrence Gray after the film's scheduling clashed with his lead role as "The Man" in Murnau's *Sunrise* (1927).

TAGLINES: "The romance of a girl who found love and faith again while fighting for life against nature's grim realities among the mountains of the north with the man who had scorned her."

"Olive Borden in the Best Picture She Has Ever Appeared in — PAJAMAS — Thrills! — Suspense! — Laughter!"

"The romance of a society girl whose smile was law and whose frown a sentence until she found herself alone with a real man among the rugged mountains of the north."

"An up to the minute romance of a daughter of the rich who found one man who didn't court her smiles or fear her frowns, but who won her in the old fashioned way by showing her who was boss when he was around."

"Thrills — Suspense — Pathos — Laughter in the most fascinating picture in which the beautiful Olive Borden has ever played."

A print of this film exists in a private collection. However, it has extensive nitrate damage and is incomplete.

Come to My House (1927)

Director: Alfred E. Green. Assistant Director: Jack Boland. Producer: William Fox. Writers: Malcolm Stuart Boylan (titles), Philip Klein, Marion Orth (writers), Arthur Somers Roche (1927 novel). Cinematographer: Joseph H. August. Release Date: December 25, 1927 (USA). Running Time: 60 minutes. Duration in Reels: 6. Duration in Feet: 5,430. Production Company–Distributor: Fox Film Corporation. Genre: Drama. Cast: **Olive Borden (Joan Century)**, Antonio Moreno (Floyd Bennings), Ben Bard (Fraylor), Cornelius Keefe (Murtaugh Pell), Doris Lloyd (Renee Parsons), Richard Maitland (Jimmy Parsons).

TAGLINES: "A Story of Society's Saints and Sinners!"

"A Girl's Battle Against Convention."

"Beautiful Olive Borden with Antonio Moreno in a thrilling drama of a woman who dared to defy convention — and the price she paid."

"Miss Borden revealed her inimitable charm and beauty anew, in a production hardly worthy of her abilities" (*Los Angeles Times*, February 21, 1928).

In *Come to My House*, Olive plays Joan, a society girl — an orphan rich and beautiful enough to do as she pleases. The *Chicago Daily Tribune* (January 11, 1928) reviewed the film favorably, giving one criticism to Olive for her over-exuberant facial expressions: "Joan (Olive Borden) becomes engaged to one man and, that same night, steals away to the home of another for a few hours. Scandal and tragedy follow, and the picture smartly points the moral that not even the chosen of the gods can the conventions be too lightly disregarded... Olive Borden gets over all right but will be better when she learns not to express emotion by grimace."

Film Daily (February 5, 1928) slammed the film, saying, "This is a case where the Fox organization succeeded only in turning out a lemon... Olive Borden is as forced and unnatural as ever and photographs even more unattractively than usual."

Box office angle: "Let the other fellow book this picture. Neither the star nor the story come up to the mark in this offering. It has nothing to recommend it, even for Saturday or Sunday trade."

Richard Arlen was loaned by Paramount to Fox for this film. However, when his home studio got wind that his name would appear underneath Olive's in the credits, they pulled him from the production. Cornelius Keefe replaced him (*Los Angeles Examiner,* September 20, 1927). Twenty years after the release of *Come to My House*, Keefe was the only known actor to attend Olive's funeral.

As of 2009, this film is presumed lost.

• Hollywood in 1928

Number of releases: 820.

Number of all-talking pictures released (all by Warners): 10.

U.S. weekly cinema attendance: 65 million.

November 18 — Disney's *Steamboat Willie* premiered. It was the first animated short to include sound effects, music and dialogue, all of it created in post-production. Olive's *Gang War* was the main feature presentation after the historical short was shown.

First hit record from a movie: Al Jolson's "Sonny Boy," from *The Singing Fool*, which sold two million copies in less than a year (*Movie Time*, Gene Brown, MacMillan, 1995).

July 31— The roar of MGM's mascot Leo the Lion was heard for the very first time.

Top male and female box office stars for the year according to a Quigley Publications poll of exhibitors:

Male: Lon Chaney.

Female: Clara Bow.

Top ten grossing films for 1928:

1. *The Singing Fool*; 2. *Lights of New York*; 3. *Street Angel*; 4. *West of Zanzibar*; 5. *Four Sons*; 6. *Noah's Ark*; 7. *Red Dance*; 8. *The Terror*; 9. *While the City Sleeps*; 10. *Laugh, Clown, Laugh*.

A studio publicity photograph signed by Olive. This shot was used as a studio mail out to fans.

The Albany Night Boat (1928)

Director: Alfred Raboch. Writers: Fanny Hatton, Frederic Hatton, Al Martin (titles), Wellyn Totman (screenplay and story). Cinematographer: Ernest Miller. Release Date: July 20, 1928 (USA). Duration in Reels: 6. Duration in Feet: 5,884. Production Company: Tiffany-Stahl Productions. Genre: Drama. Cast: **Olive Borden (Georgie)**, Ralph Emerson (Ken), Duke Martin (Steve), Nellie Bryden (Morth Crary), Helen Marlowe (The Blonde).

In his book *American Film Cycles: The Silent Era*, Larry Langman described the basic story of *The Albany Night Boat*:

"Duke Martin, the tender of a river searchlight, covets the wife of Ralph Emerson, his assistant... Both men take turns sweeping the Hudson River with the searchlight as the Albany night boat glides along carrying its lovers. While on duty, Emerson focuses on a yacht where Olive Borden, to avoid being seduced, dives into the river. Emerson jumps in and rescues her. Following a short courtship, the couple marry, with Martin befriending the couple and wishing them happiness. On another evening during which Emerson is tending the searchlight, the beam passes his apartment which overlooks the river. He sees the silhouettes that indicate his wife is in trouble. Once again, he swims toward his dwelling, enters the apartment and finds his friend, Martin, in the act of assaulting his wife. A fight breaks out and the intruder is eventually subdued."

Film Daily (September 23, 1928) wrote, "Popular film fare. Scores easily with sexy situations and melodramatic highlights. Olive Borden gives it a kick. Olive Borden as the young married girl fighting off the boarder in hubby's absence has a great scene and makes the most of it. She is splendid all the way... Olive Borden has a lot of sex lure and makes this real entertainment."

This was Olive's first independent film after her Fox contract negotiations went sour. As of 2009, this film is presumed lost.

In the conservative '20s, Olive posed for many risqué shots. This one is no exception.

Virgin Lips (1928)

Director: Elmer Clifton. Producer: Harry Cohn. Writers: Charles Beahan (story), Dorothy Howell. Cinematographer: Joseph Walker. Release Date: July 25, 1928 (USA). Running Time: 59 minutes. Duration in Reels: 6. Duration in Feet: 6,048. Production Company–Distributor: Columbia Pictures. Genre: Action-Drama. Cast: **Olive Borden (Norma),** John Boles (Barry Blake), Marshall Ruth (Slim), Alexander Gill (Garcia), Richard Alexander (Carta), Erne Veo (Nick), Harry Semels (Patron), Arline Pretty (Madge), William H. Tooker (President).

Film Daily (September 16, 1928), wrote, "Olive Borden plays the white girl in the clutches of the Mexican bandit, and is the appealing type for the part. John Boles, the aviatar hero. Richard Alexander, the Mexican bandit, is the best part of the picture... Melodrama of Mexican bandit life... Good suspense, and lots of action."

"The boudoir battle between the lady [Olive] and the bandit is too long and rather vulgar, main object being, apparently, to show as much of Olive Borden as possible" (*Chicago Daily Tribune*, September 4, 1928).

TAGLINE: "John Boles and Olive Borden in *Virgin Lips*— A Most Fascinating and Timely Plot. Adventure, Thrills and Passionate Love in Generous Quantities."

As of 2009, this film is presumed lost.

Gang War (1928)

Director: Bert Glennon. Writers: Randolph Bartlett (titles), James Ashmore Creelman (story), Fred Myton (writer), Edgar Allan Woolf (dialogue). Cinematographer: Virgil Miller. Release Date: September 2, 1928 (USA). Running Time: 70 minutes. Duration in Reels: 7. Duration in Feet: 6,365. Alternate Title: *All Square* (UK). Production Company–Distributor: Film Booking Offices of America. Genre: Crime-Drama (with some talking sequences and sound effects). Cast: Lorin Raker (Prologue), Jack McKee (Prologue), Mabel Albertson (Prologue), David Hartman (Prologue), **Olive Borden (Flowers),** Jack Pickford (Clyde Baxter), Eddie Gribbon (Blackjack), Walter Long (Mike Luego), Frank Chew (Wong).

Gang War is best known for being the main feature attached to *Steamboat Willie* (1928), the debut of Mickey Mouse in sound. It featured the debut of actress Mabel Albertson.

TAGLINE: "Gunfire! Police sirens! Gangster jargon! Machine guns in action! Bedlam! Bomb explosions!"

"Flowers (Olive) is a young girl forced to marry a gang leader who loves her more than anything in life. She, however, loves Clyde (Jack Pickford), a fine fellow, but incapable of fighting his dangerous gangster rival. Driven by fear for the one she loves, the girl is compelled to marry the gangster, only to find that she has not saved her lover at all. With the truth coming out, Blackjack (Eddie Gribbon), as the gangster, proves himself to be a real man, and chooses death beneath the flaming guns of a rival gang so that his wife may live out her life with the young man she truly loves" (*The Bee*, Danville, Virginia, Monday, November 26, 1928).

"Olive Borden as the dance hall heroine and Jack Pickford as her saxophone-playing lover are in graceful contrast to the rough and ready acting of Eddie Gribbon as the bandit chief" (*The Sheboygan Press*, November 23, 1929).

"Just another underworld story pepped up with some hectic gang fights. All right for daily change. *Gang War* follows the regular formula of the two gangs that are warring over their bootleg traffic" (*Film Daily*, August 8, 1928).

"This film is exciting in the main and well acted, Eddie Gribbon, usually cast in low comedy roles, contributes some swell pantomime... Olive Borden is charming, though almost too ladylike as the taxi dancer. Jack Pickford hasn't a very convincing role but he does his best with it" (*Chicago Daily Tribune*, December 18, 1928).

"This picture begins with a good idea: two reporters go to a dance-hall hostess who has the dope about the innocent boy's love affair with a little cabaret girl (Olive Borden). What she tells one of the reporters, constitutes the plot of a well-acted, fairly exciting picture proving principally that Olive Borden is a better actress than most people have believed" (*Time*, December 3, 1928).

Recently completed silent films were screened for spots where sound effects or bits of dialogue could be inserted in post-production. A studio unit secretary reported that "everything is more or less experimental," but many reports suggested that the sound work on *Gang War* (1928) was "the best yet to be recorded" (*Joseph P. Kennedy Presents: His Hollywood Years,* Carrie Beauchamp, Knopf, 2009).

As of 2009, this film is presumed lost.

Olive loved fashion. She spent thousands of dollars on her collection of fur coats.

Stool Pigeon (1928)

Director: Renaud Hoffman. Producer: Jack Cohn. Writers: Stuart Anthony (adaptation and screenplay), Mort Blumenstock (titles), Edward J. Meagher (story). Cinematographer: Ted Tetzlaff. Release Date: October 25, 1928 (USA). Running Time: 56 minutes. Duration in Reels: 6. Duration in Feet: 5,592. Alternate Title: *The Decoy* (UK). Production Company–Distributor: Columbia Pictures. Genre: Crime-Drama. Cast: **Olive Borden (Goldie)**, Charles Delaney (Jimmy Wells), Lucy Beaumont (Mrs. Wells), Louis Natheaux (Butch), Ernie Adams (Dropper), Al Hill (Red), Robert Wilber (Augie), Clarence Burton (Mike Shields).

"[This] is a suspenseful story of gangsters and their ruthless methods" (*Los Angeles Examiner*, February 18, 1929).

"Olive Borden inserts the heart interest with a portrayal of a scarlet woman of the underworld, who falls in love with the innocent dupe of the gang. She contributes most of the interesting scenes of the picture and should really be starred for her work" (*Syracuse Herald*, January 27, 1929).

"This one works the sentimental angle and proves moderately entertaining. Charles Delaney is the young hero who gets in bad company but reforms and helps the cops to land the gang. Olive Borden as his sweetie has little to do and fails to show with her usual sexy side" (*Film Daily*, November 4, 1928).

Lobster Films, Paris, has a print of this film.

Sinners in Love (1928)

Director: George Melford. Writers: Randolph Bartlett (titles) and J. Clarkson Miller (writer). Cinematographer: Paul P. Perry. Release Date: November 4, 1928 (USA). Running Time: 60 minutes. Duration in Reels: 6. Duration in Feet: 6,310. Production Company–Distributor: Film Booking Offices of America. Genre: Drama. Cast: **Olive Borden (Ann Hardy)**, Huntley Gordon (Ted Wells), Seena Owen (Yvonne D'Orsy), Ernest Hilliard (Silk Oliver), Daphne Pollard (Mabel), Phillips Smalley (Spencer), Henry Roquemore.

Film Daily (October 10, 1928) wrote, "Another poor girl's romance gone wrong. Modern fairy story made fantastic and impossible. Olive Borden goes from factory gal to riches overnight and stages her usual struggle to retain her honor. She goes dramatic, and the result is sad."

"The film depicts the adventures of small town girl Ann Hardy (Olive), who is the central figure, becoming involved with a gang of crooks. However, she is first introduced to the audience as a member of a large, poverty-stricken family. Disgusted and tired with supporting her worthless parents and with the squalor of the life she leads, she goes to New York where she expects to find an easier existence. Her new life doesn't go as easy as she dreamed it to be and after considerable difficulty, she obtains employment in a 'hash house' where she meets a sensational, corrupted blonde, who introduces her to a night club proprietor. Trapped into becoming a hostess in a gambling room where she lures the 'big money' clients, she soon realizes her downward trend and hates herself for it, and suddenly disappears. When the proprietor seeks her out to tell her that he will go straight if she will marry him, the action is brought to a climax and the usual happy ending ensues" (*The Lima News*, December 10, 1928).

The *Film Spectator* (September, 29, 1928) wrote, "It is just another crook story with Huntley Gordon repenting in the last reel and taking unto himself as wife Miss Olive Borden, whose good influence prompts him to close a dignified and prosperous gambling joint and go straight. However, the picture is a worthy one that will please F.B.O.'s regular patrons."

The Centre National de la Cinematographie (CNC), Paris, has a print of this film in their archive.

• **Hollywood in 1929**

Number of releases: 707.

U.S. weekly cinema attendance: 95 million.

Number of feature films using color: 60.

Average ticket price: 35 cents.

January 20: *In Old Arizona*, the first full-length talking film to be filmed outdoors, was released.

MGM releases *The Broadway Melody*, the first major Hollywood musical of the sound era.

Top male and female box office stars for the year according to a Quigley Publications poll of exhibitors:

Male: Lon Chaney

Female: Clara Bow

Judy Garland, Betty Grable, Paulette

Goddard, Jeanette MacDonald and Ginger Rogers all made their film debuts.

Top ten grossing films of 1929:

1. *Gold Diggers of Broadway*; 2. *The Broadway Melody*; 3. *Sunny Side-Up*; 4. *Welcome Danger*; 5. *The Cock-Eyed World*; 6. *Rio Rita*; 7. *Hollywood Revue of 1929*; 8. *In Old Arizona*; 9. *Coquette*; 10. *Syncopation*.

May 16 — The first Academy Awards ceremony was held in the Blossom Room of the Hollywood Roosevelt Hotel. Douglas Fairbanks and William C. DeMille presented the statues to the winners. Since Best Actor winner Emil Jannings was scheduled to travel back to his home in Germany, he could not attend the event. He was presented with the award prior to his departure, thus making him the very first person to ever receive an Academy Award.

The 1927–1928 winners were:

Best Actress — Janet Gaynor for *Seventh Heaven, Street Angel* and *Sunrise.*

Best Actor — Emil Jannings for *The Last Command* and *The Way of All Flesh.*

Best Picture: *Wings.*

Best Picture with Unique and Artistic Production: *Sunrise.*

Love in the Desert (1929)

Director: George Melford. Writers: Randolph Bartlett (titles), Paul Percy (writer), Louis Sarecky (story), Harvey F. Thew (screenplay and story). Cinematographer: Paul P. Perry. Release Date: January 27, 1929 (silent version), March 17, 1929 (sound version). Duration in Reels: 7. Duration in Feet: 6,365. Production Company–Distributor: Film Booking Offices of America. Genre: Drama (silent with some talking sequences and sound effects). Cast: **Olive Borden (Zarah),** Hugh Trevor (Bob Winslow), Noah Beery (Abdullah), Frank Leigh (Harim), Pearl Varvalle (Fatima), William H. Tooker (Mr. Winslow), Ida Darling (Mrs. Winslow), Alan Roscoe (Houdish), Hillard Karr (Briggs), Gordon Magee (Sears), Charles Brinley.

The story involves an American youth working on an irrigation project who falls in love with an Arabian princess (Olive) and saves her from a forced marriage to a bandit sheik.

Film Daily (May 5, 1929) wrote, "Olive Borden as the native princess is pretty tame, and Hugh Trevor as the hero lacks punch and uncovers no personality. All in all, the cast is mediocre, and the story is no better..."

Olive had a couple of lines in the opening and closing scenes, as did Trevor. The *Syracuse Herald* (February 3, 1929) wrote, "[Olive's] voice agreeably surprises, as does that of Mr. Trevor."

A few months after the release of this film, Olive was appointed secretary of the Catholic Motion Picture Guild. It was a position she was honored to receive. The Cineteca del Friuli, Gemona, Italy, and the Centre National de la Cinematographie, Paris, both have 35mm prints of this film in their archives.

Olive is every inch the movie star in this whimsical pose.

The Eternal Woman (1929)

Director: John P. McCarthy. Producer: Harry Cohn. Writer: Wellyn Totman (based on the short story "The Wildcat"). Cinematographer: Joseph Walker. Release Date: March 18, 1929 (USA). Duration in Reels: 6. Duration in Feet: 5,812. Production Company–Distributor: Columbia Pictures. Genre: Drama. Cast: **Olive Borden (Anita),** Ralph Graves (Hartley Forbes), Ruth Clifford (Doris Forbes), John Miljan (Gil Martin), Nina Quartero (Consuelo), Josef Swickard (Ovaldo), Julia Swayne Gordon (Mrs. Forbes).

Olive wearing a rather bizarre-looking cape and costume with an anchor theme.

Film Daily (April 7, 1929) wrote, "Strong program picture gets over nicely with good story and fine work of Ralph Graves and Olive Borden. Ralph Graves is very effective as the wronged husband. Olive Borden does her usual sexy stuff and is very attractive."

The *Chicago Daily Tribune* (April 8, 1929), wrote, "It's far-fetched and incredible in spots, but has much relief in the way of good acting, beautiful scenery, and fine photography."

In an unidentified article dated January 1929, Olive commented on her role as Anita: "Playing this fiery girl of the Argentine is different from anything I have ever attempted. This Anita is intensely emotional, vivacious, and unrestrained, but with a capacity for a great love or a great hate. Impulsive, quick in her decisions, she is unwavering in her loyalty."

TAGLINE: "A fiery tempestuous Argentine girl crosses land and sea in her quest for revenge to find love waiting for her at the end of her journey! Her thrilling series of exploits, coupled with a tender and beautiful love story, make up a picture you can not afford to miss!"

The British Film Institute has a print of this film.

Half Marriage (1929)

Director: William J. Cowen. Producer: William Le Baron. Writers: Jane Murfin (writer), George Kibbe Turner (based on his short story). Release Date: October 13, 1929 (USA). Running Time: 68 minutes. Duration in Reels: 7. Production Company–Distributor: RKO Radio Pictures (USA). Genre: Drama-Romance — Silent and Sound Versions. Cast: **Olive Borden (Judy Page)**, Morgan Farley (Dick "Dickie" Carroll), Ken Murray (Charles Turner), Ann Greenway (Ann Turner), Anderson Lawler (Tom Stribbling), Sally Blane (Sally), Hedda Hopper (Mrs. Page), Richard Tucker (Mr. Page), Henry Armetta (Henry, Hot Dog Vendor), Gus Arnheim (Himself: Bandleader), James Bradbury, Jr. (Poverty), G. Pat Collins (Detective Bob Mulhall), James Eagles (Matty), Jack Trent (Rudy).

Soundtrack: "After the Clouds Roll By," written by Sidney Clare and Oscar Levant.

Sung by Ann Greenway (part of the score). "You're Marvelous," written by Sidney Clare and Oscar Levant. Played by Gus Arnheim and His Coconut Grove Ambassadors. Sung by Ken Murray.

Half Marriage was Olive's first talkie for RKO Radio Pictures and her first all-talkie: pe-

riod! (She had already been heard briefly in *Gang War* [1928] and she had a few spoken lines at the beginning and end of *Love in the Desert* [1929].)

Director William J. Cowen installed a soundproof snoring booth for members of the cast who might need a rest in between scenes. One day, in the middle of a scene, sounds of someone "sawing wood" began to raise havoc with the recording track. The actors very professionally tuned the sound out and continued with their lines to the end of the scene. When they were done, everyone went to investigate the noise. Their ears led them to a chair behind one of the sidewalls of the set. One of the actors was taking a nap and snoring: loudly! This incident prompted the sound proof snoring booth (*Los Angeles Times*, June 9, 1929).

Film Daily (August 25, 1929) wrote, "One of the poorest samples of dialogue [the sound transfer] that has yet assailed these poor abused ears of ours... Olive Borden does her usual sexy stuff, and is good, as far as the script would allow her to be."

"A starless feature but Borden is a revelation in dialogue. She is natural and modern. She does her best screen work" (*Variety*, August 14, 1929).

"Borden has made the dialog her own in this script, and comes off completely natural" (www.tvguide.com).

The UCLA Film and Television Archive (Los Angeles, California) has an incomplete print. The original footage was 6,501 ft. The UCLA print is significantly less than this. DVD copies of this film are occasionally made available by private collectors. Author has a DVD copy.

Dance Hall (1929)

Director: Melville W. Brown. Producer: Henry Hobart. Writers: Vina Delmar (*Liberty Magazine* story "Dance Hall," March 16, 1929), Jane Murfin, J. Walter Rubin (writers). Cinematographer: Jack MacKenzie. Release Date: December 14, 1929 (New York City), December 27, 1929 (nationwide). Running Time: 65 minutes. Duration in Reels: 7. Production Company–Distributor: RKO Radio Pictures. Genre: Drama. Cast: **Olive Borden (Gracie Nolan)**, Arthur Lake (Tommy Flynn), Margaret Seddon (Mrs. Flynn), Ralph Emerson (Ted Smith), Joseph Cawthorn (Bremmer: Dance Hall Proprietor), Helen Kaiser (Bee), Lee Moran (Ernie), Tom O'Brien (Truck Driver), Natalie Joyce.

Two days of *Dance Hall* footage was completely destroyed after fire broke out at the Consolidated Film Industries vaults. One man perished in the blaze and millions of dollars in damage was reported. Several major studios lost complete films (*Los Angeles Times*, October 25, 1929).

Los Angeles Evening Express (January 22, 1930): "Olive Borden, noted for her curly, blue-black hair, turns blonde for the first time in her screen career in the talking drama."

Film Daily (December 22, 1929): "Arthur Lake does the adolescent as a genuine person and Olive Borden is capable enough as the dance hall hostess who does a love Brody for the wrong chap and then, in the last reel, finds that she's really in love with the personable shipping clerk."

New York Times (December 16, 1929): "The dialogue in this film lives up to the nature of the story. There are plenty of 'Goshes,' 'Gees,' 'Don't be sil,' and other such expressions... Such a picture would be exasperating enough in silent form, but when the characters receive the gift of speech, then it is far worse... Olive Borden plays Gracie Nolan according to the demands of the part."

Playing a small role in *Dance Hall* is Olive's cousin Natalie Joyce, who made over forty films. She voluntarily quit her Hollywood career in 1932 and died on November 9, 1992, three days after her ninetieth birthday.

A print of this film exists in a private collection. The film is clear and in good overall condition; however, it is slightly out of sync and the dialogue is often heard before the mouths of the actors move. Author has a DVD copy. The film also exists in the UCLA Film and Television Archive (Los Angeles, California).

Olive posing in yet another unusual costume.

The *Los Angeles Times* ("Olive Borden's Mother Ill," September 25, 1929) reported that Sibbie was "critically ill" in the Good Samaritan Hospital after suffering from complications from an operation she received in January of 1929. She remained in the hospital for several weeks and Olive was reported as being in an "extremely nervous state" due to the seriousness of her mother's condition. Despite her anxiety, she began work on *Dance Hall* and raced to the hospital each evening to be by her side until she recovered.

Wedding Rings (1929)

Director: William Beaudine. Producer: Robert North. Writers: Ray Harris (screenplay and titles), Ernest Pascal (based on his novel *The Dark Swan*, New York, 1924). Cinematographer: Ernest Haller. Release Date: December 29, 1929 (USA). Running Time: 74 minutes. Duration in Reels: 7. Alternate Title: *The Dark Swan* (USA). Production Company: First National Pictures. Distributors: Warner Bros. Pictures and First National Pictures. Genre: Drama. Cast: H. B. Warner (Lewis Dike), Lois Wilson (Cornelia Quinn), **Olive Borden (Eve Quinn)**, Hallam Cooley (Wilfred Meadows), James Ford (Tim Hazelton), Kathlyn Williams (Agatha), Aileen Manning (Ester Quinn).

Soundtrack: "Love Will Last Forever" and "That's My Business," lyrics by Al Bryan, music by Eddie Ward.

Wedding Rings is mostly a fashion show with beautiful clothes and stunning sets. The interesting story involves the beautiful daughter (Olive) of a wealthy family who always steals her less attractive sister's men. This heartless, selfish little wench finally attracts a millionaire, the man her sister really loves, and marries him.

On her wedding day, the scorned sister warns her sibling "bride-to-be" rival that she will win her soon-to-be husband back, for she truly loves him and she knows her sister does not. This is not so hard, for the bad sister soon gets bored with the millionaire and sets her sights on pursuing another man to appease her spoiled ways. As expected, the complicated love triangle comes to a dramatic end.

"Miss Borden is stunningly gowned throughout and looks very lovely most of the time, but has a most difficult and unsympathetic character to portray..." (*Hollywood Daily Citizen,* February 8, 1930).

"Highly entertaining domestic drama... Olive Borden does well in her characterization of the flapper who is little concerned by whose heart she breaks" (*Film Daily,* May 11, 1930).

Olive seems to have done her job in this film, her character wasn't meant to be liked, but according to the *Chicago Daily Tribune* (March 15, 1930), that wasn't the way for her to endear herself to audiences if she wanted to remain a popular actress. "If they're trying to make a star of Miss Borden they are going about it the wrong way. You thoroughly dislike and disapprove of her in *Wedding Rings* and that's no way to feel about a young lady who aspires to be a box office favorite. As Eve she's cheap; she's immoral; she's a rotten sport, and your contempt for her knows no bounds."

TAGLINES: "Sister vs. Sister in a fight for love!"

"One woman's wit against another's "IT," for the love of the same man—fighting almost recklessly for possession, ice and fire—selfishness and sacred love—three of the screen's greatest artists—Lois Wilson, H.B. Warner, Olive Borden in *Wedding Rings*."

There may be no complete print of this film. The seven reels that are known to exist show deterioration. This incomplete print is housed at the UCLA Film and Television Archive (Los Angeles, California).

The Voice of Hollywood No. 1 (1929)

Producer: Louis Lewyn. Release Date: December 1929 (USA). Running Time: 10 minutes. Production Company: Louis Lewyn Productions. Distributor: Tiffany Productions. Cast: Lloyd Hamilton (Guest Host), **Olive Borden**, Robert Frazer, Arthur Lake, Benny Rubin, Rudy Vallee, Sally Bland, Stepin Fetchit (Themselves).

"*The Voice of Hollywood No. 1*, made at the Tec Art Studio, cleverly introduces Rudy Vallee, Lloyd Hamilton, Sally Bland, Arthur Lake, Olive Borden and Stepin Fetchit with Robert Frazer announcing Station S-T-A-R and the events that take place. This is an interesting short with a novel twist" (*Hollywood Daily Citizen,* March 28, 1930).

The Library of Congress has a 35mm print. A copy also exists in a private collection.

• Hollywood in 1930

Number of releases: 595.

U.S. weekly cinema attendance: 90 million.

Number of theaters in the U.S.— 23,000 (wired for sound: 8,860).

First modern horror film: *Dracula.* Bela Lugosi's pay for *Dracula*—$3,500.

Top male and female box office stars for the year according to a Quigley Publications poll of exhibitors:

Male: William Haines.

Female: Joan Crawford.

Top ten grossing films for 1930:

1. *Whoopee!*; 2. *Common Clay*; 3. *Check and Double Check*; 4. *Feet First*; 5. *All Quiet on the Western Front*; 6. *The Big House*; 7. *Min and Bill*; 8. *Song o' My Heart*; 9. *Anna Christie*; 10. *Raffles.*

Laurence Olivier, Buster Crabbe, Rex Harrison and Ethel Merman all made their film debuts.

February 23: Mabel Normand died of tuberculosis at age thirty-five.

April 3 — The second Academy Awards ceremony was held. William C. DeMille hosted the ceremony in the Coconut Grove of the Ambassador Hotel in Los Angeles, California. The winners were:

Best Actress — Mary Pickford for *Coquette.*

Best Actor — Warner Baxter for *In Old Arizona.*

Best Picture — *The Broadway Melody.*

August 26: Lon Chaney died at 47 as a result of a throat hemorrhage. He also had advanced lung cancer.

November 5, 1930 — The third Academy Awards ceremony was held in the Coconut Grove just seven months after the second Academy Awards ceremony in an attempt to close the gap of time on the films that were eligible. Conrad Nagel hosted the ceremony. The winners were:

Best Actress — Norma Shearer for *The Divorcee.*

Best Actor — George Arliss for *Disraeli.*

Best Picture — *All Quiet on the Western Front.*

Hello Sister (1930)

Director: Walter Lang. Producer: James Cruze. Writers: Reita Lambert (serial story), Brian Marlow. Cinematographer: Harold Rosson. Release Date:

An Olive Borden paper doll designed by artist Gregg Nystrom in 2009. Photograph credit — Gregg Nystrom.

February 15, 1930. Running Time: 70 minutes. Working Title: *See You in Church.* Production Company: James Cruze Productions. Distributor: Sono Art-World Wide Pictures. Genre: Drama. Cast: **Olive Borden (Vee Newel),** Lloyd Hughes (Marshall Jones), George Fawcett (Fraser Newell), Bodil Rosing (Martha Peddie), Norman Peck ("Tivvie" Rose), Howard C. Hickman (John Stanley), Raymond Keane (Randall Carr), Wilfred Lucas (Dr. Saltus), James T. Mack (Horace Peddie), Harry McDonald (Appleby Sims), Billy Seay (Norbert).

Film Daily (September 9, 1930) was less than impressed with the picture: "Fails to click ... Olive Borden as the heroine is not in her element portraying the jazz-crazed miss who is forced to change her habits so that she can be in keeping with requirements of her father's will."

"There is a thrill when Miss Borden rides in a steeplechase, against two men, and there is a delicious touch when at a church bazaar the boys and girls put on a 'Tell Me Pretty Maiden' number in the costume of the '90s" (*The Sheboygan Press*, April 9, 1930).

"Miss Borden never quite arises to the dramatic possibilities of her role, although she has acquired much more microphone poise and her voice is greatly improved" (*Los Angeles Times*, May 1, 1930).

Hello Sister was adapted from Reita Lambert's serial story *Clipped Wings*.

TAGLINES: "A snappy, rowdy-dow story of a whoopee society girl whose creed is — yesterday is gone, tomorrow may never come, tonight is here — LET'S GO!"

"Snappy Story of a 12 O'clock Girl and a Hey, Hey, Gang in a 9 O'clock Town!"

"All Talking Hit with Olive Borden and Lloyd Hughes."

"A good story, lots of singing, interludes of dancing, a thrill or two, a motion picture in which modern youth had its fling — that's *Hello Sister.*"

Three different versions of the song "(What Good Am I) Without You" are heard on the soundtrack.

During 1930, Olive was a representative of Lux toilet soap. She appeared in several print ads for the product, saying, "Lux Toilet Soap gives my skin the special velvety smoothness we mean by 'studio skin.' I am certainly delighted with it." Her signature was printed after her endorsement (*The Bellingham Herald*, March 4, 1930).

Author has a DVD copy taken from a privately owned print.

The Social Lion (1930)

Director: A. Edward Sutherland. Writers: Octavus Roy Cohen (story "Marco, Himself"), Agnes Brand Leahy (writer), Joseph L. Mankiewicz (adaptation: dialogue). Cinematographer: Allen G. Siegler. Release Date: June 21, 1930. Running Time: 72 minutes. Working Title: *High Society*. Production Company–Distributor: Paramount Pictures Corporation. Genre: Comedy. Cast: Jack Oakie (Marco Perkins), Mary Brian (Cynthia Brown), Richard "Skeets" Gallagher (Chick Hathaway), **Olive Borden (Gloria Staunton),** Charles Sellon (Jim Perkins), Cyril Ring (Ralph Williams), E. H. Calvert (Henderson), James Gibson (Howard), Henry Roquemore (Smith), William Bechtel (Schultz), Richard Cummings (McGinnis), Jack Byron ("Knockout" Johnson), Frank Biedka, Virginia Bruce.

Los Angeles Illustrated News (June 13, 1930) wrote, in part, "It has that effervescent quality that should make it go over big with young people especially.... Olive Borden, with her ritzy manner, somehow doesn't seem quite sincere as the girl with the selfish ways. However, she is lovely to look upon."

The *Chicago Daily Tribune* (June 28, 1930) called Olive's performance "convincing." The rest of the review is also favorable: "Sound and photography are peppy and punchful. Direction is good, though perhaps there are times when there's too much play for laughs. You can rest assured that *The Social Lion* is clean, zestful entertainment which the children as well as yourselves will enjoy."

TAGLINES: "Jack Oakie and Skeets Gallagher, the screen's funniest wise-crackers making their hilarious way into *High Society*! You'll roar at the comedy — laugh at the antics of this funny pair of comics!"

"Oakie hits the upper crust with grin and gusto! Laughs and love! See and hear the happiness hit of "Hit the Deck" and "Sweetie" in a fresh and roaring romance made to order for him. He's the great grin invasion the nation's crazy over."

Author has a DVD copy taken from a privately owned print; however, it is only a 58-minute version. It appears that polo and boxing footage was edited out of the TV prints made by MCA-Universal.

• Hollywood in 1932

Number of releases: 685.

U.S. weekly cinema attendance: 60 million.

Top male and female box office stars for the year according to a Quigley Publications poll of exhibitors:

Male: Charles Farrell.

Female: Marie Dressler.

Some noted films of 1932 were director Tod Browning's *Freaks*, *A Farewell to Arms* starring Gary Cooper and Helen Hayes, *Call Her Savage* starring Clara Bow, *The Big Broadcast* starring Bing Crosby, *Horse Feathers* starring The Marx Brothers, *Grand Hotel*, with an all-star cast including Greta Garbo, Lionel Barrymore, John Barrymore, Joan Crawford and Lewis Stone, *The Mummy* starring Boris Karloff, and *Red Dust* starring Clark Gable and Jean Harlow.

August 10— Canine actor Rin Tin Tin died a month shy of his fourteenth birthday. Jean Harlow, who lived across the street from the famous dog, cradled his head in her lap as he passed away.

September 18 — Failed actress Peg Entwistle became infamous for leaping to her death from the "H" of the Hollywood (it then read Hollywoodland) sign.

November 18 — The fifth Academy Awards ceremony was held in the Fiesta Room of the Ambassador Hotel in Los Angeles. Lionel Barrymore hosted the event.

The 1931–1932 winners were:

Best Actress — Helen Hayes for *The Sin of Madelon Claudet.*

Best Actor — Wallace Beery for *The Champ* and Fredric March for *Dr. Jekyll and Mr. Hyde* (the first tie in Academy history).

Best Picture — *Grand Hotel.*

The Divorce Racket (1932)

Director: Aubrey Scotto. Writer: Daniel Kusell (continuity), James W. Poling (story). Cinematographers: William Miller and Frank Zucker. Release Date: 1932. Running Time: 66 minutes. Alternate Titles: *Divorce Decoy* and *The Divorce Market.* Production Company: Paradise Pictures. Distributor: States Rights Independent Exchanges. Genre: Drama. Cast: James Rennie (Detective Malcom "Duke" Ayres), **Olive Borden (Marie Douglas),** Judith Wood (Helen Travers alias Paula Murdock), Wilfred Jessop (Valet), Harry Tyler (John Hamilton), Adrian Rosley (Tony the Window Washer), Charles Eaton (Carl Travers), Joseph Calleia (Stephen Arnaud), Walter Fenner (Miguel Cordoba), Harry Short (Sulk), Sidney Easton (Elevator Boy), Betty Hamilton (Maid), A.J. Herbert (Bennett), Herschel Mayall (Medical Examiner), Scott Moore (Cop).

This film got little coverage in the papers. *The Hartford Courant* (November 14, 1932) provided the basic synopsis in two sentences: "*The Divorce Racket* is the usual story with a few trimmings of the crooked lawyer who extorts money from persons who wish to secure a divorce without publicity and notoriety; the poor secretary with a weak brother who has gotten into the clutches of the lawyer, and the police investigator who falls in love with the secretary and untangles the snarls in the murder mystery. It has the customary happy ending."

As of 2009, this film is presumed lost.

• Hollywood in 1933

Number of releases: 644.

U.S. weekly cinema attendance: 60 million.

Number of theaters in the U.S.—18,553 (wired for sound); 14,405.

Capacity of first drive-in: 400 cars (Camden, New Jersey).

Fred Astaire's first screen dancing partner: Joan Crawford in *Dancing Lady.*

The only two Hollywood stars "big enough" to be billed by their last name only: Garbo and Karloff.

Top stars at the box office according to a Quigley Publications poll of exhibitors:

1. Marie Dressler; 2. Will Rogers; 3. Janet Gaynor; 4. Eddie Cantor; 5. Wallace Beery; 6. Jean Harlow; 7. Clark Gable; 8. Mae West; 9. Norma Shearer; 10. Joan Crawford.

Top ten grossing films for 1933:

1. *I'm No Angel*; 2. *Roman Scandals*; 3. *42nd Street*; 4. *She Done Him Wrong*; 5. *Little Women*; 6. *Footlight Parade*; 7. *State Fair*; 8. *Damaged Lives*; 9. *King Kong*; 10. *Queen Christina.*

Leave It to Me (1933)

Director: Monty Banks. Producer: John Maxwell. Writers: Gene Gerrard (writer), Ian Hay, P.G. Wodehouse (play *Leave It to Psmith*), Cecil Lewis (writer), Frank Miller (writer). Release Date: April 1933 (UK). Running Time: 76 minutes. Production Company: British International Pictures (BIP). Distributor: Wardour Films (UK: theatrical). Genre: Comedy. Cast: Gene Gerrard (Sebastian Help), **Olive Borden (Peavey),** Molly Lamont (Eve Halliday), George K. Gee (Coots), Gus McNaughton (Baxter), Clive Currie (Lord Emsworth), Toni Edgar-Bruce (Lady Constance), Peter Godfrey (Siegffied Velour), Syd Crossley (Beach), Melville Cooper (Honorable Freddie), Wylie Watson (Client), Monty Banks.

As of 2009, this film is presumed lost.

Several newspaper clippings refer to this picture and another picture, *Help!*, that Olive was supposed to have filmed in the U.K. The *Syracuse Herald* (December 30, 1932) reported that British International had signed Olive for *Help!* Gene Gerrard was named as her co-star, along with Syd Crossley, one of the original Keystone Cops. Since both actors, and Olive, all ap-

pear in the cast of *Leave It to Me*, one would assume that *Help!* was a working title. Furthermore, *The British Film Catalogue v.1—Fiction
Film 1895–1994 e.* by Denis Gifford, published
in 1998 by Fitzroy Dearborn, lists *Leave It to Me*
as the *only* Olive Borden picture released during
this period.

Hotel Variety (1933)

Director: Raymond Cannon. Producer: Arthur
Hoerl. Writer: Arthur Hoerl (story). Cinematographers: G. W. "Billy" Bitzer, Marcel Le Picard,
William O. Steiner. Production Dates: Mid–August–August 25, 1932 (Fox-Case Studio, New York).
Release Date: January 7, 1933. Duration in Reels:
7. Duration in Feet: 6, 391. Running Time: 71 minutes. Alternate Title: *The Passing Show* (UK). Production Company: Screencraft Productions. Distributor: Capitol Film Exchange Inc. Genre:
Drama. Cast: Hal Skelly, **Olive Borden,** Charlotte
Walker, Sally Rand, Glorian Gray, Shannon Day,
Martin Burton, Marshall Montgomery, Ned Nor-
worth, Lilya Vallon, Herschel Mayall, Alan Brooks,
Bernard Randall, Jackie Jordan, Judith Wood.

Soundtrack — "Wrapped Up in Nothing at
All" — words by Al Koppell; music by Lou Her-
scher and Paul Vincent. "I Gave the Right Kind
of Love to the Wrong Kind of Man": words by
Allan Taub and Ben Gordon; music by Lou Her-
scher.

"A dancer and singer working in a neighborhood
speakeasy witnesses the murder of a federal officer in
a private room. She takes refuge in the nearby 'Hotel
Variety,' a boardinghouse for vaudevillians, where,
unknown to her, the murderer also has a room. At
the boardinghouse, she falls in love with a 'hoofer,'
who, like the other tenants, is waiting for the chance
to be in a big show.

"When the hoofer, who lives with his young
son, finally gets a job through his agent, the other
boarders celebrate, but the job falls through. The
hoofer's ex wife then comes and says that her new
husband, who is wealthy, can provide a good education for the boy. Feeling that he is a failure, the
hoofer agrees to give the boy up.

"The owner of the speakeasy who is after the
speakeasy performer to save herself, is dragged over
the fire escape by the murderer, and they both crash
to their death. After one of the boarders sells a scenario to a film producer, the hoofer is hired to play
the lead, and he persuades the director to hire most
of the other boarders. The boy returns, saying that
he does not want to live apart from his father, and
the hoofer and speakeasy performer are united in
love" [American Film Institute: Catalog of Entries].

Since this film is considered "lost," I must
assume that the speakeasy dancer-singer is played
by Olive and the hoofer by Hal Skelly.

A speakeasy was an establishment that sold
alcoholic beverages during Prohibition, which
lasted from 1920 to 1932 and longer in some
states. During this time, the sale and manufac-
ture of alcohol was illegal. The term speakeasy
came from a patron's manner in ordering an alcoholic drink without raising suspicion; bar-
tenders would tell patrons to be quiet and "speak
easy" (*The City in Slang: New York Life and Popular Speech,* Allen Irving, Oxford University
Press, 1995). Speakeasies became more popular
and numerous as the Prohibition years progressed. More and more of them came to be operated by people connected to organized crime.
Although police and Bureau of Prohibition
agents would raid them and arrest the owners
and patrons, the business of running speakeasies
was so lucrative that they continued to flourish.
In major cities, speakeasies were often quite elaborate, offering food, live music, floorshows, and
striptease dancers. Speakeasy operators routinely
bribed policemen to leave them alone or to give
them advance notice of raids.

This was the first film produced by Screencraft Productions. Director Raymond Cannon
had assisted D.W. Griffith during the silent era
and also acted in some of his films. *Hotel Variety* was the last feature film for Griffith's main
cameraman, G. W. "Billy" Bitzer, one of the first
and most well-known cameramen in film history.

A number of well-known vaudevillians
played boarders at the Hotel Variety. The opening shots of New York City landmarks Central
Park and George Washington Bridge and tall
buildings establish the setting within the first
few frames.

Film Daily (August 13, 1932) panned the
film, saying the script was "rambling and care-
lessly prepared." *Variety* (January 10, 1933), not-
ing that it was "another wrangle with the *Grand
Hotel* idea," further commented, "All told there's
about three reels of real footage in nearly eight
reels of film."

As of 2009, this film is presumed lost.

Gobs of Fun (1933)

Director: Ray McCarey. Release Date: December
1933. Filmed at Warners' Vitaphone Studio in
Brooklyn, New York. Cast —**Olive Borden,**
Charles Judels, George Givot.

Film Daily (September 9, 1933) wrote,
"Rather hackneyed material holds this Big V

comedy down in spite of a cast that is capable of much better things... The principal charmer role is played by Olive Borden, who, by the way, looks swell."

A review by J. J. Medford, manager of the Orpheum Theatre in Oxford, North Carolina, said, "This is a good comedy with plenty of laughs and some good music. Vitaphone certainly has improved this series of shorts over last season and practically the entire product show 100 percent improvement" (*Motion Picture Herald*, February 17, 1934).

In stark contrast Warren L. Weber, manager of the Ellinwood Theatre, Ellinwood, Kansas, loathed it, saying, "Lay off this one and refuse to look at it. Another very terrible so-called comedy. The day of this type of comedy has passed. Nobody likes them, not even the kiddies!" (*Motion Picture Herald*, March 3, 1934). Walter Beymer, manager of the Lido Theatre in Providence, Kentucky, wasn't quite as harsh; however he wasn't thrilled about it either. "Not up to the standard of Broadway Brevities," he said (*Motion Picture Herald*, March 24, 1934).

Louis Peretta, manager of the Crescent Theatre in Mahoningtown, Pennsylvania, said, "It's a Big V comedy and it's good." (*Motion Picture Herald*, April 14, 1934).

Rounding out the mixed reviews was the opinion of A. N. Miles of the Eminence Theatre, Eminence, Kentucky: "Not funny, not good, not anything!" (*Motion Picture Herald*, August 8, 1934).

This little known short exists in the Turner Library. A copy is also held at the Library of Congress.

The Mild West (1933)

Director: Joseph Henabery. Writers: A. Dorian Otvos, Cyrus Wood. Cinematographer: Edwin B. DuPar. Release Date: November 18, 1933. Running Time: 21 minutes. Production Company: The Vitaphone Corporation. Genre: Musical/Western. Cast: Janet Reade (LuLu), **Olive Borden (Baby Doll)**, Paul Keast (Gentleman Joe), Helene Denizon, Philip Ryder, Philip Loeb, The Vikings (Male Vocalists).

Soundtrack — "My Pony Boy" by Bobby Heath and Charley O'Donnell. Performed by studio orchestra as opening theme and bridge music. "I'll Take 'Em Every Time" by Cliff Hess and sung by Janet Reade. "Way Down in Texas" by Cliff Hess and sung by The Vikings. "West-

ward Ho" by Cliff Hess. Performed by Paul Keast (vocal) and dancers. "Broadway Bubble" by Cliff Hess. Performed by Janet Reade (vocal) and dancers. "Moonlight Memories" by Cliff Hess. Performed by unidentified male vocalist. "A Little Too Late" by Cliff Hess. Sung by Janet Reade and Paul Keast.

Film Daily (November 17, 1933) wrote, "This is a rather curious mixture, starting in an old Western saloon, then jumping to a jazz age and face-lifting atmosphere, with a romance between Janet Reade, torch singer, and Lyle Evans, another singer, holding things together. Olive Borden plays the role of a vamp in competition with Janet, and some chorus numbers are worked into the proceedings. Just fairly entertaining."

J. J. Medford, manager of the Orpheum Theatre in Oxford, North Carolina, said, "This is another issue of the Broadway Brevity series with good music, pretty girls and everything you could expect of a musical comedy. There are several good dance numbers and this is good entertainment for any type of audience."

The Turner Library and the Library of Congress have copies of this short.

The Fisherman (1933)

Director: Marshall Neilan. Filmed on location at Sun Haven Studios on Weedon Island in St. Petersburg, Florida. Cast: **Olive Borden**, Buster Keaton, Reed Howes, Ford Sterling.

The film was never completed and (obviously) was never released. As of 2009, no scene stills, production reports or footage has been recovered.

On June 23, 1933, E.B. Ring, a local Florida general contractor, was awarded a contract to construct the new sound stage for the Kennedy Productions at the Kennedy City motion picture studios on Weedon Island. The new project had an estimated cost of $35,000, which included all furnishings and necessary equipment, with a four-week completion time. The building was to be constructed principally of steel and fabricated in Tampa. The inside dimensions of the sound stage were 91×108 feet and 35 feet high. The catwalk had an eleven-foot clearance around the top in order to hang drops and stage scenery.

Flamingo Films, the company formed by Buster Keaton, would begin comedy productions for Aubrey Kennedy upon completion of the studio. Unfortunately, Buster did most of his work in the local bar, where he was known to entertain the locals by taking off his pants and sweeping the floor with them! (*The Evening Independent*, June 24, 1933).

The new studio, dubbed "Hollywood East," was far from successful and plans to film there were abandoned after several lackluster productions. In an undated article, William G. Wiley of the *St. Petersburg Independent* gave insight into the promise and failure surrounding Sun Haven Studios: "Before its demise, Sun Haven Studios managed to turn out three films and the city held its breath waiting for the great new prosperity the film industry would bring. Olive Borden starred in the first film, an item entitled *Chloe*—a very topical title for that period. The second and third pictures were called *Playthings of Desire* and *Hired Wife*.

The second picture was released before the first, and the hullaballoo surrounding the premiere showing of that turkey kept the town in a tizzy for weeks. Searchlights were to probe the sky around the Capitol Theater, and notables of the movie outfit, city officials and civic leaders were to speak to radio listeners from the theater lobby. It was to be what was described as a "gala" event. The town turned out en masse and an air of intense excitement pervaded the audience until the operator started the film flickering on the screen. Without any question, *Playthings of Desire* was among the worst motion pictures ever produced. It was a combination of lousy writing, atrocious acting, foul direction, dismal photography, and hopeless sound recording. Most of the time the photography was so bad no one could tell what was happening on the screen, which after all was probably fortunate. A death scene acted by James Kirkwood sounded like the snorting and growling of the MGM lion!

The production quality of *Chloe* and *Hired Wife* wasn't much better and that was the end of Sun Haven Studios. Olive subsequently continued her promotional appearances across the country.

A July 28, 1933 edition of *The Alton Iowa Democrat* published a photograph of a wide-eyed, surprised-looking Olive, pretending to be scared. A man dressed in a gorilla suit is clutching her tightly, his hand on her thigh. Beauty and the beast were publicizing the 1933 classic *King Kong*, at the Chicago's World Fair: A Century of Progress.

• Hollywood in 1934

Number of releases: 662.

U.S. weekly cinema attendance: 70 million.

Top stars at the box office according to a Quigley Publications poll of exhibitors:

1. Will Rogers; 2. Clark Gable; 3. Janet Gaynor; 4. Wallace Beery; 5. Mae West; 6. Joan Crawford; 7. Bing Crosby; 8. Shirley Temple; 9. Marie Dressler; 10. Norma Shearer.

March 16 — The sixth Academy Awards ceremony was held in the Fiesta Room of the Ambassador Hotel in Los Angeles. Will Rogers hosted the event.

The 1932–1933 winners were:

Best Actress — Katharine Hepburn for *Morning Glory*.

Best Actor — Charles Laughton for *The Private Life of Henry VIII*.

Best Picture: *Cavalcade*.

June 13: In yet another change to the film industry, an amendment to the Production Code established the Production Code Administration. All films now required a certificate of approval before their release.

December 11: Shirley Temple sang "On the Good Ship Lollipop" in the film *Bright Eyes*. The following year she won the first-ever Academy Award given to a child; the Special Juvenile Academy Award was given to her "in grateful recognition of her outstanding contribution to screen entertainment during the year 1934."

The Inventors (1934)

Director–Producer: Al Christie. Writers: Sig Herzig, William Watson (story), Budd Hulick, F. Chase Taylor (additional material). Cinematographer: George Webber. Release Date: February 2, 1934. Production Company: Educational Films Corporation of America (Coronet Comedies). Distributor: Fox Film Corporation. Genre: Comedy. Cast: F. Chase Taylor (Colonel Lemuel Q. Stoopnagle), Budd Hulick (Budd), Harry Short (Professor), Evelyn Dall (Miss Brown), Lucile Watson (Miss Tiddlebaum), Winifred Law (Miss Hogan), **Olive Borden**.

Film Daily (January 8, 1934) reported on the completion of this short, saying, "Cutting on *The Inventors*, which Stoopnagle and Budd make their debut in Educational's Coronet Comedies, has been completed at the Eastern Service studio in Astoria. Olive Borden appears as their leading lady..." By October 1, 1934, *The Inventors* was in theaters and *Film Daily* called it an "Excellent Comedy." This enjoyable comedy shows Stoopnagle and Budd at their best as nutty inventors. They receive their diplomas in their dormitory, then show the committee some of their inventions. A school for girls, being taught by Olive Borden, vote Stoopnagle and Budd as the outstanding inventors of the year. As a result they are invited to the school to give a talk. The girls want them to demonstrate their ability as inventors, but having no equipment they send the girls out to get it, which results in some very funny situations. They wind up by building a "Stupenstein" which scares everyone in the place, turning the school into an asylum from the result of phone calls to the authorities. If you are looking for belly laughs, this has them.

This short survives (unpreserved) in 11mm format at the International Museum of Photography and Film at George Eastman House in Rochester, New York. A print also exists in a private collection.

Chloe, Love Is Calling You (1934)

Director: Marshall Neilan. Producer: J. D. Trop. Writer: Marshall Neilan (story). Cinematographer: Max Stengler. Release Date: April 1, 1934. Duration in Reels: 7. Duration in Feet: 5,802. Running Time: 64 minutes. Alternate Title: *Chloe*. Production Company: Pinnacle Productions Inc. Distributor: State Rights Pinnacle Productions Inc. Genre: Drama-Horror. Cast: **Olive Borden (Chloe aka Betty Ann Gordon),** Reed Howes (Wade Carson), Molly O'Day (Joyce), Philip Ober (Jim Strong), Georgette Harvey (Mandy), Francis Joyner (Colonel Gordan), Reed Howes (Wade Carson), Augustus Smith (Moses), Jess Cavin (Jill), Richard Huey (Ben), Shreveport Home Wreckers (Blues Band).

Mandy (Georgette Harvey), a voodoo-practicing nursemaid, leaves the swamps of the Everglades with her half-white daughter Chloe (Olive) and helper Jim Strong (Philip Ober) to exact revenge on Colonel Gordon (Francis Joyner), the man she believes is responsible for the lynching of her husband Sam some fifteen years earlier. Gordon, whose daughter Betty Ann drowned in the swamps at the same time that Sam was killed, lives with his niece Joyce (Molly

O'Day) and oversees the family turpentine factory.

As Chloe, Mandy and Jim near the colonel's home, Chloe expresses doubts about her black heritage and rejects the proposal of the devoted Jim. Wade Carson (Reed Howes), the new "Yankee" foreman of the turpentine factory, impresses the colonel when he discovers shortages at the factory and establishes that Moses (Augustus Smith), one of his employees, has been stealing. Fired Moses swears revenge and then tries to force his attentions on Chloe. Wade comes to Chloe's rescue, further aggravating Moses and confusing Chloe with his obvious romantic interest. Later, while Mandy and Moses join forces and plan their voodoo revenge, Chloe and Jim argue about Chloe's attraction to the "white northerner." On the anniversary of Betty Ann's disappearance, Mandy leaves voodoo switches on the colonel's doorstep and initiates a drum-beating ceremony. During the ceremony, Mandy, who is also concerned about Chloe's interest in Wade, drugs her tea and orders Jim to take advantage of her subsequent stupor to assure their marriage. Jim refuses to seduce Chloe, but confronts Wade and tells him that she is half-black and therefore "off limits." Although Wade is reluctant to believe Jim about Chloe, he takes seriously his warning that Mandy and Moses are plotting against him and the colonel.

Mandy is hired by the colonel to wash clothes and, while in his house, steals a photograph of the young Betty Ann. The colonel and Wade then break into Mandy's cabin and discover clothes that the colonel is sure belonged to Betty Ann. While Chloe identifies the clothes as ones she wore as a child, the colonel becomes convinced she is his daughter.

Mandy, however, denies that she kidnapped Chloe to replace her own dead child, and Joyce, who is attracted to Wade, also expresses doubts about Chloe's white parentage. Confused and distraught, Chloe flees into the swamps, while the colonel and Wade, determined to prove their hunch, dig up a grave that the colonel believes contains Mandy's black baby. After they discover "kinky" hair in the gravesite, Wade and the colonel arrest Mandy and rush to save Chloe from an imminent voodoo sacrifice. Her life saved and at last assured of her "whiteness," Chloe is free to pursue her romance with Wade. (1934 New York State Censor Board and author's notes.)

Chloe was filmed on location at the short-lived Sun Haven Studios in St. Petersburg, Florida. Locals were cast to keep production costs to a minimum. Production began May 22, 1933. On Friday night, May 26, scenes of a lawn party were filmed at Mrs. Karl Jungbluth's home at 630 20th Avenue Northeast. The public were permitted to view these scenes; however, the rest of the production was shot under a tight rein and no one was permitted on or off the set without a pass ("First *Chloe* Scenes Shot," *Evening Independent*, May 22, 1933).

On May 18, Olive arrived in St. Petersburg on the Atlantic Coast Line to begin work on *Chloe*, the first picture produced in St. Petersburg. The papers said she was as "beautiful as her many pictures have portrayed her to be." She was met at the train station by Aubrey Kennedy, producer of the picture, Marshall Neilan, director, and Fred V. Blair, official of the Kennedy Productions, Inc. "Smiling in her gracious and charming manner, Miss Borden exclaimed, 'Oh! I know I shall love this place. The flowers and trees in Florida are so lovely. I am so glad to be able to see for myself this lovely city'" ("Olive Borden Here to Start Work on Kennedy Film, Falls in Love with City's Charms," *Evening Independent,* May 19, 1933).

The Evening Independent reported on May 27 that Olive had a double, Madolyn Ketchell of Morristown, New Jersey, for her water scenes. Olive knew how to swim; however, the producers deemed the scenes too risky for Olive to undertake herself. Olive's leading man, Reed Howes, did his own swimming stunt. He was a swim coach at the University of Harvard in Massachusetts and was well equipped to handle himself in the water.

A local Florida paper printed a lengthy article and interview with Olive while she was getting ready to shoot scenes. In Olive's opinion, St. Petersburg would become, in a very short time, a decidedly important center of motion picture production, a distant rival of Hollywood. Olive also talked entertainingly about the subject of pictures and declared that she liked St. Petersburg so much that she hoped to spend an additional month there, just resting and enjoying the sunshine and wonderfully invigorating air. She said the local people were very respectful of the production and she complimented them on their cooperation: "The people are not only willing to aid in every way they can and remarkably courteous and considerate, but they are also intelli-

gent," said Olive. She said they seemed to know what to do and what not to do when pictures were being made and they helped a lot in the success of scenes from *Chloe* that were shot away from the studio.

The writer complimented Olive's strong work ethic, saying she had worked the day before from 7 a.m. until midnight and never for a moment lost her enthusiasm and pep. She was said to be vitally alive all the time, on or off the set, giving everything she had to making the picture a success.

Her co-star, Philip Ober, said, "Miss Borden is the star of the piece and is really the star with all of the company here." He said nobody could be nicer to work with than Olive, who had endeared herself to the whole company by the way she had always been thoughtful and helpful to all of the cast and crew around her.

The article continues with a brief background of Olive's career, saying she has played many parts, such as half-caste, Mexican, gypsy and South Seas girls, and for a time she was in what the profession calls "clothes films" where she wore fine clothes and acted with due repression to fit the costumes. "I did not like those parts," said Olive. "I much prefer the role of a half-caste or South Seas woman. I feel much more comfortable in old clothes and ragged shoes such as I wear most of the time in *Chloe* in which picture I am supposed to be a mulatto though it finally turns out that I am the colonel's daughter. Such a part gives me a chance to display the exuberance I feel and I do not have to be sedate or repressed. I enjoy these parts and can romp and be myself." When asked what role she liked best, she replied "Eve" promptly and decidedly. "I was not hampered by clothes in that picture as about all I wore was a fig leaf."* The reporter noted that as he spoke with Olive in her dressing room, she was getting her makeup done for a night scene; he said that every so often a member of the company would come in, always to be greeted by a delightfully cordial smile. Eventually there were calls from Marshall Neilan so he had to let her finish dressing. Later he saw Olive work some scenes that would eventually appear in the finished picture. When he left the lot, he said, she was "still at work and was as

*Olive was scantily clad, albeit briefly, in the prehistoric scenes in Fig Leaves (1926), but for the most part she was dressed in fine clothing designed by leading Hollywood costumer Adrian.

lively as ever" ("St. Petersburg Will Become Important Picture Center in Opinion of Screen Star," *Evening Independent,* June 3, 1933).

"In a natural setting that would take thousands of dollars to reproduce in Hollywood, the voodoo scene of *Chloe,* Kennedy City's first full-length picture, was shot on a balmy Saturday night on Weedon's Island. As a great fire burned in the center of a natural amphitheater walled in by ancient oaks and monkey palms heavily draped in Spanish moss. The weird chant of a 'negro' chorus; the hypnotic tom-tom of kettle drums could be heard for almost half a mile. And a three-quarter moon rode high. About 75 voodoos circled around the open fire, their bronze bodies glistening in the glare of the Klieg lights, and swayed in an abandoned frenzy to the rhythmic beat of tom-toms. To one side was Wheeton's colored chorus, and farther down the line stood another company of 'negroes' under a tree, waving their hands and apparently on their way to the great feast. Behind the circling voodoos stood an altar upon which were five human skulls, a sword and a snake, mute evidence of former sacrifices to the voodoo religion. A young redhead by the name of Jack Chapin assisted in the direction of the 'negroes' and almost succeeded in stealing the show, so compelling was the power of his enthusiasm and sincerity. He was known as 'Red-bug' to intimates and had just recently arrived from California — in fact so recently that he made the mistake once of addressing Marshall Neilan as 'Mr. DeMille.' Which he corrected, however, immediately" ['Voodoo Scenes for *Chloe* Made with 75 Local Negroes,' Hazel Wilton, *Evening Independent*, June 5, 1933].

In May, 1934, Kodascope Libraries Inc., one of the largest 16mm film lending libraries, listed *Chloe* in their new catalogue ("Film Made Here Gets Big Boost — *Chloe* Now Available in Small Prints For Use in Home Machine," *Evening Independent*, May 16, 1934). In June 1963, Ash Greeley, stage manager for a Florida theatre, who was one of the movie staff on *Chloe*, remembers Olive lost in the swamps, gamely fighting whole clouds of mosquitoes, her body and clothing drenched in some kind of obnoxious mosquito repellent that chased away some of the skeeters, and almost overcame the movie crew ("Our Town," *Evening Independent,* June 29, 1963).

The movie's taglines included "Strange secrets never before revealed!," "See the virgin dance of death!" and "She was doomed to Die!" *Chloe* was considered "lost" until a print turned up in 1997. Alpha Video released *Chloe* on DVD on August 23, 2005, on a double feature with another voodoo-inspired bomb, *The Devil's Daughter* (1939). The DVD is widely available for under $8 and is worth the investment, if only for the curiosity factor.

Appendix 1: Stage Work

April 27 and 28, 1923— The *Writer's Review of 1923* at the Philharmonic Auditorium was billed as a "musical-comedy extravaganza." Olive starred in the "Shadow of the Pyramids" number and, for a newcomer, she was in good company: Anna May Wong, Colleen Moore, May MacAvoy, Laura La Plante and Virginia Fox, among others, were part of the same act (*Los Angeles Times*, April 26, 1923).

February 22, 1930— At the *Hollywood Midnight Frolic* at Grauman's Chinese Theater, the Dodge Sisters were the feature star act and Olive was billed as making a special appearance (*Los Angeles Times,* February 20, 1930).

October 4, 1930: Olive was signed for a Lee Shubert play entitled *On the Spot*. It never eventuated (*Joplin Globe*, October 1930).

December 20, 1930— *The Devil Is a Lady* was produced by Jack White and starred Olive, Frieda Inescort, Ara Gerald, Victor Morley, Leonard Wiley, and Edward Crandall. The preliminary run began in Great Neck, Long Island, New York. It ran for seven weeks in the outer New York area. It was originally slated for Broadway for the week of January 5, 1931. It never made it. One critic called Olive's voice "charming" and said that she had acquired "poise" and "polish." This favorable review did nothing to bolster the popularity of the play (unidentified newspaper clipping, December 22, 1930).

1931: Olive appeared in the comedic romp *A Modern Virgin* at the Locust Street Theatre in Philadelphia (unidentified clipping).

1932: Olive appeared in *Hollywood Revels of 1933* at the Hollywood Cabaret Restaurant (clipped ad in multiple newspapers).

1932— The newspaper *The Oil City Derrick* (February 25, 1932) promoted Olive's in-person appearance at the Drake Theatre in Pennsylvania, saying, "On the stage — Olive Borden — Beautiful movie star in person. Miss Borden will charm you with her pleasant and vivacious personality. If you want to see how beautiful a girl must be to achieve fame as a movie actress — see Miss Borden!" Appearing with Olive were Dickinson and Tempest, Deluxe Laugh Makers; De Latour, Dancing Sextette; and Siem, Internationally Famous Card and Coin Juggler.

February 5, 1935: Olive appeared in *Hollywood Revue* at the Sheboygan Theatre. In *The Sheboygan Press* (February 5, 1935) ran an advertisement: "Olive Borden — Screen Idol — Stage Star — Now in Person and Her Hollywood Revue (35 People) featuring Earl Faber: Paramount Picture comedian as master of ceremonies." They appeared at the Sheboygan on February 6 and 7.

1935: A personal appearance tour in the Midwest was Olive's final work as a professional performer. Several theatres billed her as a "Film and Broadway Star." It was a desperate attempt to fill seats. By 1935, Olive was almost a decade past her peak, and she hadn't even celebrated her thirtieth birthday! (clipped ad from multiple newspapers, 1935).

1946: Olive's last acting performance was on the stage at the Sunshine Mission. She planned the 1946

Christmas pageant and taught the children who called the Mission their home how to act and remember their lines. Olive also performed in the play. It was her last acting — ever. Shortly before her death, she had begun planning the 1947 Christmas show. The children performed the 1947 Christmas play in Olive's honor. Sibbie sat in the front row, clutching Olive's scrapbook. It wasn't yet three months since Olive's passing. Emotions were still very raw. Understandably, as the children took their bows, there wasn't a dry eye in the house (*Joplin Globe*, January 2, 1948).

Radio — April 26, 1929 — *Los Angeles Times* — "Olive Borden to Face 'Mike' in KEJK Studio."

"KEJK calls particular attention to its night program when, at 10 o'clock, Olive Borden, film actress, is scheduled to be the center of syncopation half-hour with the song hits from popular musical comedies."

Appendix 2: Addresses

1926: 627 Hillcrest Road, Beverly Hills, California (bought from actor Hobart Bosworth for $65,000 in 1926). Sold in February of 1928. As of 2009 the house is still standing and in beautifully restored condition. It recently sold for over $4 million.

1928: 905 Ocean Front, Santa Monica, California. (Following the loss of her Fox contract, Olive and her mother rented the beachside home for several months.)

1930 census: 1301-1309 North Harper Avenue, Hollywood, California, aka Romanesque Villa Apts.

Early 1931: 59 West 10th Street, New York, New York.

1931: Following her March 28, 1931, marriage to Theodore Spector, Olive moved to her new husband's place of residence (as noted on their marriage license) at 105 Graham Avenue, Paterson, New Jersey. The Victorian home and the neighboring houses have since been demolished to make way for a city park. Graham Avenue has been renamed Rosa Parks Boulevard.

Olive doesn't mention her New York City address as her place of residence on the marriage license; rather a Norfolk, Virginia, address is noted as her residential address: 708 Yarmouth Avenue. Once again, this address is now parkland.

1932: 160 Central Park South, New York, New York. The *New York Times* (April 21, 1932) announced that Olive recently leased an apartment at the prestigious Essex House, overlooking Central Park.

Early 1934: 313 W. 91st Street, New York, New York. A beautiful limestone construction; still standing in 2009.

Late 1934: After Olive's November 2, 1934, marriage to her second husband, John Moeller, the newlyweds moved to a small, three-room apartment on Long Island, New York. She shared the home (according to the marriage license the address was 30-11 92nd Place, Richmond Hill, Long Island, New York) with her husband, and his father (William Moeller) until their divorce (1941).

Note: The residential address on the marriage license is slightly wrong for John Moeller. The 1930 census shows him living at 130-13 92nd Avenue, Richmond Hill, Long Island, New York. He is listed as "brother-in-law" in the household. The head of the household is Norbert Schaeffer, the husband of John's older sister Marie.

On the same census, John's father, William Moeller, is living at 130-11: same address (92nd Avenue), different apartment number, probably neighboring (130–11 and 130–13). By 1934 (as per the marriage license), John is now living in his father's apartment (130-11). The marriage license address is written as: 30-11 92nd Place, Richmond Hill, Long Island, New York.

The actual address was 130-11 92nd Avenue, Richmond Hill, Long Island, New York.

That address is now 13011 92nd Avenue.

Late 1942: Olive was living in Brentwood, Long Island, New York. Her mailing address was 341 W. 45th Street, New York City: c/o Barr.

1945–1947: The Sunshine Mission (aka Casa de Rosas) is registered with the U.S. National Register of Historic Places (No. 241). The address (a shelter to homeless women and their children since 1942) is 2600 S. Hoover Street, Los Angeles, California (in West Adams district).

Sibbie Borden's Addresses After Olive's Death

1947–1949: The Sunshine Mission, 2600 S. Hoover Street, Los Angeles, California (in West Adams district)/

1950: 8631 La Tuna Canyon, Malibu, California.

1952: 10743 Millbank Street, North Hollywood/Studio City, California.

1954–1959: The Sunshine Mission, 2600 S. Hoover Street, Los Angeles, California (in West Adams district).

Bibliography

Books

Anthony, Brian, and Andy Edmonds. *Smile When the Raindrops Fall: The Story of Charley Chase.* Lanham, MD: Scarecrow Press, 1998.

Basinger, Jeanine. *Silent Stars.* New York: Knopf, 1999.

Baxter, John. *Stunt: The Story of the Great Movie Stunt Men.* Garden City, NY: Doubleday, 1974.

Beauchamp, Cari. *Joseph P. Kennedy Presents: His Hollywood Years.* New York: Knopf, 2009.

Bogdanovich, Peter. *Allan Dwan: The Last Pioneer.* New York: Praeger, 1971.

Brown, Gene. *Movie Time: A Chronology of Hollywood and the Movie Industry from Its Beginnings to the Present.* New York: Macmillan, 1995.

Bruskin, N. David. *The White Brothers: Jack, Jules & Sam White.* Lanham, MD: Scarecrow Press, 1990.

Carey, Harry, Jr. *Company of Heroes: My Life as an Actor in the John Ford Stock Company.* Lanham, MD: Madison Books, 1994.

Cut! Hollywood Murders, Accidents and Other Tragedies. Hauppauge, NY: Global, 2005.

Everson, William K. *A Pictorial History of the Western Film.* Secaucus, NJ: Citadel Press, 1969.

Eyman, Scott. *Print the Legend: The Life and Times of John Ford.* New York: Johns Hopkins University Press, 2001.

Fleming, E.J. *Paul Bern: The Life and Famous Death of the MGM Director and Husband of Harlow.* Jefferson, NC: McFarland, 2009.

Ford, Dan. *Pappy: The Life of John Ford.* New York: Prentice-Hall, 1979.

Gifford, Denis. *The British Film Catalogue, v.1—Fiction Films 1895–1994.* London: Fitzroy Dearborn, 1998.

Herman, Hal. *How I Broke Into the Movies.* Yesteryear Press, 1984.

Kalinak, Kathryn. *How the West Was Sung: Music in the Westerns of John Ford.* Berkeley: University of California Press, 2007.

Kent, David. *The Lizzie Borden Sourcebook.* Boston: Branden Books, 1992.

Klepper, Robert K. *Silent Films, 1877–1996: A Critical Guide to 646 Movies.* Jefferson, NC: McFarland, 1999.

Langman, Larry. *American Film Cycles: The Silent Era.* Westport, CT: Greenwood Press, 1998.

Lanza, Joseph, and Dennis Penna. *Russ Columbo and the Crooner Mystique.* Los Angeles: Feral House, 2002.

Lee, Betty. *Marie Dressler: The Unlikeliest Star.* Lexington: University Press of Kentucky, 1997.

Lowe, Denise. *An Encyclopedic Dictionary of Women in Early American Films: 1895–1930.* New York: Routledge, 2004.

Marx, Samuel, and Joyce Vanderveen. *Deadly Illusions.* New York: Random House, 1990.

McCarthy, Todd. *Howard Hawks: The Grey Fox of Hollywood.* New York: Grove Press, 2000.

Oderman, Stuart. *Talking to the Piano Player: Silent Film Stars, Writers and Directors Remember.* Boalsburg, PA: Bear Manor Media, 2005.

Philips, Gene D. *Major Film Directors of the American and British Cinema,* Bethlehem, PA: Lehigh University Press, 1999.

Porter, Darwin. *The Secret Life of Humphrey Bogart: The Early Years (1899–1931).* New York: Blood Moon Productions, 2003.

Price, Michael. *Forgotten Horrors: The Definitive Edition.* Baltimore: Midnight Marquee Press, 2009.

Robertson, Patrick. *Film Facts.* New York: Aurum Press, 2001.

Robertson, Patrick. *Guinness Book of Film Facts.* New York: Sterling Publishing, 1985.

Senn, Bryan. *Drums of Terror: Voodoo in the Cinema,* Baltimore: Luminary Press, 2003.

Slide, Anthony. *Silent Players: A Biographical and Autobiographical Study of 100 Silent Film Actors and Actresses,* Lexington: University Press of Kentucky, 2002.

Soister, John. *Up from the Vault: Rare Thrillers of the 1920s and 1930s,* Jefferson, NC: McFarland, 2004.

Vance, Jeffrey, and Suzanne Lloyd. *Harold Lloyd: Master Comedian.* New York: Harry N. Abrams, 2002.

Wagner, Walter. *You Must Remember This.* New York: Putnam's, 1975.

Ward, Lewis Richard. *A History of Hal Roach Studios.* Carbondale: Southern Illinois University Press, 2005.

Wray, Fay. *On The Other Hand: A Life Story.* New York: St. Martin's Press, 1989.

Newspapers

"Actresses on Trip Eastward." *Ogden Standard Examiner,* July 20, 1930.

Appleton Post-Crescent, 3 Bad Men review, June 27, 1927.

Appleton Post-Crescent, The Monkey Talks review, April 6, 1927.

Bahn, Chester. *Yankee Señor* review. *Syracuse Herald,* March 28, 1926.

"Beauties and Broker Figure in Bigamy Fight: Olive Borden Leaves Her Husband, Learning He's Married." *Mansfield News,* August 26, 1932.

Bee (Danville, VA), *Gang War* review, November 26, 1928.

Bellingham Herald, March 4, 1930.

Bridgeport Telegram, November 4, 1927.

Capital Times, October 30, 1929.

Chapman, John. "Looking at Hollywood." *Chicago Daily Tribune,* March 7, 1941.

Charleroi Mail, Wedding Rings review, February 28, 1930.

Charleston Daily Mail, The Monkey Talks review, July 24, 1927.

Charleston Gazette, May 3, 1931.

Chicago Daily Tribune, July 27, 1925.

Chicago Daily Tribune, March 21, 1926.

Chicago Daily Tribune, February 1, 1927.

Chicago Daily Tribune, August 27, 1929.

Chicago Daily Tribune, January 7, 1930.

Chicago Daily Tribune, April 5, 1931.

Chicago Daily Tribune, November 8, 1931.

Chicago Daily Tribune, Come to My House review, January 11, 1928.

Chicago Daily Tribune, Gang War review, December 18, 1928.

Chicago Daily Tribune, The Eternal Woman review, April 8, 1929.

Chicago Daily Tribune, The Royal Razz review, December 27, 1924.

Chicago Daily Tribune, The Social Lion review, June 28, 1930.

Chicago Daily Tribune, Virgin Lips review, September 4, 1928.

Chicago Daily Tribune, Wedding Rings review, March 15, 1930.

Chicago Sun Times, undated, 1926.

Cumberland Evening Times, January 28, 1926.

Daily News (Frederick, MD), January 27, 1925.

Davenport Democrat and Leader, Yellow Fingers review, June 13, 1926.

"Desert Heat Makes Film Players Ill." *Los Angeles Times,* October 6, 1925.

"Designer for Stars Dies at 56." *Corpus Christi Times,* September 14, 1959.

"Ex-Screen Star Olive Borden Dies in Los Angeles Mission." *Amarillo Daily News,* October 3, 1947.

"Fashion Designer Gilbert Adrian Dies." *Oakland Tribune,* September 14, 1959.

Fidler, Jimmie. "In Hollywood." *Chronicle-Telegram,* September 19, 1938.

"Film Actress Olive Borden Succumbs to WAAC Lure." unidentified, undated Iowa article.

Film Daily, July 11, 1927.

Film Daily, January 8, 1934.

Film Daily, The Albany Night Boat review, September 23, 1928.

Film Daily, Come to My House review, February 5, 1928.

Film Daily, The Country Beyond review, October 24, 1926.

Film Daily, Dance Hall review, December 22, 1929.

Film Daily, The Eternal Woman review, April 7, 1929.

Film Daily, Gang War review, August 8, 1928.

Film Daily, Gobs of Fun review, September 9, 1933.

Film Daily, Half Marriage review, August 25, 1929.

Film Daily, Hello Sister review, September 9, 1930.

Film Daily, Hotel Variety review, August 13, 1932.

Film Daily, The Inventors review, October 1, 1934.

Film Daily, The Joy Girl review, September 11, 1927.

Film Daily, Love in the Desert review, May 5, 1929.

Film Daily, The Mild West review, November 17, 1933.

Film Daily, The Monkey Talks review, February 27, 1927.

Film Daily, The Monkey Talks review, June 26, 1927.

Film Daily, Pajamas review, November 13, 1927.

Film Daily, Sinners in Love review, October 10, 1928.

Film Daily, Stool Pigeon review, November 4, 1928.

Film Daily, 3 Bad Men review, October 17, 1926.

Film Daily, Virgin Lips review, September 16, 1928.

Film Daily, Wedding Rings review, May 11, 1930.

Film Daily, The Yankee Señor review, March 21, 1926.

Film Daily, Yellow Fingers review, April 4, 1926.

"Film Made Here Gets Big Boost—*Chloe* Now Available in Small Prints for Use in Home Machine." *St. Petersburg Evening Independent,* May 16, 1934.

Film Spectator, March 20, 1926.

Film Spectator, Sinners in Love review, September, 29, 1928.

"Film Star Discovered in Hospital." *Los Angeles Times,* undated, 1926.

"Film Stars Feet Grow Larger in Ten Years." *Oakland Tribune,* March 10, 1930.

"First *Chloe* Scenes Shot." *St. Petersburg Evening Independent,* May 22, 1933.

"Fox Buys Story for Star." *Los Angeles Times*, August 18, 1927.

"Frank Lloyds Plan Ranch Festivity." *Los Angeles Examiner*, June 1, 1930.

Fresno Bee, 3 Bad Men review, November 7, 1926.

"Friends at Mission Pay Olive Borden Tribute." *Los Angeles Times*, October 5, 1947.

"Great Russian Drive Aids Allies in North Africa." *Evening Standard,* January 21, 1943.

"Guild Plans Gay Gambol." *Los Angeles Examiner,* January 28, 1927.

Hall, Mordaunt. *Dance Hall* review. *New York Times,* December 16, 1929.

Hamilton Daily News (Hamilton, OH), *The Yankee Señor* review, August 14, 1926.

Hamilton Evening Journal, June 5, 1926.

Hamilton Evening Journal, June 26, 1926.

Hamilton Evening Journal, August 21, 1926.

Hamilton Evening Journal, October 2, 1926.

Hamilton Evening Journal, October 9, 1926.

Hamilton Evening Journal, December 31, 1926.

Hamilton Evening Journal, May 24, 1930.

Hamilton Evening Journal, Yellow Fingers review, June 25, 1926.

Hartford Courant, May 25, 1930.

Hartford Courant, The Divorce Racket review, November 14, 1932.

Hollywood Daily Citizen, The Social Lion review, March 10, 1930.

Hollywood Daily Citizen, The Voice of Hollywood No. 1 review, March 28, 1930.

Hollywood Daily Citizen, Wedding Rings review, February 8, 1930.

"A Hollywood Party." *Los Angeles Times*, November 25, 1928.

Houston Press, April 23, 1928.

"How the Stars Will Greet Santa Claus." *Los Angeles Times*, December 23, 1928.

"Introducing Olive Borden — Flapper." *Los Angeles Times*, March 13, 1927.

Jefferson City Post Tribune, January 31, 1929.

Joplin Globe, October 12, 1947.

Joplin Globe, January 2, 1948.

Joplin Globe, October 1930.

Lathrop, Monroe. Untitled article. *Los Angeles Evening Express,* January 9, 1930.

Lima News, My Own Pal review, April 15, 1926.

Lima News, Sinners in Love review, December 10, 1928.

Long Beach Independent, October 2, 1947.

Loring, Helen. "Olive in Quest of Her Soul." *Photoplay,* December 1929.

Los Angeles Evening Express, Dance Hall review, January 22, 1930.

Los Angeles Evening Herald Express, undated, 1947.

Los Angeles Examiner, October 16, 1927.

Los Angeles Examiner, October 4, 1930.

Los Angeles Examiner, Stool Pigeon review, February 18, 1929.

Los Angeles Illustrated News, The Social Lion review, June 13, 1930.

Los Angeles Times, April 26, 1923.

Los Angeles Times, May 4, 1926.

Los Angeles Times, February 3, 1927.

Los Angeles Times, June 3, 1927.

Los Angeles Times, June 7, 1927.

Los Angeles Times, July 10, 1927.

Los Angeles Times, November 30, 1927.

Los Angeles Times, October 19, 1928.

Los Angeles Times, December 25, 1928.

Los Angeles Times, April 11, 1929.

Los Angeles Times, June 9, 1929.

Los Angeles Times, October 25, 1929.

Los Angeles Times, February 20, 1930.

Los Angeles Times, April 27, 1930.

Los Angeles Times, July 12, 1931.

Los Angeles Times, September 10, 1938.

Los Angeles Times, January 15, 1945.

Los Angeles Times, Come to My House review, February 21, 1928.

Los Angeles Times, Hello Sister review, May 1, 1930.

Los Angeles Times, The Monkey Talks review, April 10, 1927.

Los Angeles Times, The Monkey Talks review, March 1, 1927.

Los Angeles Times, The Monkey Talks review, March 13, 1927.

Los Angeles Times, The Royal Razz review, December 10, 1924.

Los Angeles Times, Too Many Mammas review, October 8, 1924.

Los Angeles Times, Why Men Work review, August 6, 1924.

Lusk, Norbert. Untitled article. *Los Angeles Times*, February 13, 1927.

Lusk, Norbert. Untitled article. *Los Angeles Times*, June 19, 1927.

Merrick, Mollie. "Hollywood in Person." *Atlanta Constitution*, November 23, 1929.

"Miss Borden Has Narrow Escape in Film Scene." *Daily News* (New York), July 12, 1926.

Morning Herald (Hagerstown, MD), April 29, 1926.

Moser, MacMillan Stephen. "Gowns by Adrian." *Austin Chronicle*, June 29, 2001.

Motion Picture Herald, February 17, 1934.

Motion Picture Herald, March 3, 1934.

Motion Picture Herald, March 24, 1934.

Motion Picture Herald, April 14, 1934.

Motion Picture Herald, August 8, 1934.

Motion Picture News, Should Husbands Be Watched? review, March 11, 1925.

Motion Picture News, Too Many Mammas review, October 11, 1924.

"Movie Stars to Attend Premiere in Hollywood." *Illustrated Daily News*, July 16, 1927.

Moving Picture News, The Royal Razz review, December 20, 1924.

Moving Picture World, Neck and Neck review, January 26, 1924.

Moving Picture World, The Royal Razz review, December 20, 1924.

Moving Picture World, Why Men Work review, September 6, 1924.

"New Club Plans for Gay Opening." *Los Angeles Examiner,* September 20, 1927.

"New Studio Will Open Sunday." *Los Angeles Times,* August 24, 1926.

New York Times, May 13, 1932.

New York Times, The Happy Warrior review, July 7, 1925.

New York Times, The Monkey Talks review, June 15, 1927.

"News Notes from Movieland." *Kingsport Times* (Kingsport, TN), May 17, 1925.

Nye, Myra. Untitled article. *Los Angeles Times,* May 8, 1927.

Oakland Tribune, May 4, 1925.

"Odds-and-Ends of Stage-News." *Chicago Daily Tribune,* September 19, 1926.

Ogden-Standard Examiner, August 31, 1927.

Ogden Standard Examiner, January 22, 1930.

Oil City Derrick, February 25, 1932.

"Olive Borden Former Film Star Dies in Poverty." *Coshocton Tribune,* October 2, 1947.

"Olive Borden Here from Vacation in Minnesota." *Chicago Daily Tribune,* July 30, 1930.

"Olive Borden Here to Start Work on Kennedy Film, Falls in Love with City's Charms." *St. Petersburg Evening Independent,* May 19, 1933.

"Olive Borden Now in Critical Condition." *Los Angeles Times,* October 23, 1926.

"Olive Borden Quits Husband." *Oakland Tribune,* April 18, 1932.

"Olive Borden to Face 'Mike' in KEJK Studio." *Los Angeles Times,* April 26, 1929.

"Olive Borden's Mother Ill." *Los Angeles Times,* September 25, 1929.

"One-Time Bathing Beauty Ends Life with Barbiturates." *Eureka Humboldt Standard,* November 21, 1960.

Oshkosh NorthWestern, February 27, 1935.

"Our Town." *St. Petersburg Evening Independent,* June 29, 1963.

"Pageant of Fashion at F.W. Murnau's *Sunrise* Premiere." *Los Angeles Examiner,* November 30, 1927.

Parsons, Louella O. *The Monkey Talks* review. *Los Angeles Examiner,* April 30, 1927.

Parsons, Louella O. Untitled article. *Los Angeles Examiner,* October 12, 1927.

Parsons, Louella O. Untitled article. *Los Angeles Examiner,* September 2, 1930.

Parsons, Louella O. Untitled article. *Los Angeles Examiner,* September 30, 1930.

Parsons, Louella O. Untitled article. *Los Angeles Examiner,* December 10, 1930.

Pharos-Tribune, The Dressmaker from Paris ad, May 23, 1925.

St. Petersburg Evening Independent, May 27, 1933.

St. Petersburg Evening Independent, June 24, 1933.

St. Petersburg Times, Olive Borden interview, May 19, 1933.

"St. Petersburg Will Become Important Picture Center in Opinion of Screen Star." *St. Petersburg Evening Independent,* June 3, 1933.

San Antonio Express, June 29, 1930.

San Antonio Express, The Country Beyond review, December 12, 1926.

San Antonio Light, February 27, 1935.

"Sennett's Bathing Beauties: Filmland's Forgotten Women." *Olean Times-Herald,* February 3, 1937.

Shaw, Edna. "Society in Filmland." *Hollywood Daily Citizen,* August 4, 1927.

"She Can Take It: Olive Borden Has Character as Well as Curves." *Motion Picture Classic,* November, 1929.

Sheboygan Press, November 26, 1926.

Sheboygan Press, February 5, 1935.

Sheboygan Press, The Country Beyond review, November 24, 1926.

Sheboygan Press, Gang War review, November 23, 1929.

Sheboygan Press, Half Marriage review, December 9, 1929.

Sheboygan Press, Hello Sister review, April 9, 1930.

"'The Show Must Go On,' Cries Olive Borden, Injured During Filming of *The Monkey Talks.*" *Daily News,* 1927.

"The Society of Cinemaland." *Los Angeles Times,* February 19, 1928.

"Star May Return to Fox Films." *Los Angeles Times,* February 19, 1928.

"Star of 30's Adopts Missionary Career." *Los Angeles Times,* June 16, 1946.

"Sun as Klieg Light Shines on Brilliant Hollywood Easter." *Chicago Daily Tribune,* April 1, 1929.

Syracuse Herald, January 2, 1927.

Syracuse Herald, August 18, 1927.

Syracuse Herald, December 30, 1932.

Syracuse Herald, Love in the Desert review, February 3, 1929.

Syracuse Herald, Pajamas review, January 27, 1928.

Syracuse Herald, Stool Pigeon review, January 27, 1929.

"That Old Sweetheart O'Mine!" *Modesto News-Herald,* February 11, 1928.

"Theodore Spector Held." *New York Times,* May 9, 1934.

Tinee, Mae. Untitled article. *Chicago Daily Tribune,* June 21, 1927.

Tinee, Mae. Untitled article. *Chicago Daily Tribune,* September 21, 1927.

"To Aid Actors Dinner Club." *New York Times,* May 19, 1932.

Underhill, Harriet. *The Monkey Talks* review. *New York Herald-Tribune,* April 2, 1927.

Washington Post, undated, late 1927.
Weekly Kansas City Star, July 29, 1925.
Wells, Hal. "The Most Misunderstood Girl in Hollywood." *Motion Picture Classic,* July 1928.
Wiley, William. Article on Sun Haven Studios. *St. Petersburg Independent,* undated.
"Will Be Seen As Woodley." *Los Angeles Record,* October 20, 1927.
Williams, Alan. "Olive Borden's Last Starring Role." *American Weekly,* February 15, 1948.
Wilton, Hazel. "Voodoo Scenes for *Chloe* Made with 75 Local Negroes." *St. Petersburg Evening Independent,* June 5, 1933.
Yeaman, Elizabeth. "Society in Filmland." *Hollywood Daily Citizen,* February 5, 1930.
Zanesville Signal, The Joy Girl review, January 4, 1928.

Magazines and Periodicals

Ankerich, Michael. "Olive Borden: The Joy Girl of the Silent Screen — Part I." *Classic Images* #185, November 1990.
Ankerich, Michael. "Olive Borden: The Joy Girl of the Silent Screen — Part II." *Classic Images* #187, January 1991.
Ankerich, Michael. "Olive Borden: The Sybil Tinkle Connection." *Classic Images* #209, November 1992.
"Chicken Southern-Style." *Photoplay,* March 1926.
"If You Love Your Work." *Motion Picture Magazine,* June 1926.
"A Letter from Location." *Picture–Play,* June 1926.
Manners, Dorothy. Untitled article. *Lowell Sun,* November 2, 1944.
Motion Picture Classic, July 1928.
Motion Picture Magazine, Fig Leaves review, June 1926.
Movie Life Magazine, Dance Hall review, 1929.
Moving Picture World, December 10, 1927.
Photoplay, April 26, 1928.
Photoplay, December 1929.
Photoplay, 3 Bad Men review, October 1926.
Picture Play, 3 Bad Men review, November 1926.
Pylant, James. "The Bewitching Family Tree of Elizabeth Montgomery." *Genealogy Magazine* (2004).
"Seventy-Five Cents and a Made-Over Dress." *Motion Picture Magazine,* July 1927.
Sidelights of the Stage and Screen, January 18, 1928.
"Tell It to Bern." *Picture Play,* 1925.
Time, Gang War review, December 3, 1928.
Time, Olive Borden obituary, October 13, 1947.
Variety, Half Marriage review, August 14, 1929.
Variety, Hello Sister review, March 12, 1930.
Variety, Hotel Variety review, January 10, 1933.

Several newspaper and magazine snippets that were trimmed and therefore undated came from the following publications:

American, Appleton-Crescent, Billboard, Daily Mirror, Evening Journal, Hartford Courant, Hollywood Daily Citizen, Morning Telegraph, Motion Picture News, Motion Pictures Today, Movie Fans' News, Moving Picture World, New York Graphic, New York Telegram, New York Times, Photoplay, Variety.

Other Sources

Ankerich, Michael, emails to the author, January, 2008–June 2009.
Baptismal certificate of Olive Borden (September 9, 1906).
Brownlow, Kevin, emails and letters to the author, March–April 2009.
Cappello, Bill, emails to the author, March 2007–June 2009.
Census records from various states, 1860–1930.
S.S. *Champlain* ship manifest (Olive Borden — passenger from Plymouth, England, to New York City, February 9–16, 1933).
Comstock, Ned (USC Library), emails, letters, Hal Roach payroll ledgers, magazine articles to the author, March–June 2009.
Death certificates (Borden, Shields).
Doros, Dennis, emails to the author, May–June 2009.
Drew, William, emails to the author, January 2008–May 2009.
Educational Films press sheets.
Fleming, E. J., emails to the author and phone conversation, January 2008–May 2009.
Fox Films, miscellaneous studio documents and promotional material.
Graves, Ralph, Jr., letters to and phone conversations with the author, January 2007–June 2009.
Hatch, Susan, emails to the author, February 2008–June 2009.
History's Mysteries: The Strange Case of Lizzie Borden (DVD), The History Channel, 2005.
Kalat, David, emails to the author, May 2009.
The Legend of Lizzie Borden, 1975 made-for-TV movie.
Mank, Charles, Jr., personal letters to and from Olive Borden, 1926.
Marriage licenses (Shields-Borden, Borden-Spector, Borden-Moeller)
Massa, Steve, emails to the author, June 2009.
Model, Ben, emails to the author, May 2008–June 2009.

Narine, Dr. Levica, emails to and phone conversation with the author, June 2009.

New York State Censor Board.

Personal appearance ads clipped from unidentified publications, 1926–1935.

Roberts, Richard, emails to the author, May–June 2009.

Solan, Yair, emails to the author, May–June 2009.

Wood, Benjie, emails to the author, March 2008–May 2009.

WWII Records, Borden, O'Brien, Spector, Moeller.

Yeager, Caroline, emails to the author, May 2009.

Websites

www.afi.com
www.ancestry.com
www.filmreference.com
www.findagrave.com
www.goldensilents.com
www.grapevinevideo.com
www.hollywoodchamber.net
www.ibdb.com
www.imdb.com
www.measuringworth.com
www.movielanddirectory.com
www.newspaperarchive.com
www.oliveborden.com
www.rudolph-valentino.com
www.sacredheartnorfolk.org
www.silentsaregolden.com
www.silentfilmstillarchive.com
www.tcm.com
www.tvguide.com
www.wikipedia.org

Index

Numbers in *bold italics* indicate pages with photographs.